Practising Quarkus 2.x

Quarkus

Antonio Goncalves

2021-11-29

Table of Contents

Practising Quarkus 2.x

- www.antoniogoncalves.org
- agoncal.teachable.com
- www.amazon.com/author/agoncal

You can find two different formats of this fascicle:

- eBook (PDF/EPUB) at https://agoncal.teachable.com/p/ebook-practising-quarkus
- Paper book (ISBN: 9798775794774) and eBooks at https://www.amazon.com/gp/product/B0993RBKKR

Version Date: 2021-11-29

To my wonderful kids, Eloise, Ligia and Ennio, who are the best thing life has given me.

Foreword

I started learning Java in 1999. Over the past 20 years, I have witnessed the journey that Java and its ecosystem have been on. But 20 years is a long time, especially for software. Many trends have been called the "next big thing" only to then fade away. How many times have we read about the supposed death of Java? But it is still very much alive!

Corba, Applet, JavaEE, Spring, OSGi, Android, OpenJDK, etc. all of these technologies have shaped the Java we know today. All of these technologies have pushed the limits of Java and have led to an increase in its versatility. That's how Java has endured across the ages: by adapting itself.

Nowadays, Java is facing another challenge. The rise of the Cloud, Containers and Serverless has pushed Java away from the spotlight. Until now, until Quarkus.

And, there is no better way to start with Quarkus than with this fascicle (and its companion fascicle *Understanding Quarkus 2.x*). The extensive expertise of Antonio is the perfect tool to guide you towards new horizons. You are going to see *live* how Quarkus mutates Java to make it relevant in Containers, on Kubernetes and in Serverless environments. From the first line of code to production monitoring, this fascicle is your companion. Fasten your seat belt, and get ready to take off!

Clement Escoffier
Vert.x and Quarkus Core Developer at Red Hat
@clementplop

[1] **KDP** https://kdp.amazon.com
[2] **MIT licence** https://opensource.org/licenses/MIT

About the Author

I am a senior software architect living in Paris. Having been focused on Java development since the late 1990s, my career took me to many different countries and companies where I now work as a recognised consultant. As a former employee of BEA Systems (acquired by Oracle), I developed a very early expertise on distributed systems. I am particularly fond of open source and I am a member of the OSSGTP[3] (*Open Source Solution Get Together Paris*). I love to create bonds with the community. So, I created the Paris Java User Group[4] in 2008 and co-created Devoxx France[5] in 2012 and Voxxed Microservices in 2018[6].

I wrote my first book on Java EE 5[7], in French, in 2007. I then joined the JCP[8] to become an Expert Member of various JSRs (Java EE 8, Java EE 7, Java EE 6, CDI 2.0, JPA 2.0, and EJB 3.1) and wrote *Beginning Java EE 6* and *Beginning Java EE 7* with Apress[9]. Still hooked on sharing my knowledge, I decided to then self-publish my later fascicles as well as on-line video courses.

For the last few years, I have given talks at international conferences, mainly on Java, distributed systems and microservices, including JavaOne, Devoxx, GeeCon, The Server Side Symposium, Jazoon, and many JUGs (*Java User Groups*). I also wrote numerous technical papers and articles for IT websites (DevX) and IT magazines (Java Magazine, Programmez, Linux Magazine). Since 2009, I have been part of the French Java podcast called *Les Cast Codeurs*[10].

In recognition of my expertise and all of my work for the Java community, I was elected **Java Champion**[11].

I am a graduate of the *Conservatoire National des Arts et Métiers*[12] (CNAM) in Paris (with an engineering degree in IT), *Brighton University*[13] (with an MSc in object-oriented design), *Universidad del Pais Vasco*[14] in Spain, and *UFSCar University*[15] in Brazil (MPhil in Distributed Systems). I also taught for more than 10 years at the Conservatoire National des Arts et Métiers where I previously studied.

Follow me on Twitter (@agoncal) and on my blog (www.antoniogoncalves.org).

[3] OSSGTP https://www.ossgtp.org

[4] Paris JUG https://www.parisjug.org

[5] Devoxx France https://devoxx.fr

[6] Voxxed Microservices https://voxxeddays.com/microservices

[7] Amazon https://www.amazon.com/author/agoncal

[8] JCP https://jcp.org

[9] Amazon https://www.amazon.com/author/agoncal

[10] **Les Cast Codeurs** https://lescastcodeurs.com

[11] **Java Champions** https://developer.oracle.com/javachampions

[12] **CNAM** https://www.cnam.eu/site-en

[13] **Brighton University** https://www.brighton.ac.uk

[14] **Universidad del Pais Vasco** https://www.ehu.eus/en/en-home

[15] **UFSCar** https://www.ufscar.br

Acknowledgments

In your hands, you have a technical fascicle that comes from my history of writing, learning and sharing. When writing, you need a dose of curiosity, a glimpse of discipline, an inch of concentration, and a huge amount of craziness. And of course, you need to be surrounded by people who help you in any possible way (so you don't get totally crazy). And this is the space to thank them.

First of all, it is a great honour to have **Clement Escoffier** writing the foreword of this book. Thank you for this difficult exercise that is writing foreword for a technical book.

Then, I really want to thank my proofreading team. I was constantly in contact with them during the writing process. They reviewed the book and gave me precious advice. I have to say, it was a real pleasure to work with such knowledgeable developers.

Clement Escoffier[16] is a software engineer at Red Hat. He has had several professional lives, from academic positions to management. Currently, he is mainly working as a Quarkus and Vert.x developer. He has been involved in projects and products touching many domains and technologies such as OSGi, mobile app development, continuous delivery, DevOps, etc. His main area of interest is software engineering, processes, methods and tools that make the development of software more efficient and also more fun. Clement is an active contributor to many open source projects such as Apache Felix, iPOJO, Wisdom Framework, Eclipse Vert.x, SmallRye, Eclipse MicroProfile and, of course, Quarkus.

Youness Teimouri[17] is currently a Senior Software Developer in Silicon Valley with over 15 years of development experience, particularly in Java, across various countries. He has utilised Java stack to help numerous companies scale in a variety of industries such as Telecoms, ERP systems, Mobile Banking, and Payment systems, etc. He has co-authored and contributed to some papers on Cloud-Computing and some of my previous books. Youness is fascinated by the endless possibilities of Java in different industries and enjoys mentoring junior developers, inspiring them to develop their own Java skill-set.

Mike François[18] is a senior solution architect specialising in Java technology oriented API, Edge and Cloud architecture. He started with Java from 2005 and was heavily involved in different communities as technical writer for Developpez.com and Dzone. After several years as a developer, he moved to various places to learn more about dev/ops, testing, methodologies and all kinds of architecture (enterprise, solution, api, technical, cloud, edge).

Thanks to my proofreader, **Gary Branigan**, who added a Shakespearean touch to this fascicle.

And thanks to Emmanuel Bernard and Clement Escoffier for working with me on the original Quarkus workshop[19] at which this fascicle had its genesis.

I could not have written this fascicle without the help and support of the Java community: blogs, articles, mailing lists, forums, tweets etc.

The fascicle you have in your hands uses a rich Asciidoctor[20] toolchain, making it possible to create PDF, EPUB and MOBI files. I am really grateful to the entire Asciidoctor community, and to Dan Allen[21] and Marat Radchenko in particular, who helped me in sorting out a few things so that the end result looks so great. PlantUML[22] is an amazing tool with a very rich syntax for drawing diagrams, etc. and sometimes, you need a bit of help. So, thanks to the PlantUML community. As for the text editor used to write this fascicle, you might have guessed: it's an IDE! Thank you JetBrains for providing me with a free licence for your excellent IntelliJ IDEA[23].

Living in Paris, I also have to thank all the bars who have given me shelter so that I could write while drinking coffee and talking to people: La Fontaine, Le Chat Bossu, La Grille, La Liberté and Bottle Shop.

As you might have guessed, I have a passion for IT. But I have other passions such as science, art, philosophy, cooking, Tango dancing and music (I even play jazz guitar). I cannot work without listening to music, so while I was writing this fascicle, I spent most of my time listing to the best radio ever: FIP[24]. Thank you FIP.

And a big kiss to my wonderful kids, **Eloise**, **Ligia** and **Ennio**. They are the best present life has given me.

Thank you all!

[16] **Clement Escoffier** https://twitter.com/clementplop

[17] **Youness Teimouri** http://www.youness-teimouri.com

[18] **Mike François** https://twitter.com/mike_francois

[19] **Quarkus Workshop** https://quarkus.io/quarkus-workshops/super-heroes

[20] **Asciidoctor** http://asciidoctor.org

[21] **Dan Allen** https://twitter.com/mojavelinux

[22] **PlantUML** http://plantuml.com

[23] **IntelliJ IDEA** https://www.jetbrains.com/idea

[24] **FIP** https://www.fip.fr

Introduction

In the late 90s, I was working on J2EE 1.2: the very first release of the *Java Enterprise Edition*. It was also the time where companies started to realise the potential of the Internet for their business. For a few months, I worked for a famous English airline company setting up their e-commerce website. Yes, it was a time where you would usually buy a flight or train ticket at a travel agency. This revolutionary move (buying flights online) came at a technical cost: a cluster for static content (HTML, CSS, images), a cluster for the web tier (Servlets and JSPs), a cluster for Stateless EJBs, a cluster for Entity Beans, and a cluster for the database. And as you can imagine, load balancing, failover and sticky sessions for every tier were loaded with application servers. This e-commerce website went live... and it worked!

Then came Struts, Spring and Hibernate. Full J2EE application servers shrank down to servlet containers such as Tomcat or Jetty. We could see things moving, such as architectures becoming stateless, failover being abandoned, migrations from SOAP to REST and mobile devices taking over web crawling. Then came the *Internet of Things* (IoT), the cloud, microservices, *Function as a Service* (FaaS), and it never stops moving. Other things didn't change, like the good old *Gang of Four* design patterns, architecture design patterns, unit testing frameworks and building tools. We reinvented some wheels and gave them different names, but we also learnt dozens of new promising programming languages (running on top of the JVM or not) and agile techniques. Thanks to these evolutions that I have witnessed, today you can sit down, read this fascicle and write some code.

Where Does This Fascicle Come From?

Involved in J2EE since 1998, I followed its evolution and joined the Java EE expert group from version 6 to version 8. During that time, I wrote a book in French called "*Java EE 5*"[25]. The book was published by a French editor and got noticed. I was then contacted by Apress, an American editor, to work on an English version. I liked the challenge. So, I changed the structure of the book, updated it, translated it, and I ended up with a "*Beginning Java EE 6*" book. A few years later, Java EE 7 was released, so I updated my book, added a few extra chapters, and ended up with a "*Beginning Java EE 7*"[26] that was 500 pages long. This process of writing got a bit painful (some text editors shouldn't be used to write books), inflexible (it's hard to update a paper book frequently) and I also had some arguments with my editor[27].

Parallel to that, the history of Java EE 8 was also somewhat painful and long[28]. I was still part of the Expert Group, but nobody really knew why the experts' mailing list was so quiet. No real exchange, no real vision, no real challenges. That's when I decided not to work on a Java EE 8 book. But the community said otherwise. I started receiving emails about updating my book. I used to always meet someone at a conference going "*Hey, Antonio, when is your next book coming out?*" My answer was "*No way!*"

I decided to take stock. What was holding me back from writing? Clearly it was my editor and Java EE 8. So, I decided to get rid of both. I extracted the chapters I wanted from my Java EE 7 book and updated them. That's where the idea of writing "*fascicles*", instead of an entire book, came from. Then, I looked at self-publishing, and here I am on my own publishing platform[29] as well as on Amazon Kindle Publishing[30].

After self-publishing a few fascicles, I saw that Red Hat was working on a game changer: Quarkus. I started to look at it at a very early stage, and got the idea of creating a workshop. I contacted the Quarkus team to submit my idea: Emmanuel Bernard and Clement Escoffier liked it, and we put together a workshop[31] and gave it at a few conferences. This workshop inspired me to write this fascicle. I did with the Quarkus team and is thus structured in a different way and easier to read.

I hope you'll find this fascicle useful.

Who Is This Fascicle For?

Quarkus has its genesis in the JBoss community. JBoss has extensive experience of running applications on application servers (JBoss EAP, WildFly) and building reactive applications on the JVM (with Eclipse Vert.x for example). Due to its extension mechanism, Quarkus supports several Java frameworks (e.g. Hibernate, Camel, etc.) as well as specifications (e.g. a subset of Jakarta EE, or MicroProfile which is a set of specifications to develop microservices in Java).

So, this fascicle is for the Java community as a whole and for those of you interested in microservice architectures. The only requirements to follow and understand this fascicle are having a knowledge of Java and having some knowledge of relational databases and Docker.

How Is This Fascicle Structured?

This fascicle uses Quarkus 2.5.0.Final. Its structure will help you to discover this technology as well as helping you to further dive into it if you already have some experience of it.

This fascicle starts with Chapter 1, *First Look at Quarkus* by showing a few lines of Quarkus code. That's because, as developers, we like to read code first when learning a new technology.

Chapter 2, *Understanding Quarkus* briefly presents Quarkus, the problems it addresses and explains the common concerns discussed throughout the fascicle. This chapter also looks at the standardisation side of MicroProfile and where it comes from.

Chapter 3, *Getting Started* is all about getting your environment ready so you can develop the entire microservice architecture.

In Chapter 4, *Developing the REST Number Microservice* you will develop a first microservice named Number which is just a REST endpoint that generates ISBN book numbers and exposes OpenAPI documentation on Quarkus.

In Chapter 5, *Developing the REST Book Microservice* you will develop a second microservice. The *Book* microservice allows transactional create/read/update/delete operations on a PostgreSQL relational database.

Chapter 6, *Installing the Vintage Store User Interface* is about packaging and installing an already-developed Angular application in Quarkus. This user interface allows us to interact graphically with the microservices.

In Chapter 7, *Adding Communication and Fault Tolerance* you will make all of the components communicate with each other. Communication in a distributed environment can be challenging as you need to deal with network failure and latency. That's when fault-tolerance comes into play.

The more microservices you have in an architecture, the harder it is to monitor them. In Chapter 8, *Monitoring the Microservices* you will develop health checks to both microservices so you know they are up and running. You'll also add metrics and visualise them with Prometheus so you can visualise the throughput of each microservice.

Chapter 9, *Deploying the Application* is used to create native executables for each microservice. You will package these executables with Docker so they can be portable across servers.

Chapter 10, *Summary* wraps up with a summary of what you've learnt in this fascicle.

Appendix A, *Setting up the Development Environment on macOS* highlights the tools used throughout the fascicle and how to install them.

Appendix B, *Quarkus Versions* lists all the Quarkus releases.

Appendix C, *Eclipse MicroProfile Specification Versions* lists all the revisions of the MicroProfile specification.

Appendix D points to some external references which are worth reading if you want to know more about Quarkus.

Thanks to self-publication and electronic format, I can update this fascicle regularly when typos or bugs are discovered. Appendix E, *Revisions of the Fascicle* gives you the revision notes of each version of this fascicle.

This is not the only fascicle I have written. You'll find a description of the other fascicles I wrote and online courses I created in Appendix F:

- *Understanding Bean Validation 2.0*
- *Understanding JPA 2.2*
- *Understanding Quarkus 2.x*
- *Practising Quarkus 2.x*

Conventions

This fascicle uses a diverse range of languages, mostly Java, but also JSON, XML, YAML or shell scripts. Each code example is displayed appropriately and appears in `fixed-width font`. All the included code comes from a public Git repository and is continuously tested. Therefore, you shouldn't have any problem with code that is not syntactically correct. In some cases, the original source code has been specially formatted to fit within the available page space, with additional line breaks or modified indentation. To increase readability, some examples omit code where it is seen as unnecessary. But always remember that you can find the entire code online at https://github.com/agoncal/agoncal-fascicle-quarkus-pract/tree/2.0.

Italics are used to *highlight an important word for the first time,* or to give the definition of an abbreviation or *acronym*. Bold is **rarely used**.

 Some useful information.

Something you really should do if you want the code to work properly.

 Warns you of a possible technical problem.

🖵 Call to Action

This is an incremental number to help you reference a Call to Action **(1)**

You need to do something

The Sample Application

Throughout the book, you will see snippets of code all belonging to the Vintage Store application. I created this application for my very first book a long time ago, and I still use it as an example. This application is an e-commerce website allowing users to browse a catalogue of vintage stuff (vinyl, tapes, books and CDs). Using a shopping cart, they can add or remove items as they browse the catalogue and then check out so that they can pay and obtain a purchase order. The application has external interactions with a bank system to validate credit card numbers.

The actors interacting with the system are:

- *Employees* of the company who need to manage both the catalogue of items and the customers' details. They can also browse the purchase orders.

- *Users* who are anonymous persons visiting the website and who are consulting the catalogue of books and CDs. If they want to buy an item, they need to create an account to become customers.

- *Customers* who can login to the system, browse the catalogue, update their account details, and buy items online.

- The external *Bank* to which the system delegates credit card validations.

Figure 1 depicts the use case diagram which describes the system's actors and functionalities.

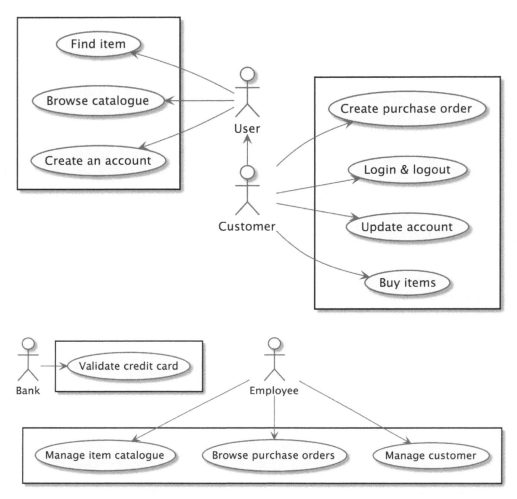

Figure 1. Use case diagram of the Vintage Store application

The Vintage Store application manipulates a few domain objects that are described in Figure 2. Vinyl, tapes, books and CDs, of course, but also chapters, authors, purchase orders, invoices and shopping carts. Don't spend too much time on this diagram for now as you will come across most of these objects throughout this fascicle.

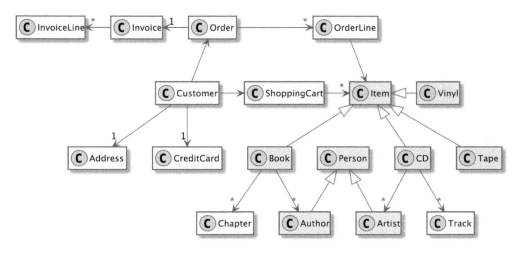

Figure 2. Class diagram of the Vintage Store application

 The code you'll see in this fascicle gets its inspiration from the Vintage Store application, but it's not the original application per-se. You can download the code of the original application if you want, but it's not necessary in order to follow the code[32] of this fascicle.

Downloading and Running the Code

The source code of the examples in the fascicle is available from a public Git repository and can be cloned, downloaded or browsed online at https://github.com/agoncal/agoncal-fascicle-quarkus-pract/tree/2.0. The code has been developed and tested on the macOS platform but should also work on Windows or Linux. The examples used in this fascicle are designed to be compiled with Java 11, to be built with Maven 3.8.3 and to be tested with JUnit 5.x and to store data in a relational database (H2 and PostgreSQL). GraalVM 21.3.0 is used to build native images. Appendix A shows you how to install all of these software packages which will be used in most of the chapters to build, run and test the code.

Getting Help

Having trouble with the code, the content or the structure of the fascicle? Didn't understand something? Not clear enough? I am here to help! Do not hesitate to report issues or any questions at https://github.com/agoncal/agoncal-fascicle-quarkus-pract/issues. I'll do my best to answer them. This will also allow me to improve the content of this fascicle, and upload a new version through Amazon Kindle Publishing.

Contacting the Author

If you have any questions about the content of this fascicle, please use the instructions above and use the GitHub issue tracker. But if you feel like contacting me, drop me an email at agoncal.fascicle@gmail.com or a tweet at @agoncal. You can also visit my blog at:

- www.antoniogoncalves.org

- agoncal.teachable.com

[25] **Antonio's books** http://amazon.com/author/agoncal

[26] **Antonio's Books** https://antoniogoncalves.org/category/books

[27] **The Uncensored Java EE 7 Book** https://antoniogoncalves.org/2014/09/16/the-uncensored-java-ee-7-book

[28] **Opening Up Java EE** https://blogs.oracle.com/theaquarium/post/opening-up-java-ee-an-update

[29] **Antonio Goncalves** https://antoniogoncalves.org

[30] **Amazon Kindle Publishing** https://kdp.amazon.com

[31] **Quarkus workshop** https://quarkus.io/quarkus-workshops/super-heroes

[32] **Code of the Vintage Store application** https://github.com/agoncal/agoncal-application-cdbookstore

Chapter 1. First Look at Quarkus

If you are reading this fascicle, it's because you are a developer. And like most developers, when you learn a new technology or framework, you like to see some code first. So here is the very first step with Quarkus.

Listing 1 shows a Java class representing an Author REST resource. This resource "*listens*" to HTTP requests on the /authors URL and has two methods: one returning the entire list of sci-fi authors, and another one returning a single author giving the index of the array.

Listing 1. Java Class with JAX-RS Annotations

```java
@Path("/authors")
@Produces(MediaType.TEXT_PLAIN)
public class AuthorResource {

  String[] scifiAuthors = {"Isaac Asimov", "Nora Jemisin", "Douglas Adams"};

  @GET
  public String getAllScifiAuthors() {
    return String.join(", ", scifiAuthors);
  }

  @GET
  @Path("/{index}")
  public String getScifiAuthor(@PathParam("index") int index) {
    return scifiAuthors[index];
  }
}
```

If you look carefully at Listing 1, you can see a few JAX-RS annotations (@Path, @Produces, @GET, and @PathParam) but no specific Quarkus code. So where is Quarkus?

Actually, you can find a little bit of Quarkus in Listing 2 (because most of the code is from REST Assured). Here, we use the @QuarkusTest annotation to let Quarkus test the *Author* REST resource. We target the URL /authors with an HTTP GET method (with and without an index parameter), and we make sure the HTTP status code is 200-OK and that the content of the HTTP body is correct.

Listing 2. Test Class with a Quarkus Annotation

```java
@QuarkusTest
public class AuthorResourceTest {

  @Test
  public void shouldGetAllAuthors() {
    given()
      .header(ACCEPT, TEXT_PLAIN).
    when()
      .get("/authors").
    then()
      .assertThat()
        .statusCode(is(200))
      .and()
      .body(is("Isaac Asimov, Nora Jemisin, Douglas Adams"));
  }

  @Test
  public void shouldGetAnAuthor() {
    given()
      .header(ACCEPT, TEXT_PLAIN)
      .pathParam("index", 0).
    when()
      .get("/authors/{index}").
    then()
      .assertThat()
        .statusCode(is(200))
      .and()
      .body(is("Isaac Asimov"));
  }
}
```

You didn't understand all the code? You did understand it but you feel there is more to it than that? The fascicle you have in your hands is all about Quarkus. Thanks to the chapters that follow, you will understand the basics of this technology and will have plenty of examples so that you can dive into more complex topics.

Chapter 2. Understanding Quarkus

In the previous *First Step with Quarkus* chapter, you've already seen some code. But before going further into more code, we need to step back and define some concepts. This *Understanding* chapter gives you some terminology that will be used in the rest of the fascicle so you don't get lost.

2.1. Understanding Quarkus

Quarkus[33] is *A Kubernetes Native Java stack tailored for OpenJDK HotSpot & GraalVM, crafted from the best of breed Java libraries and standards.* In practice, Quarkus is an Open Source stack for writing Java applications, specifically back end applications. So Quarkus is not limited to microservices, even though it is highly suited for it.

Java was born in 1995 and, at the time, was mostly used to write GUI applications and Applets. The language was based on the available hardware using single cores and multi-threads. Quickly, the language moved to the servers, and we started developing monolithic applications, designed to run on huge machines 24/7 for months (even years), with lots of CPU and memory. The JVM startup time was not an issue, the memory used by the JVM was huge, but we just let the JIT optimise the execution over time and left the GC manage the memory efficiently. Slow startup time and resource consumption don't fit well in our new environment where we need to deploy hundreds of microservices into the cloud, move them around and stop and start them quickly. Instead of scaling an application by adding more CPU and memory, we now scale microservices dynamically by adding more instances. That's where Quarkus, GraalVM, Kubernetes and other projects come into play.

Quarkus tailors applications for HotSpot and GraalVM. The result is that your application will have amazingly fast boot time and incredibly low RSS memory (*Resident Set Size*[34]) offering high density memory utilisation in container orchestration platforms like Kubernetes.

From a developer's point of view, Quarkus proposes a nice developer experience: it gives you fast live reload, unified configuration and hides the complexity of GraalVM, allowing you to easily generate native executables. All this without reinventing the wheel by proposing a new programming model, Quarkus leverages your experience in standard libraries that you already know (e.g. CDI, JPA, Bean Validation, JAX-RS, etc.) as well as many popular frameworks (e.g. Eclipse Vert.x, Apache Camel, etc.).

 If you like the format of this fascicle and are interested in Quarkus, check out the references for my *Understanding Quarkus 2.x* fascicle in Appendix F. In this *Understanding* fascicle, you will learn about Quarkus' architecture, Microservices, MicroProfile GraalVM, Reactive Systems and much more.

2.2. Understanding MicroProfile

Having an extension mechanism, Quarkus implements many features and integrates with many external frameworks. But being microservices-oriented, Quarkus implements the entire set of specifications of MicroProfile.

Eclipse MicroProfile[35] addresses the need for enterprise Java microservices. It is a set of specifications for handling microservices design patterns. MicroProfile enables Jakarta EE developers to leverage their existing skill set while shifting their focus from traditional monolithic applications to microservices. MicroProfile APIs establish an optimal foundation for developing microservices-based applications by adopting a subset of the Jakarta EE standards and extending them to address common microservices patterns. *Eclipse MicroProfile* is specified under the *Eclipse Foundation* and is implemented by *SmallRye*.

Compliant implementations of Eclipse MicroProfile 4.1 must provide at least the following APIs:

- *Context and Dependency Injection* (CDI) is a standard dependency injection framework included in Java EE and MicroProfile.

- *Java API for RESTful Web Services* (JAX-RS) is a standard Java API that provides support for creating web services according to the *Representational State Transfer* (REST) architectural style.

- *JSON Binding* (JSON-B) is a standard binding layer for converting Java objects to/from JSON documents.

- *JSON Processing* (JSON-P) is a Java API to process (parse, generate, transform and query) JSON messages.

- *Common Annotations* is a set of annotations for common semantic concepts in the Java SE, Java EE and MicroProfile platforms.

- *Configuration* injects configuration property values directly into an application that comes from different sources.

- *Fault Tolerance* provides a simple and flexible solution to build fault tolerant microservices (e.g. timeouts, retries, fallbacks, etc.), which is easy to use and configurable.

- *Health* allows applications to provide information about their state to external viewers.

- *JWT* provides *Role-Based Access Control* (RBAC) using OpenID Connect (OIDC) and JSON Web Tokens (JWT).

- *Metrics* provides a unified way for servers to export monitoring data to management agents.

- *OpenAPI* provides a unified Java API for the OpenAPI v3 specification to expose API documentation.

- *OpenTracing* defines an API that allows services to easily participate in a distributed tracing environment.

- *REST Client* provides a type safe approach using proxies and annotations for invoking RESTful services over HTTP.

MicroProfile 4.1 specifications are described in Table 1. You'll find specifications that come from Jakarta EE (e.g. CDI, JAX-RS, etc.) as well as brand new specifications that were created with microservices in mind.

Table 1. MicroProfile 4.1 Specifications

Specification	Version	URL
Context and Dependency Injection (CDI)	2.0	https://jcp.org/en/jsr/detail?id=365

Specification	Version	URL
Java API for RESTful Web Services (JAX-RS)	2.1	https://jcp.org/en/jsr/detail?id=370
JSON Binding (JSON-B)	1.0	https://jcp.org/en/jsr/detail?id=367
JSON Processing (JSON-P)	1.1	https://jcp.org/en/jsr/detail?id=374
Common Annotations	1.3	https://jcp.org/en/jsr/detail?id=250
Configuration	2.0	https://microprofile.io/project/eclipse/microprofile-config
Fault Tolerance	3.0	https://microprofile.io/project/eclipse/microprofile-fault-tolerance
Health	3.1	https://microprofile.io/project/eclipse/microprofile-health
JSON Web Token (JWT)	1.2	https://microprofile.io/project/eclipse/microprofile-jwt-auth
Metrics	3.0	https://microprofile.io/project/eclipse/microprofile-metrics
OpenAPI	2.0	https://microprofile.io/project/eclipse/microprofile-open-api
OpenTracing	2.0	https://microprofile.io/project/eclipse/microprofile-opentracing
REST Client	2.0	https://microprofile.io/project/eclipse/microprofile-rest-client

SmallRye[36] is an open source project that implements the Eclipse MicroProfile specifications. It is community-driven and everyone is welcome to contribute to it. SmallRye implementations are tested against the Eclipse MicroProfile TCKs (*Technology Compatibility Kits*). Several open source projects integrate SmallRye such as Thorntail, WildFly, WebSphere Liberty and Quarkus.

2.3. Summary

This *Understanding* chapter gave you most of the required terminology around Quarkus. There is less code in this chapter than in the following ones, but we needed to make sure you understand all the concepts around Quarkus before going any further.

Quarkus is an Open Source stack for writing Java applications, specifically microservices, that's why it implements MicroProfile, etc. but also much more. That's what you are about to discover in the following chapters.

[33] **Quarkus** https://quarkus.io
[34] **RSS memory** https://en.wikipedia.org/wiki/Resident_set_size
[35] **MicroProfile** https://microprofile.io
[36] **SmallRye** https://github.com/smallrye

Chapter 3. Getting Started

This fascicle offers an intro-level, hands-on experience with Quarkus, from the first line of code to making microservices, consuming them, and finally to assembling everything in a consistent system. It should give you a practical introduction to Quarkus. But if you feel that you first need some theory on Quarkus, please check out the references for my *Understanding Quarkus 2.x* fascicle in Appendix F.

In this fascicle, you will first install all the required tools to then develop an entire microservice architecture, mixing HTTP microservices with transactions, database access and monitoring. What you will learn with this fascicle is:

- What Quarkus is and how you can use it,
- How to build an HTTP endpoint (REST API) with Quarkus,
- How to access a relational database in a transactional way with JTA and Hibernate ORM with Panache,
- How you can use Swagger UI and OpenAPI to provide a clearer picture of your microservice,
- How to test your microservices,
- How you can improve the resilience of your services,
- How to monitor the health of the entire systems and check some metrics,
- How to build native executables,
- How to package your microservices into Docker images and execute them.

This fascicle is as self-explanatory as possible. So your job is to follow the instructions by yourself, do what you are supposed to do (following the 🖳 **Call to Action** sections), and do not hesitate to ask for any clarification or assistance at https://github.com/agoncal/agoncal-fascicle-quarkus-pract/ issues.

3.1. What Will You Build in This Fascicle?

In this fascicle, you will develop an application that allows CRUD (*Create/Read/Update/Delete*) operations on books. Reading a fascicle about microservices, you will be developing several microservices communicating synchronously via REST. You will get an Angular application with the downloaded code so you can visually interact with the microservices.

3.1.1. Overall Architecture

The Vintage Store application is made up of several microservices and a user interface, all monitored by Prometheus:

- Vintage Store UI: the Angular application allowing you to visually pick up a random book, create/read/delete a book and generate ISBN numbers,
- *Number* REST API: Simple HTTP microservice generating ISBN numbers,
- *Book* REST API: Allows CRUD operations on Books which are stored in a PostgreSQL database,

• Load Vintage Store: Generates load on the Vintage Store application.

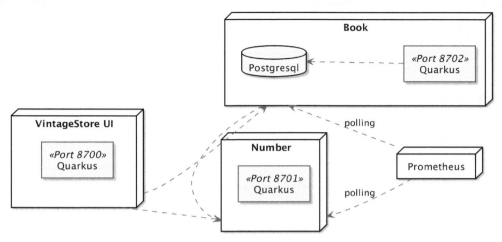

Figure 3. Overall architecture

3.1.2. User Interface

The main page of the Angular application in Figure 4 displays a random book which comes from the *Book* microservice.

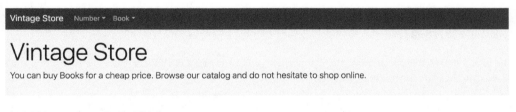

Figure 4. Main page displaying a random book

By clicking on the **Book** menu you'll get access to a list of all the books (see Figure 5) which has several buttons to allow CRUD operations on a specific book.

Vintage Store

You can buy Books for a cheap price. Browse our catalog and do not hesitate to shop online.

Books

+Create new Book

ID	Isbn	Title	Author		
997	9781980399025	Understanding Bean Validation	Antonio Goncalves	⊙View	✕Delete
998	9781093918977	Understanding JPA	Antonio Goncalves	⊙View	✕Delete
1001	1931182310	Advanced Java EE Development for Rational Applicat	Roger Kitain	⊙View	✕Delete
1002	1931182311	Advanced Java EE Development for Rational Applicat	Kinman Chung	⊙View	✕Delete
1003	1931182312	Advanced Java EE Development for Rational Applicat	Lincoln Baxter	⊙View	✕Delete
1004	1514210959	Advanced Java EE Development with WildFly	Antoine Sabot-Durand	⊙View	✕Delete
1005	8894038912	Advanced Jax-Ws Web Services	Antonio Goncalves	⊙View	✕Delete
1006	0071763929	Mike Meyers' Guide to Supporting Windows 7 for Com	Lincoln Baxter	⊙View	✕Delete
1007	1849512442	Apache Maven 3 Cookbook (Quick Answers to Common P	Adam Bien	⊙View	✕Delete
1008	2746062399	Apache Tomcat 7 - Guide d'administration du serveu	Antonio Goncalves	⊙View	✕Delete

Figure 5. List of books

Figure 6 shows the component that generates book numbers (ISBNs, ASIN and EAN numbers) by invoking the *Number* microservice.

Vintage Store

You can buy Books for a cheap price. Browse our catalog and do not hesitate to shop online.

Book Numbers

⟳Generate

Asin	B000A143NO
EAN 8	12577842
EAN 13	8245028822117
ISBN 10	1-08-219071-3
ISBN 13	978-1-9760933-6-4

Figure 6. Generating book numbers

3.2. Setting up the Development Environment on macOS

In this section, you will check that all the required tools are installed by executing a set of commands. You will also download some code so you can start developing with some guidelines.

3.2.1. Installing the Required Tools

First of all, make sure you have a 64-bit computer with admin rights (so you can install all the required tools) and at least 16Gb of RAM (as some tools need some resources such as compiling to native executables). This fascicle makes use of the following software, tools and frameworks. You should install and know (more or less) how they work:

- Any IDE you feel comfortable with (e.g. IntelliJ IDEA, Eclipse IDE, VS Code, etc.),
- JDK 11.0.13,
- GraalVM 21.3.0,
- Maven 3.8.3,
- Docker,
- cURL (or any other command line HTTP client),
- NodeJS (optional, can be installed with Maven),
- Git (optional, helps you to commit and rollback your code if needed).

 Make sure your development environment is set up to execute the code in this chapter. You can go to Appendix A to check that you have all the required tools installed, in particular JDK 11.0.13, GraalVM 21.3.0 and Maven 3.8.3.

💻 Call to Action

(1)

To make sure your environment is setup, the following commands should work on your machine:

```
$ java -version
$ $GRAALVM_HOME/bin/native-image --version
$ mvn -version
$ curl --version
$ docker version
$ git --version
```

3.2.2. Checking Listening Ports

Each microservice listens to a port, as well as the containers of the infrastructure. You need to make sure the ports used by out application are free so you don't run into any conflicts later.

🖥 Call to Action

(2)

On macOS you can use `lsof` command to check if a process is listening on a specific port:

```
$ lsof -i tcp:5005    // Quarkus debug port
$ lsof -i tcp:8080    // Quarkus default port
$ lsof -i tcp:8081    // Quarkus default test port
$ lsof -i tcp:8700    // UI
$ lsof -i tcp:8701    // Book REST API
$ lsof -i tcp:8702    // Number REST API
$ lsof -i tcp:5432    // PostgreSQL
$ lsof -i tcp:9090    // Prometheus
```

3.3. Installing the Startup Code

You will have to develop most of the code but some pieces (like the user interface or the parent `pom.xml` file for example) are given to you in a zip file.

🖥 Call to Action

(3)

Download the zip file https://raw.githubusercontent.com/agoncal/agoncal-fascicle-quarkus-pract/2.0/dist/agoncal-fascicle-quarkus-practising-2.0.zip, and unzip it wherever you want on your machine. Open the project with your favourite IDE.

3.3.1. Directory Structure

Once you've downloaded the zip file and unzip it, you should see the following directories:

```
.
├── first-step        The code from Chapter 1
├── infrastructure    All the required infrastructure (PostgreSQL, Prometheus)
├── load-vintagestore Stress tool loading books
└── ui-vintagestore   Angular application
```

As you can see, the code of the microservices is not in the zip file, you will have to develop it entirely. Most of these subdirectories are Maven projects and follow the default Maven directory structure:

```
first-step/
├── src
│   ├── main
│   │   ├── java
│   │   └── resources
│   └── test
│       └── java
└── pom.xml
```

You will have to create the rest-book and rest-number directories that will follow the same Maven structure. The infrastructure directory contains all the Docker images' source files that you need. You won't have to change it. Same for the stress tool (under load-vintagestore) and the Angular user interface (directory ui-vintagestore) that you will just have to package and install.

3.3.2. Root Maven POM

At the root you will find a pom.xml file. The pom.xml is the fundamental unit of work in Maven and will be used to build our project. This root pom.xml just declares the modules of our project, nothing more (see Listing 3). I am using Maven parent POM to ease the development of the Vintage Store application. Bear in mind that microservices are intended to be developed separately, therefore it is good practice not to have POM inheritance. First, shows the header of the pom.xml with just the groupId and artifactId.

Listing 3. Root Maven pom.xml

```xml
<project xmlns="http://maven.apache.org/POM/4.0.0" xmlns:xsi=
"http://www.w3.org/2001/XMLSchema-instance"
         xsi:schemaLocation="http://maven.apache.org/POM/4.0.0
http://maven.apache.org/xsd/maven-4.0.0.xsd">
  <modelVersion>4.0.0</modelVersion>

  <groupId>org.agoncal.fascicle</groupId>
  <artifactId>quarkus-practising</artifactId>
  <version>2.0.0-SNAPSHOT</version>
  <packaging>pom</packaging>
  <name>Practising Quarkus</name>

  <modules>
    <module>first-step</module>
    <module>infrastructure</module>
    <module>load-vintagestore</module>
    <module>ui-vintagestore</module>
  </modules>

</project>
```

Listing 3 lists all the Maven modules in the project. This indicates that under each sub-directory you will find a child pom.xml.

3.4. Warming up Local Caches

Now that you have the initial structure in place, let's warm up the local caches of your machine so we are sure you are ready to go. Be aware that Maven, Docker and npm download plugins, project dependencies, images, etc. that take network bandwidth and a few Gigabits of local storage on your machine.

3.4.1. Warming up Maven

Our microservice application uses Maven extensively. Each microservice uses several Maven dependencies and plugins, all stored in a local Maven repository that needs to be warmed up.

🖳 Call to Action

(4)

Navigate to the root directory where you've unzipped the startup code, and run:

```
$ mvn install
```

By running this command, Maven downloads all the required dependencies and builds the initial code. You should have the following output:

```
[INFO] ------------------------------------------------------------
[INFO] Reactor Summary for Practising Quarkus 2.0.0-SNAPSHOT:
[INFO]
[INFO] Practising Quarkus ............................... SUCCESS
[INFO] Practising Quarkus :: First Step ................. SUCCESS
[INFO] Practising Quarkus :: Infrastructure ............. SUCCESS
[INFO] Practising Quarkus :: Load VintageStore .......... SUCCESS
[INFO] Practising Quarkus :: UI VintageStore ............ SUCCESS
[INFO] ------------------------------------------------------------
[INFO] BUILD SUCCESS
[INFO] ------------------------------------------------------------
```

Notice the BUILD SUCCESS end result. If your build is not successful, please look for a similar problem at https://github.com/agoncal/agoncal-fascicle-quarkus-pract/issues and create a new issue if you can't find any.

🖳 Call to Action

(5)

To add some load, we will use the code inside the load-vintagestore directory. Start the *Load* application using the following commands:

```
load-vintagestore$ ./mvnw compile
load-vintagestore$ ./mvnw exec:java
```

Stop it by hitting `Ctrl` + `C` to kill the process.

We will bootstrap our microservices with the Quarkus Maven plugin. So we have to make sur the generation works.

🖳 Call to Action

(6)

Bootstrap a *Dummy* Quarkus application by using the Quarkus Maven plugin and executing the following commands:

```
$ mkdir dummy
$ cd dummy
mvn io.quarkus:quarkus-maven-plugin:2.5.0.Final:create \
    -DplatformVersion=2.5.0.Final \
    -DprojectGroupId=org.agoncal.fascicle.quarkus-practising \
    -DprojectArtifactId=dummy
$ cd ..
$ rm -rf dummy/
```

Once again, make sure to follow the maven installation notes in Appendix A before going any further, in case there is an error.

3.4.2. Warming up Docker

Any microservice system is going to rely on a set of technical services. For the Vintage Store application, we are going to use:

- A PostgreSQL database for the REST *Book* microservice,
- Prometheus to monitor all the components of the application.

We will use Docker to start all these services, so you don't have to worry about installing or setting them up. For that, navigate to the infrastructure sub-directory. Here, you will find a postgresql.yaml file (see Listing 4) which defines the PostgreSQL Docker container.

Listing 4. Docker Compose File Defining a PostgreSQL Container

```
services:
  database:
    image: "postgres:14.1"
    container_name: "vintage_store_books_database"
    ports:
      - "5432:5432"
    environment:
      - POSTGRES_DB=books_database
      - POSTGRES_USER=book
      - POSTGRES_PASSWORD=book
```

Listing 5 shows a Docker compose file for Prometheus. Don't worry for now if you don't understand it all, all this will be explained later.

Listing 5. Docker Compose File Defining a Prometheus Container

```
services:
  monitoring:
    image: "prom/prometheus:v2.31.1"
    container_name: "vintage_store_monitoring"
    ports:
      - 9090:9090
    volumes:
      - ./monitoring/prometheus.yml:/etc/prometheus/prometheus.yml
```

🖥 Call to Action

(7)

To run the entire infrastructure, make sure Docker is up and running (docker version), and navigate to the infrastructure directory to execute the following Docker command:

```
infrastructure$ docker compose -f postgresql.yaml up -d
infrastructure$ docker compose -f prometheus.yaml up -d
```

This will download all the Docker images and start the containers. Then, run the docker container ls command. You should see all the running containers. The output should look like this:

```
$ docker container ls
CONTAINER ID    IMAGE                   PORTS                     NAMES
94fe93e795be    postgres:14.1           0.0.0.0:5432->5432/tcp
vintage_store_books_data
bb051ab4dd57    prom/prometheus:v2.31.1 0.0.0.0:9090->9090/tcp
vintage_store_monitoring
```

Once all the containers are up and running, shut them down with the following command:

```
infrastructure$ docker compose -f postgresql.yaml down
infrastructure$ docker compose -f prometheus.yaml down
```

Again, if you can't start your infrastructure, check out https://github.com/agoncal/agoncal-fascicle-quarkus-pract/issues for help.

3.5. Summary

In this chapter, you've downloaded a zip file with all the quick start code to build and run the Vintage Store application, made of several microservices. There is no need to install Quarkus per-se. It is just a Maven dependency that will ultimately execute our code. Thanks to Docker, installing a database such as PostgreSQL or a monitoring tool such as Prometheus is as easy as writing a few YAML lines.

In the coming chapters, you will have to fill in the gaps: developing the entire code of our microservice, making the microservices talk to each other in a reliable way, installing an Angular application, configuring, monitoring and building native executables.

🖥 Call to Action

(8)

If you want, you can use Git to commit your code at each chapter so you can come back to a previous version of the code if needed. Now that you have your environment set up and that the code is installed, create a local Git repository and commit what you've done so far:

```
$ git init
$ git add .
$ git commit -m "getting started"
```

If in the next chapter, for some reason, you want to reset all your changes and come back to this commit, you can use the following commands:

```
$ git reset --hard
$ git clean -f -d
```

Chapter 4. Developing the REST Number Microservice

At the heart of the Vintage Store application comes ISBN numbers. We need to expose a REST API that generates ISBN numbers so that, when we create a new book, we can have ISBN numbers. For that, we will create a *Number* microservice. It uses HTTP to expose a REST API and will then be used by another microservice named *Book*. The *Number* microservice generates all sorts of numbers: ISBN (*International Standard Book Number*), ASIN (*Amazon Standard Identification Number*) and EAN (*European Article Number*). In this chapter, you will create a JAX-RS endpoint running inside Quarkus. Nothing outstanding but a good first step to discovering Quarkus.

4.1. What Will You Build in This Chapter?

In this chapter, you will:

- Bootstrap a new Quarkus application using its Maven plugin,
- Implement a REST API using JAX-RS,
- Inject external configuration,
- Customise the JSON Output with JSON-B,
- Enable OpenAPI and Swagger UI on the *Number* endpoint,
- Display a banner when Quarkus starts up,
- Configure Quarkus logging and HTTP port listening.

4.1.1. Overall Architecture

Figure 7 shows the architecture of what you will be building in this chapter. The *Number* REST API runs on Quarkus, on port 8701, and exposes an OpenAPI contract.

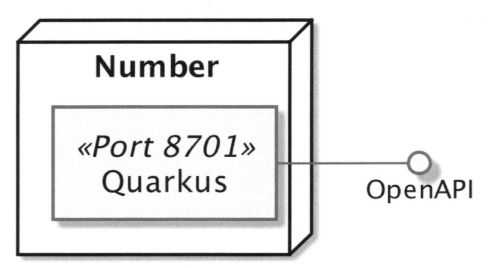

Figure 7. Overall architecture

4.2. Bootstrapping the REST Number Microservice

Let's first bootstrap a new Quarkus application to host the code of our *Number* microservice For that we use the Quarkus plugin[37] which is based on the following Maven coordinates: `io.quarkus:quarkus-maven-plugin`. It has several available goals, but we will use the `create` goal for now.

⌨ Call to Action

(9)

Bootstrap the *Number* microservice by using the Quarkus plugin and executing the following Maven command from the root directory:

```
mvn -U io.quarkus:quarkus-maven-plugin:2.5.0.Final:create \
    -DplatformVersion=2.5.0.Final \
    -DprojectGroupId=org.agoncal.fascicle.quarkus-practising \
    -DprojectArtifactId=rest-number \
    -DprojectVersion=2.0.0-SNAPSHOT \
    -DclassName="org.agoncal.fascicle.quarkus.number.NumberResource" \
    -Dpath="/api/numbers" \
    -Dextensions="resteasy, resteasy-jsonb, smallrye-openapi"
```

Once the `rest-number` module created, you should see it declared in the Parent Maven POM with the other modules:

```
<modules>
    <module>first-step</module>
    <module>infrastructure</module>
    <module>load-vintagestore</module>
    <module>rest-number</module>
    <module>ui-vintagestore</module>
</modules>
```

4.2.1. Directory Structure

The Quarkus plugin command generates a new Maven module called `rest-number` with a REST endpoint called `NumberResource` located at the `/api/numbers` path. Below the directory structure with all the generated artifacts:

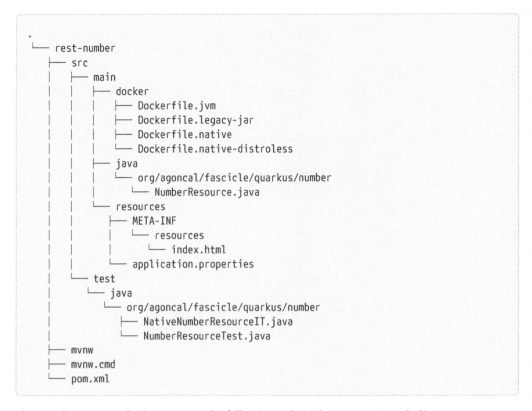

```
.
└── rest-number
    ├── src
    │   ├── main
    │   │   ├── docker
    │   │   │   ├── Dockerfile.jvm
    │   │   │   ├── Dockerfile.legacy-jar
    │   │   │   ├── Dockerfile.native
    │   │   │   └── Dockerfile.native-distroless
    │   │   ├── java
    │   │   │   └── org/agoncal/fascicle/quarkus/number
    │   │   │       └── NumberResource.java
    │   │   └── resources
    │   │       ├── META-INF
    │   │       │   └── resources
    │   │       │       └── index.html
    │   │       └── application.properties
    │   └── test
    │       └── java
    │           └── org/agoncal/fascicle/quarkus/number
    │               ├── NativeNumberResourceIT.java
    │               └── NumberResourceTest.java
    ├── mvnw
    ├── mvnw.cmd
    └── pom.xml
```

The Quarkus Maven plugin generates the following code in the `rest-number` sub-directory:

- Dockerfile files for both native and JVM modes in `src/main/docker` (more on Docker in Chapter 9),

- An `org.agoncal.fascicle.quarkus.number.NumberResource` REST endpoint,

- The landing page `index.html` that is accessible on `http://localhost:8080` after starting the application,

- An empty `application.properties` configuration file under the `resources` directory,

- A native test (`NativeNumberResourceIT`) and a JVM test (`NumberResourceTest`),

- Maven wrappers (`mvnw` for Linux/macOS and `mvnw.cmd` for Windows),

- The Maven structure with a `pom.xml`.

4.2.2. Maven Dependencies

Once generated, look at the `pom.xml` at the root of the `rest-number` directory (see Listing 6). It has a set of properties with plugins, dependencies and Quarkus versions. You will also find the import of the Quarkus BOM (*Bill of Materials*), allowing you to omit the version on the different Quarkus dependencies.

Listing 6. Header of the pom.xml

```xml
<project xsi:schemaLocation="http://maven.apache.org/POM/4.0.0
https://maven.apache.org/xsd/maven-4.0.0.xsd" xmlns="
http://maven.apache.org/POM/4.0.0"
        xmlns:xsi="http://www.w3.org/2001/XMLSchema-instance">
  <modelVersion>4.0.0</modelVersion>

  <groupId>org.agoncal.fascicle.quarkus-practising</groupId>
  <artifactId>rest-number</artifactId>
  <version>2.0.0-SNAPSHOT</version>
  <name>Practising Quarkus :: Numbers REST Microservice</name>

  <properties>
    <compiler-plugin.version>3.8.1</compiler-plugin.version>
    <maven.compiler.parameters>true</maven.compiler.parameters>
    <maven.compiler.source>11</maven.compiler.source>
    <maven.compiler.target>11</maven.compiler.target>
    <project.build.sourceEncoding>UTF-8</project.build.sourceEncoding>
    <project.reporting.outputEncoding>UTF-8</project.reporting.outputEncoding>
    <quarkus.platform.artifact-id>quarkus-bom</quarkus.platform.artifact-id>
    <quarkus.platform.group-id>io.quarkus</quarkus.platform.group-id>
    <quarkus.platform.version>2.5.0.Final</quarkus.platform.version>
    <surefire-plugin.version>3.0.0-M5</surefire-plugin.version>
  </properties>
  <dependencyManagement>
    <dependencies>
      <dependency>
        <groupId>${quarkus.platform.group-id}</groupId>
        <artifactId>${quarkus.platform.artifact-id}</artifactId>
        <version>${quarkus.platform.version}</version>
        <type>pom</type>
        <scope>import</scope>
      </dependency>
    </dependencies>
  </dependencyManagement>
```

The dependencies section in Listing 7 gives us all the required dependencies to compile and execute the *Number* REST API for now. This section only declares the dependencies, not the versions, as they are defined on the parent POM:

- quarkus-resteasy: REST framework implementing JAX-RS.

- quarkus-resteasy-jsonb: JSON-B serialisation support for RESTEasy.

- quarkus-smallrye-openapi: Documents the REST APIs with OpenAPI and comes with Swagger UI.

- quarkus-arc: Context and Dependency Injection implementation.

As you will see, testing an application with Quarkus is very easy. For that, we need a few dependencies such as the one listed in Listing 7:

- `quarkus-junit5`: JUnit 5 support in Quarkus.

- `rest-assured`: Framework to easily test REST endpoints.

Listing 7. Maven Dependencies

```xml
<dependencies>
  <dependency>
    <groupId>io.quarkus</groupId>
    <artifactId>quarkus-smallrye-openapi</artifactId>
  </dependency>
  <dependency>
    <groupId>io.quarkus</groupId>
    <artifactId>quarkus-resteasy-jsonb</artifactId>
  </dependency>
  <dependency>
    <groupId>io.quarkus</groupId>
    <artifactId>quarkus-resteasy</artifactId>
  </dependency>
  <dependency>
    <groupId>io.quarkus</groupId>
    <artifactId>quarkus-arc</artifactId>
  </dependency>
  <dependency>
    <groupId>io.quarkus</groupId>
    <artifactId>quarkus-junit5</artifactId>
    <scope>test</scope>
  </dependency>
  <dependency>
    <groupId>io.rest-assured</groupId>
    <artifactId>rest-assured</artifactId>
    <scope>test</scope>
  </dependency>
</dependencies>
```

If you want to know more about JUnit and REST Assured, you can check out Appendix A.

💻 Call to Action

(10)

We will use Java Faker to generate fake ISBN, ASIN and EAN numbers. For that you need to edit the rest-number/pom.xml file and add the javafaker dependency:

```xml
<dependency>
    <groupId>com.github.javafaker</groupId>
    <artifactId>javafaker</artifactId>
    <version>1.0.2</version>
</dependency>
```

The last part of the generated pom.xml shows in Listing 8 the plugins required to execute and test our code:

- quarkus-maven-plugin: The Quarkus plugin is responsible for creating the final JAR and for running the development mode.

- maven-compiler-plugin: The Maven compiler plugin is used to compile the sources of the project.

- maven-surefire-plugin: The Surefire plugin is used during the test phase to execute the unit tests of the application.

Listing 8. Building Steps

```xml
<build>
  <plugins>
    <plugin>
      <groupId>${quarkus.platform.group-id}</groupId>
      <artifactId>quarkus-maven-plugin</artifactId>
      <version>${quarkus.platform.version}</version>
      <extensions>true</extensions>
      <executions>
        <execution>
          <goals>
            <goal>build</goal>
            <goal>generate-code</goal>
            <goal>generate-code-tests</goal>
          </goals>
        </execution>
      </executions>
    </plugin>
    <plugin>
      <artifactId>maven-compiler-plugin</artifactId>
      <version>${compiler-plugin.version}</version>
      <configuration>
        <parameters>${maven.compiler.parameters}</parameters>
      </configuration>
    </plugin>
    <plugin>
      <artifactId>maven-surefire-plugin</artifactId>
      <version>${surefire-plugin.version}</version>
      <configuration>
        <systemPropertyVariables>
          <java.util.logging.manager>
org.jboss.logmanager.LogManager</java.util.logging.manager>
          <maven.home>${maven.home}</maven.home>
        </systemPropertyVariables>
      </configuration>
    </plugin>
  </plugins>
</build>
```

Notice that the `java.util.logging.manager` system property is set to make sure that the tests use the correct logging manager.

🖥 Call to Action

(11)

With all these test dependencies and plugins in place, let's make sure that the code compiles and the tests pass with:

```
rest-number$ ./mvnw compile
rest-number$ ./mvnw test
```

Everything is ready: let's write our *Number* REST endpoint.

4.3. Exposing the Number REST Endpoint

Quarkus integrates JAX-RS through the RESTEasy implementation. In this section we will use JAX-RS APIs and annotations to develop our *Number* REST endpoint. The *Number* endpoint is a REST web service that uses JAX-RS annotations to generate all sorts of book numbers.

Java API for RESTful Web Services[38] (JAX-RS) is a specification that provides support for creating web services according to the Representational State Transfer (REST) architectural style. JAX-RS provides a set of annotations and classes/interfaces to simplify the development and deployment of REST endpoints. It also brings a client API to programmatically invoke REST endpoints.

The Java API for RESTful Web Services APIs and annotations are all defined under the javax.ws.rs. Table 2 lists the main subpackages defined in JAX-RS 2.1 (under the root javax.ws.rs package[39]).

Table 2. Main javax.ws.rs Subpackages

Subpackage	Description
root	Root package of the CDI APIs
client	Classes and interfaces of the new JAX-RS client API
container	Container-specific JAX-RS API
core	Low-level interfaces and annotations used to create RESTful web resources
ext	APIs that provide extensions to the types supported by the JAX-RS API

Along with APIs, JAX-RS comes with a set of annotations. Table 3 lists a subset of the most commonly used annotations.

Table 3. Main JAX-RS Annotations

Annotation	Description
@GET, @POST, @PUT, @DELETE	Indicates that the annotated method responds to HTTP GET, POST, PUT or DELETE requests
@Path	Identifies the URI path that a resource class or class method will serve requests for

Annotation	Description
@PathParam	Binds the value of a URI template parameter or a path segment
@QueryParam	Binds the value(s) of an HTTP query parameter to a resource method parameter
@Produces, @Consumes	Defines the media types that the methods of a resource can produce or accept
@Context	Injects information into a field, a property or a method parameter

4.3.1. The Number Resource

The NumberResource in Listing 9 uses some of these JAX-RS annotations. As you can see, NumberResource is a very simple REST endpoint, returning a JSON representation of random numbers on the /api/numbers path. It returns a BookNumbers object containing ISBN, ASIN and EAN numbers all randomly generated by the Java Faker. The generation date is set using the Java time Instant class

The *Java Faker*[40] library is a port of Ruby's faker[41] gem that generates fake data. It's useful when you're developing a project and need some pretty data for a showcase. Here, we use it to generate some random data.

Listing 9. REST Endpoint Generating Book Numbers

```
@Path("/api/numbers")
public class NumberResource {

  @Inject
  Logger LOGGER;

  boolean separator;

  @GET
  @Produces(MediaType.APPLICATION_JSON)
  public Response generateBookNumbers() throws InterruptedException {
    LOGGER.info("Generating book numbers");
    Faker faker = new Faker();
    BookNumbers bookNumbers = new BookNumbers();
    bookNumbers.isbn10 = faker.code().isbn10(separator);
    bookNumbers.isbn13 = faker.code().isbn13(separator);
    bookNumbers.asin = faker.code().asin();
    bookNumbers.ean8 = faker.code().ean8();
    bookNumbers.ean13 = faker.code().ean13();
    bookNumbers.generationDate = Instant.now();
    return Response.ok(bookNumbers).build();
  }
}
```

💻 Call to Action

Edit the `org.agoncal.fascicle.quarkus.number.NumberResource.java` class (leave the generated method `hello()`, we will need it later) and add the code shown in Listing 9. Make sure to resolve your `import` statements:

```
import com.github.javafaker.Faker;
import org.jboss.logging.Logger;
import javax.inject.Inject;
import javax.ws.rs.GET;
import javax.ws.rs.Path;
import javax.ws.rs.Produces;
import javax.ws.rs.core.MediaType;
import javax.ws.rs.core.Response;
```

4.3.2. The Book Numbers Class

The `NumberResource` returns the `BookNumbers` object defined in Listing 10. As you can see, `BookNumbers` is just a simple POJO (*Plain Old Java Object*) with attributes, getters and setters. It holds the values of several generated book numbers.

Listing 10. Java Class Holding Book Numbers

```java
public class BookNumbers {

  public String isbn10;
  public String isbn13;
  public String asin;
  public String ean8;
  public String ean13;
  public Instant generationDate;
}
```

Create the new class org.agoncal.fascicle.quarkus.number.BookNumbers and add the code shown in Listing 10. Now, you can start Quarkus with the command

```
rest-number$ ./mvnw compile quarkus:dev
```

Now cURL the *Number* REST endpoint. You should have a similar output:

```
$ curl -X GET -H "Accept: application/json" http://localhost:8080/api/numbers |
jq

{
  "asin": "B0000AB07P",
  "ean13": "6615352338240",
  "ean8": "13354022",
  "generationDate": "2020-01-11T09:25:18.541227Z",
  "isbn10": "1932563601",
  "isbn13": "9791961975483"
}
```

> ⓘ The previous cURL command pipes the output to jq. jq is a nice tool to manipulate JSON in the shell. If you want to know more about jq and install it, see Appendix A.

4.4. Injecting Configuration Value

If you look carefully at Listing 9 you will notice that the generateBookNumbers() method of the NumberResource uses a separator variable. separator is a boolean that indicates to Java Faker whether ISBN numbers should be generated with a separator or not. We could manually set it to true or false depending on our needs, but there is a better way to do it: use an external property. For that purpose, Quarkus uses the Eclipse MicroProfile Configuration.

In a microservice architecture, the fact that there is no central runtime implies that there is no single point of configuration, but several points. Each microservice has its own configuration. But sometimes two microservices might want to share a common configuration. In that case, it can be helpful that they access configurations from multiple sources homogeneously and transparently. *Eclipse MicroProfile Configuration*[42] provides applications and microservices with the means to obtain configuration properties through several sources (internal and external to the application), through dependency injection or lookup.

The Eclipse MicroProfile Configuration APIs and annotations are all defined under the org.eclipse.microprofile.config package. Table 4 lists the main subpackages defined in Eclipse MicroProfile Configuration version 2.0 (under the root org.eclipse.microprofile.config package[43]).

Table 4. Main org.eclipse.microprofile.config Subpackages

Subpackage	Description
root	Root package of the Configuration APIs
inject	CDI support
spi	Internal SPIs (*Service Provider Interfaces*) implemented by the provider

Along with APIs, Configuration comes with a set of annotations. Table 5 lists a subset of the most commonly used annotations.

Table 5. Main Configuration Annotations

Annotation	Description
@ConfigProperty	Binds the injection point with a configured value

So when we generate new ISBN numbers, we want to be able to have separators, or not, depending on the value that can be configured. For that, MicroProfile Configuration can inject the configuration in the application thanks to the @ConfigProperty annotation.

💻 Call to Action

(14)

Edit the NumberResource REST endpoint, and annotate the separator attribute with the @ConfigProperty annotation:

```
@ConfigProperty(name = "number.separator", defaultValue = "false")
```

Make sure you get the right import statement:

```
import org.eclipse.microprofile.config.inject.ConfigProperty;
```

 When injecting a configured value, you can use @Inject @ConfigProperty or just @ConfigProperty. The @Inject annotation is not necessary for members annotated with @ConfigProperty.

If you do not provide a value for a property in the application.properties, the application startup would fail with a javax.enterprise.inject.spi.DeploymentException. That's why we use a default value (using the property defaultValue). If we don't declare a value in the application.properties it would not fail and pick up the defaultValue. Or we can set it up in the application.properties file.

Edit the src/main/resources/application.properties file and add the following content:

```
number.separator=true
```

Now execute the following command (at the root of the rest-number project folder) to start Quarkus:

```
rest-number$ ./mvnw compile quarkus:dev
```

Now cURL the api/numbers URL like shown below: You should see separators on the ISBN numbers.

```
$ curl -X GET -H "Accept: application/json" http://localhost:8080/api/numbers |
jq

{
  "asin": "B0000AB07P",
  "ean13": "6615352338240",
  "ean8": "13354022",
  "generationDate": "2020-01-11T09:25:18.541227Z",
  "isbn10": "1-932563-60-1",
  "isbn13": "979-1-9619754-8-3"
}
```

You can also overwrite the value of the number.separator using the command line:

```
rest-number$ ./mvnw compile quarkus:dev -Dnumber.separator=false
rest-number$ ./mvnw compile quarkus:dev -Dnumber.separator=true
```

4.5. Customising the JSON Output

The JSON output from the *Number* REST endpoint is not exactly what we want. We would like to change the name of some keys (e.g. isbn_13 instead of isbn13), and prevent sending back the generationDate. To change the JSON binding, Quarkus uses the JSON-B specification.

JSON Binding[44] (JSON-B) is a standard binding layer for converting Java objects to/from JSON documents. It defines a default mapping algorithm for converting existing Java classes to JSON while enabling developers to customise the mapping process through the use of Java annotations.

The JSON Binding APIs are all defined under the javax.json.bind package. Table 6 lists the main subpackages defined in JSON-B 1.0 (under the root `javax.json.bind` package[15]).

Table 6. Main javax.json.bind Subpackages

Subpackage	Description
root	Root package of the JSON-B APIs
adapter	APIs to define a custom mapping for a given Java type
annotation	JSON-B mapping annotations
config	Classes and interfaces to configure the mapping provider
serializer	JSON-B internals for custom serialisers
spi	Internal SPIs (*Service Provider Interfaces*) implemented by the provider

Along with APIs, JSON-B comes with a set of annotations. Table 7 lists a subset of the most commonly used annotations.

Table 7. Main JSON-B Annotations

Annotation	Description
@JsonbDateFormat	Customises the date format of a field
@JsonbProperty	Allows customisation of a field name
@JsonbNumberFormat	Customises the number format of a field
@JsonbTransient	Prevents mapping of a field

Listing 11 shows the `BookNumbers` class with some JSON-B mapping annotations. For example, the `@JsonbProperty` tells the JSON-B provider to change the name `isbn10` to `isbn_10`. As for `@JsonbTransient`, it prevents the generation date from being present on the JSON output.

Listing 11. BookNumbers Class with JSON-B Annotations

```java
public class BookNumbers {

    @JsonbProperty("isbn_10")
    public String isbn10;
    @JsonbProperty("isbn_13")
    public String isbn13;
    public String asin;
    @JsonbProperty("ean_8")
    public String ean8;
    @JsonbProperty("ean_13")
    public String ean13;
    @JsonbTransient
    public Instant generationDate;
}
```

Edit BookNumbers and add the JSON-B annotations as shown in Listing 11. Make sure you resolve your import statements:

```
import javax.json.bind.annotation.JsonbProperty;
import javax.json.bind.annotation.JsonbTransient;
```

Without any other change to the Quarkus runtime or configuration, if you execute ./mvnw quarkus:dev and go back to the same URL, you will see that the JSON has changed and looks like the following (e.g. isbn_13 instead of isbn13):

```
$ curl -X GET -H "Accept: application/json" http://localhost:8080/api/numbers | jq

{
  "asin": "B000A3PI3G",
  "ean_13": "7438504344437",
  "ean_8": "38833700",
  "isbn_10": "1-383-10381-X",
  "isbn_13": "978-0-929138-68-8"
}
```

4.6. Documenting with OpenAPI

Quarkus applications can expose an API description through the OpenAPI specification. The OpenAPI specification helps you to describe your RESTful APIs to the consumers by available endpoints, allowed operations on each endpoint, input/output parameters for each operation, etc. For that it's just a matter of adding the smallrye-openapi extension in a pom.xml, and that's exactly what we did in Listing 7.

Exposing RESTful APIs has become an essential part of all modern applications. From the microservices developer's point of view, it is important to understand how to interact with these APIs and how to test that they are still valid and backward compatible. For that, there needs to be a clear and complete contract. Therefore a standard API documentation mechanism is required and can also be used for API testing. That's when *OpenAPI*[46] comes along.

Eclipse MicroProfile OpenAPI[47] provides a Java API for the OpenAPI v3 specification that all application developers can use to expose their API documentation. It aims to provide a set of Java interfaces and programming models which allow Java developers to natively produce OpenAPI v3 documents from their JAX-RS endpoints.

The Eclipse MicroProfile OpenAPI APIs and annotations are all defined under the main org.eclipse.microprofile.openapi package, either at the root, or under the other subpackages. Table 8 lists the main subpackages defined in Eclipse MicroProfile OpenAPI version 2.0 (under the root `org.eclipse.microprofile.openapi` package[48]).

Table 8. Main org.eclipse.microprofile.openapi Subpackages

Subpackage	Description
root	Root package of the OpenAPI APIs
annotations	Set of annotations to produce a valid OpenAPI document
models	Interfaces to define OpenAPI document programmatically
spi	Internal SPIs (*Service Provider Interfaces*) implemented by the provider

Along with APIs, OpenAPI comes with a set of annotations. Table 9 lists a subset of the most commonly used annotations.

Table 9. Main OpenAPI Annotations

Annotation	Description
@APIResponse	Describes the endpoint's response (response code, data structure, types, etc.)
@Operation	Describes a single API operation on a path
@OpenAPIDefinition	Root document object of the OpenAPI document
@Parameter	The name of the method parameter
@RequestBody	A brief description of the request body
@Schema	Allows the definition of input and output data types
@Tag	Used to add tags to the REST endpoint contract to provide more description

💻 Call to Action

(17)

To visualise the default OpenAPI documentation, start the application (execute the `./mvnw quarkus:dev` command at the root of `rest-number` module) and execute the following cURL command:

```
$ curl http://localhost:8080/q/openapi
$ curl -H "Accept: application/json" http://localhost:8080/q/openapi
```

You should get a YAML representation of the OpenAPI contract, similar to the one in Listing 12.

As you can see in Listing 12, Quarkus automatically generates the OpenAPI documentation for the *Number* REST endpoint. This is an example of what we call an OpenAPI contract for a REST endpoint.

Listing 12. Default OpenAPI YAML Contract

```
openapi: 3.0.3
info:
  title: rest-number API
  version: 2.0.0-SNAPSHOT
paths:
  /api/numbers:
    get:
      responses:
        "200":
          description: OK
```

You can use cURL to change the HTTP header and to retrieve the OpenAPI document in several formats:

- YAML: curl http://localhost:8080/q/openapi
- JSON: curl -H "Accept: application/json" http://localhost:8080/q/openapi

But this contract lacks documentation. The Eclipse MicroProfile OpenAPI allows you to customise the methods' description of your REST endpoints as well as the entire application itself.

4.6.1. Documenting the Number REST Endpoint

Eclipse MicroProfile OpenAPI has a set of annotations to customise each REST endpoint class, method and parameter to make the OpenAPI contract richer and clearer for consumers. Listing 13 shows what the NumberResource endpoint looks like once annotated.

Listing 13. Documenting the REST endpoint

```java
@Path("/api/numbers")
@Tag(name = "Number Endpoint")
public class NumberResource {

  @Inject
  Logger LOGGER;

  @ConfigProperty(name = "number.separator", defaultValue = "false")
  boolean separator;

  @Operation(summary = "Generates book numbers", description = "These book numbers
have several formats: ISBN, ASIN and EAN")
  @APIResponse(responseCode = "200", content = @Content(mediaType = MediaType
.APPLICATION_JSON, schema = @Schema(implementation = BookNumbers.class)))
  @GET
  @Produces(MediaType.APPLICATION_JSON)
  public Response generateBookNumbers() throws InterruptedException {
    LOGGER.info("Generating book numbers");
    Faker faker = new Faker();
    BookNumbers bookNumbers = new BookNumbers();
    bookNumbers.isbn10 = faker.code().isbn10(separator);
    bookNumbers.isbn13 = faker.code().isbn13(separator);
    bookNumbers.asin = faker.code().asin();
    bookNumbers.ean8 = faker.code().ean8();
    bookNumbers.ean13 = faker.code().ean13();
    bookNumbers.generationDate = Instant.now();
    return Response.ok(bookNumbers).build();
  }
}
```

The @Tag annotation gives some information about the entire endpoint. On the other hand, @Operation focuses on each method while @APIResponse lists all the possible HTTP status code that can be returned by a method (here, a 200 when the method is invoked successfully). The implementation attribute of the @Schema annotation is important here. It provides the real implementation of the Response and allows the OpenAPI to reference ($ref) the BookNumbers class (as you will see in Listing 16).

💻 Call to Action

(18)

Edit the NumberResource class and add the OpenAPI annotations on the class (@Tag) as well as on the generateBookNumbers() method (@Operation, @APIResponse, @Content and @Schema) as shown in Listing 13.

```
import org.eclipse.microprofile.openapi.annotations.Operation;
import org.eclipse.microprofile.openapi.annotations.media.Content;
import org.eclipse.microprofile.openapi.annotations.media.Schema;
import org.eclipse.microprofile.openapi.annotations.responses.APIResponse;
import org.eclipse.microprofile.openapi.annotations.tags.Tag;
```

4.6.2. Documenting the BookNumber POJO

The generateBookNumbers() method returns a BookNumbers object. As you can see in Listing 14, this object can also be annotated with @Schema to provide a more textual description. For example, we can inform the consumers which attributes are required in the JSON document (@Schema(required = true)).

Listing 14. Documenting the BookNumber Class

```
@Schema(description = "Several formats of book numbers")
public class BookNumbers {

  @Schema(required = true)
  @JsonbProperty("isbn_10")
  public String isbn10;
  @Schema(required = true)
  @JsonbProperty("isbn_13")
  public String isbn13;
  public String asin;
  @JsonbProperty("ean_8")
  public String ean8;
  @JsonbProperty("ean_13")
  public String ean13;
  @JsonbTransient
  public Instant generationDate;
}
```

4.6.3. Documenting the Application

The previous annotations allow you to customise the contract for a given REST endpoint. But it's also important to customise the contract for the entire application. Eclipse MicroProfile OpenAPI also has a set of annotations to serve that purpose. The difference is that these annotations cannot be used on the endpoint itself, but instead on another Java class which is meant to be configuring the entire application as shown in Listing 15.

Listing 15. Custom OpenAPI Documentation for the Application

```
@ApplicationPath("/")
@OpenAPIDefinition(
    info = @Info(title = "Number API",
        description = "This API allows to generate all sorts of numbers",
        version = "2.0",
        contact = @Contact(name = "@agoncal", url = "https://twitter.com/agoncal")),
    externalDocs = @ExternalDocumentation(url = "https://github.com/agoncal/agoncal-
fascicle-quarkus-pract", description = "All the Practising Quarkus code"),
    tags = {
        @Tag(name = "api", description = "Public API that can be used by anybody"),
        @Tag(name = "numbers", description = "Anybody interested in numbers")
    }
)
public class NumberApplication extends Application {
}
```

💻 Call to Action

Create the new class `src/main/java/org/agoncal/fascicle/quarkus/number/NumberApplication` with the content described in Listing 15. Add the appropriate OpenAPI annotations as well as some Java API for RESTful Web Services APIs Make sure you use the following import statements as some classes and interfaces are present with the same names in other libraries:

```
import org.eclipse.microprofile.openapi.annotations.ExternalDocumentation;
import org.eclipse.microprofile.openapi.annotations.OpenAPIDefinition;
import org.eclipse.microprofile.openapi.annotations.info.Contact;
import org.eclipse.microprofile.openapi.annotations.info.Info;
import org.eclipse.microprofile.openapi.annotations.tags.Tag;

import javax.ws.rs.ApplicationPath;
import javax.ws.rs.core.Application;
```

4.6.4. The Customised OpenAPI Contract

After applying all the previous modifications to the contract meta-data, you will see the customised OpenAPI contract described in Listing 16.

Listing 16. Customised OpenAPI YAML Contract

```yaml
openapi: 3.0.3
info:
  title: Number API
  description: This API allows to generate all sorts of numbers
  contact:
    name: '@agoncal'
    url: https://twitter.com/agoncal
  version: "2.0"
externalDocs:
  description: 'All the Practising Quarkus code'
  url: https://github.com/agoncal/agoncal-fascicle-quarkus-pract
tags:
  - name: api
    description: Public API that can be used by anybody
  - name: numbers
    description: Anybody interested in numbers
  - name: Number Endpoint
paths:
  /api/numbers:
    get:
      tags:
        - Number Endpoint
      summary: Generates book numbers
```

```
       description: "These book numbers have several formats: ISBN, ASIN and EAN"
       responses:
         "200":
           description: OK
           content:
             application/json:
               schema:
                 $ref: '#/components/schemas/BookNumbers'
components:
  schemas:
    BookNumbers:
      description: Several formats of book numbers
      required:
        - isbn_10
        - isbn_13
      type: object
      properties:
        asin:
          type: string
        ean_13:
          type: string
        ean_8:
          type: string
        isbn_10:
          type: string
        isbn_13:
          type: string
```

🖥 Call to Action

(21)

If Quarkus is still up and running, cURL the http://localhost:8080/q/openapi endpoint and you will see the customised contract as shown in Listing 16. If you have stopped Quarkus, just execute a ./mvnw quarkus:dev command to start it in development mode.

The contract in Listing 16 is much richer than the one in Listing 12. There is information about the entire *Number* application, as well as all the paths that are accessible through HTTP. In the contract in Listing 16, notice the reference to the BookNumbers ($ref: '#/components/schemas/BookNumbers') on the generateBookNumbers method. For the consumer of this contract, the returned structure is much clearer that the one defined in Listing 12.

4.6.5. Swagger UI

Visualising an OpenAPI contract in YAML or JSON can be cumbersome if the contract is too large. Instead, we can use Swagger UI. In fact, the Quarkus extension smallrye-openapi comes with a swagger-ui extension embedding a properly configured Swagger UI page.

When building APIs, developers want to analyse them quickly. *Swagger UI*[49] is a great tool that permits you to visualise and interact with your APIs. It's automatically generated from the OpenAPI contract, with the visual documentation making it easy for back end implementation and client side consumption.

💻 Call to Action

(22)

By default, Swagger UI is accessible at the URL /q/swagger-ui. So, once your application is started, you can go to http://localhost:8080/q/swagger-ui, and you will see the contract in a visual format as shown in Figure 8.

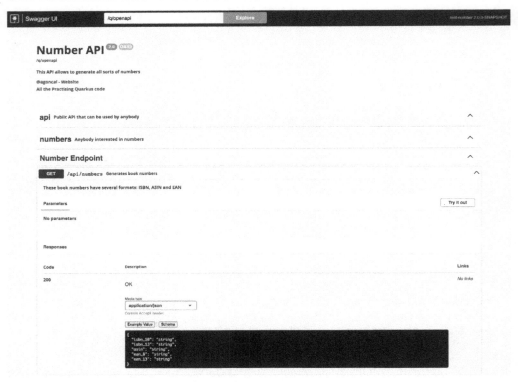

Figure 8. Swagger UI contract of the Number endpoint

You can visualise your API's operations and schemas, but you can also invoke them by simply clicking on the *GET* button and then the *Execute* button as shown in Figure 9.

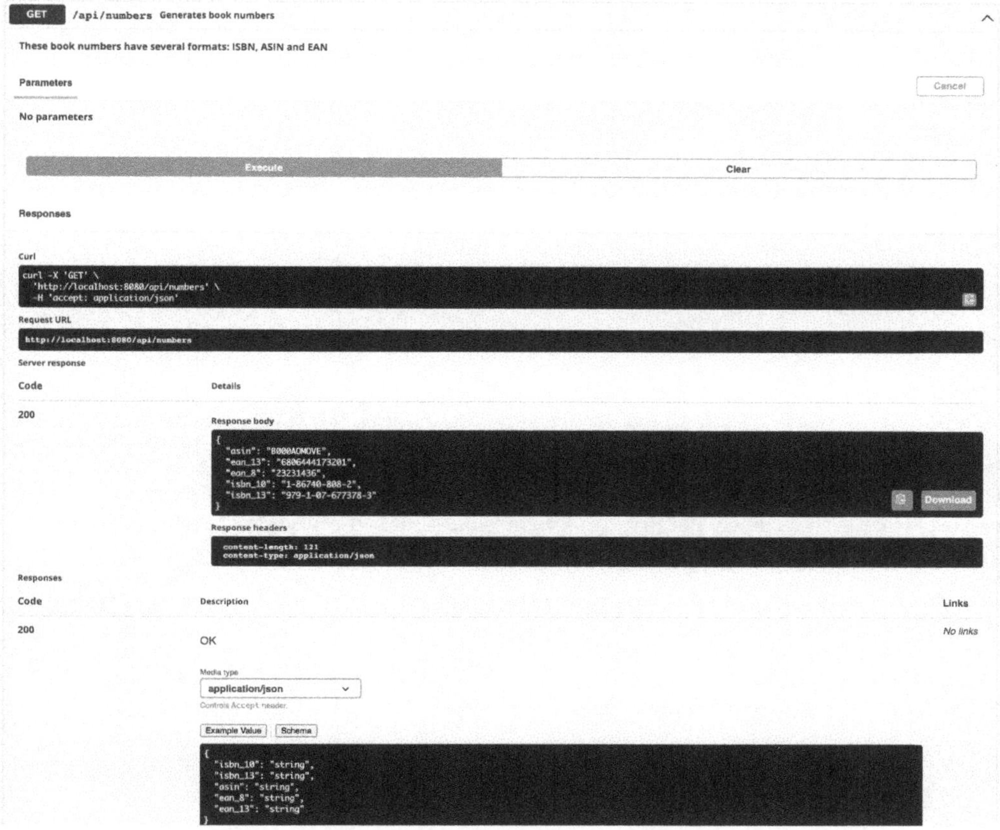

Figure 9. Invoking the generateBookNumbers method

4.7. Application Startup and Shutdown

You often need to execute custom actions when the application starts and clean up everything when the application stops. For example, up to now, when our application starts, the logs are pretty plain (see Listing 17) and show a "Quarkus" banner.

Listing 17. Original Startup and Shutdown Quarkus Logs

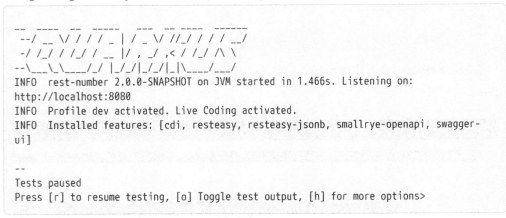

```
INFO  rest-number 2.0.0-SNAPSHOT on JVM started in 1.466s. Listening on:
http://localhost:8080
INFO  Profile dev activated. Live Coding activated.
INFO  Installed features: [cdi, resteasy, resteasy-jsonb, smallrye-openapi, swagger-
ui]


--
Tests paused
Press [r] to resume testing, [o] Toggle test output, [h] for more options>
```

So what we want to do is to add a nice "Number" text banner when Quarkus starts up, and display a message when it shuts down. But first of all, we need to disable the original "Quarkus" banner.

🖵 Call to Action

(23)

To disable the original "Quarkus" banner, edit the `application.properties` file and set the `banner.enabled` to `false`.

```
quarkus.banner.enabled=false
```

If you now start Quarkus again, you will see that the "Quarkus" banner is gone.

Now that the original banner is disabled, it's time to add a new one with some ASCII Art[50] as shown in Listing 18.

Listing 18. Displaying a Banner at Startup

```
@ApplicationScoped
class NumberApplicationLifeCycle {

  @Inject
  Logger LOGGER;

  void onStart(@Observes StartupEvent ev) {
    LOGGER.info(" _    _                         _                      ");
    LOGGER.info("| \\ | |                       | |                    ");
    LOGGER.info("|  \\| |_    _ _ __ ___   ___| |__    ___ _ __");
    LOGGER.info("| . ` | | | | | '_ ` _ \\| '_ \\ / _ \\ '__|");
    LOGGER.info("| |\\  | |_| | | | | | | | | |_) |  __/ |    ");
    LOGGER.info("\\_| \\_/\\__,_|_| |_| |_|.__/ \\___|_|    ");
    LOGGER.info("                    Powered by Quarkus");
  }

  void onStop(@Observes ShutdownEvent ev) {
    LOGGER.info("The application Number is stopping...");
  }
}
```

🖳 Call to Action

(24)

Go to the http://patorjk.com/software/taag website and pick up your favourite "Number" text banner. Then, create a new class named NumberApplicationLifeCycle in the org.agoncal.fascicle.quarkus.number package, and copy your banner so you end up with content similar to Listing 18. You need to import some classes specific to Quarkus, as well as some CDI APIs:

```
import org.jboss.logging.Logger;
import io.quarkus.runtime.ShutdownEvent;
import io.quarkus.runtime.StartupEvent;
import io.quarkus.runtime.configuration.ProfileManager;
import javax.enterprise.context.ApplicationScoped;
import javax.enterprise.event.Observes;
import javax.inject.Inject;
```

Notice the @ApplicationScoped annotation in Listing 18. It's a CDI annotation (more on this in Chapter 5) allowing Quarkus to register this class when the application starts. Thanks to the CDI @Observes annotation, the NumberApplicationLifeCycle can observe events and react in a certain way. That's because Quarkus fires CDI events, including at startup and shutdown.

CDI events allow beans to interact with no compile time dependency at all. One bean can define an event (using the `javax.enterprise.event.Event` interface), another bean can fire the event (by calling the `fire()` method), and yet another bean can handle the event (using the `@Observes` annotation). The beans can be in separate packages and even in separate JARs of the application. This basic schema follows the observer/observable design pattern[51] from the *Gang of Four*.

Thanks to CDI events, the `NumberApplicationLifeCycle` is automatically invoked:

- On startup with the `StartupEvent` so it can execute code (here, displaying the banner) when the application is starting,
- On shutdown with the `ShutdownEvent` when the application is terminating.

⌨ Call to Action

(25)

Run the application with `./mvnw clean quarkus:dev`, and check that a banner similar to Listing 19 is printed to the console. Then, stop the application: the message in the `onStop()` method should be printed.

Listing 19. Custom Banner

```
INFO    _   _                           _
INFO   | \ | |                         | |
INFO   |  \| |_   _ _  _ __   ___  | |__    ___ _ __
INFO   | . ` | | | | | '_ ` _ \| '_ \ / _ \ '__|
INFO   | |\  | |_| | | | | | | | |_) | __/ |
INFO   \_| \_/\__,_|_| |_| |_|_.__/ \___|_|
INFO                         Powered by Quarkus
INFO   rest-number 2.0.0-SNAPSHOT on JVM started in 1.466s. Listening on:
http://localhost:8080
INFO   Profile dev activated. Live Coding activated.
INFO   Installed features: [cdi, resteasy, resteasy-jsonb, smallrye-openapi, swagger-
ui]

--
Tests paused
Press [r] to resume testing, [o] Toggle test output, [h] for more options>
(...)
INFO   The application Number is stopping...
INFO   Quarkus stopped in 0.002s
```

4.7.1. Displaying the Current Profile

Quarkus supports the notion of configuration profiles. This allows you to have multiple configurations in the same file and to select them via a profile name.

By default, Quarkus has three profiles, although it is possible to create your own, as many as you like. The built-in profiles are:

- dev: Activated when in development mode (when running `mvn quarkus:dev`).

- test: Activated when running tests.

- prod: The default profile when not running in development or test mode.

If we want to display the current profile, we can use the `ProfileManager` API from Quarkus.

🖵 Call to Action

(26)

To add the current profile, update the `NumberApplicationLifeCycle` class (the one in Listing 18) and add a log invoking `ProfileManager.getActiveProfile()` in the `onStart()` method:

```
LOGGER.info("The application Number is starting with profile " + ProfileManager
.getActiveProfile());
```

When we run `./mvnw quarkus:dev` the log displays "*The application Number is starting with profile dev*" as shown in Listing 20. Later on, we will see how the *test* profile will be used when running some tests. In Chapter 9 we will build a native image of our microservices and will run the application in production mode (the profile will show "*prod*" instead of "*dev*" when run in production mode).

Listing 20. Custom Banner with Profile

```
INFO    _   _                              _
INFO   | \ | |                            | |
INFO   |  \| |_     _ _ __ ___  | |__    ___ _ __
INFO   | . ` | | | | | '_ ` _ \| '_ \ / _ \ '__|
INFO   | |\  | |_| | | | | | | | |_) |  __/ |
INFO   \_| \_/\__,_|_| |_| |_|_.__/ \___|_|
INFO                        Powered by Quarkus
INFO   The application Number is starting with profile dev
INFO   rest-number 2.0.0-SNAPSHOT on JVM started in 1.466s. Listening on:
http://localhost:8080
INFO   Profile dev activated. Live Coding activated.
INFO   Installed features: [cdi, resteasy, resteasy-jsonb, smallrye-openapi, swagger-
ui]

--
Tests paused
Press [r] to resume testing, [o] Toggle test output, [h] for more options>
(...)
INFO   The application Number is stopping...
INFO   Quarkus stopped in 0.002s
```

4.8. Running the Application

By now you've already executed the *Number* REST endpoint by starting Quarkus and invoking some cURL commands. But let's go further by hot reloading the application, configuring it, and of course, testing our endpoint.

4.8.1. Live Reload

So far we've been using `mvn quarkus:dev` to execute our application. This command runs Quarkus in development mode. This enables hot reload with background compilation, which means that when you modify your Java files and/or your resource files and invoke a REST endpoint, these changes will automatically take effect. This works also for resource files like the configuration property and HTML files. Invoking a cURL command or refreshing the browser triggers a scan of the workspace, and if any changes are detected, the Java files are recompiled and the application is redeployed; your request is then serviced by the redeployed application. Let's see this live reload in action. For that, make sure `mvn quarkus:dev` is still running.

🖥 Call to Action

With Quarkus running, cURL the path /api/numbers and you should see something like this:

```
$ curl -X GET -H "Accept: application/json" http://localhost:8080/api/numbers |
jq

{
  "asin": "B000A3PI3G",
  "ean_13": "7438504344437",
  "ean_8": "38833700",
  "isbn_10": "1-383-10381-X",
  "isbn_13": "978-0-929138-68-8"
}
```

Now, update the method NumberResource.generateBookNumbers() by setting a dummy ASIN number with bookNumbers.asin = "dummy". Save the NumberResource file if your IDE does not do it automatically, and execute the cURL command again. As you can see, the output has changed without you having to stop and restart Quarkus:

```
{
  "asin": "dummy",
  "ean_13": "7438504344437",
  "ean_8": "38833700",
  "isbn_10": "1-383-10381-X",
  "isbn_13": "978-0-929138-68-8"
}
```

Undo your changes so the asin number is generated as before, cURL the same URL, Quarkus restarts and you should get back an ASIN number instead of dummy. You can also change the application.properties file by setting the number.separator to false. Execute the cURL command again, and you will notice that the ISBN numbers do not use separators anymore.

4.8.2. Configuring the Application

Talking about configuration, let's go further. Up to now we've used the application.properties file to externalise and configure the number.separator property. Now, let's use the application.properties file to change the HTTP listening port and configure the logs

Configuring the Quarkus Listening Port

Because we will end-up running several microservices, let's configure Quarkus so it listens to a different port than 8080.

⌨ Call to Action

(28)

To change the HTTP listening port, you just need to add one property in the `application.properties` file:

```
quarkus.http.port=8701
```

Now restart the application to change the port and check the endpoint at http://localhost:8701/api/numbers **instead of** http://localhost:8080/api/numbers.

Configuring Logging

Quarkus comes with default logging properties. It displays the timestamp of the message, the package, the thread, etc.:

```
2020-01-15 15:56:19,218 INFO  [io.quarkus] (main) Quarkus started in 1.125s. Listening
on: http://localhost:8701
2020-01-15 15:56:19,219 INFO  [io.quarkus] (main) Profile dev activated. Live Coding
activated.
2020-01-15 15:56:19,219 INFO  [io.quarkus] (main) Installed features: [cdi, resteasy,
resteasy-jsonb, smallrye-openapi, swagger-ui]
```

But we might want to change this default logging mechanism. Runtime configuration of logging is also done through the `application.properties` file. The configuration can be done at several levels. It comes with different properties so you can have the logging that suits you the best[52]. Let's change the log format.

⌨ Call to Action

(29)

Edit the `application.properties` and add the following properties.

```
quarkus.log.console.enable=true
quarkus.log.console.format=%d{HH:mm:ss} %-3p [%c{1.}] %s%e%n
quarkus.log.console.level=DEBUG
quarkus.log.console.darken=5
```

Execute a cURL command so Quarkus reloads the configuration and displays the new log format.

The log level is set to DEBUG, the timestamp only displays the time, not the date, and the packages are written with only one letter. The end result looks like this:

```
16:02:28 INFO [i.quarkus] Quarkus started in 1.125s. Listening on:
http://localhost:8701
16:02:28 INFO [i.quarkus] Profile dev activated. Live Coding activated.
16:02:28 INFO [i.quarkus] Installed features: [cdi, resteasy, resteasy-jsonb,
smallrye-openapi, swagger-ui]
```

4.8.3. Testing the Application

So far so good, but wouldn't it be better with a few tests, just in case? If you look back at the pom.xml file in Listing 7, you can see 2 test dependencies:

- quarkus-junit5: Quarkus supports JUnit 5 tests.

- rest-assured: We now want to test our *Number* REST endpoint and REST Assured is a nice library to do it.

As shown in Listing 8, the Surefire Maven plugin is also setup to make the tests work. The version of the Surefire plugin must be set, as the default version does not support JUnit 5 yet. The java.util.logging.manager system property to make sure tests will use the correct log manager.

Testing the Business Logic

In Listing 21 we use the QuarkusTest runner to instruct JUnit to start the application before the tests. Then, the shouldGenerateBookNumber() method checks the HTTP response status code and the JSON content. Notice that these tests use REST Assured[53].

Listing 21. Testing the Generation of Book Numbers

```java
@QuarkusTest
public class NumberResourceTest {

  @Test
  void shouldGenerateBookNumber() {
    given()
      .header(ACCEPT, MediaType.APPLICATION_JSON).
    when()
      .get("/api/numbers").
    then()
      .statusCode(OK.getStatusCode())
      .body("$", hasKey("isbn_10"))
      .body("$", hasKey("isbn_13"))
      .body("$", hasKey("asin"))
      .body("$", hasKey("ean_8"))
      .body("$", hasKey("ean_13"))
      .body("$", not(hasKey("generationDate")));
  }
}
```

💻 Call to Action

(30)

Edit the `NumberResourceTest` class, remove the existing test method, and add the `shouldGenerateBookNumber()` method as shown in Listing 21. Make sure you use the following JAX-RS imports as well as the static imports:

```
import javax.ws.rs.core.MediaType;

import static io.restassured.RestAssured.given;
import static javax.ws.rs.core.HttpHeaders.ACCEPT;
import static javax.ws.rs.core.MediaType.APPLICATION_JSON;
import static javax.ws.rs.core.Response.Status.NOT_FOUND;
import static javax.ws.rs.core.Response.Status.OK;
import static org.hamcrest.CoreMatchers.is;
import static org.hamcrest.Matchers.hasKey;
import static org.hamcrest.Matchers.not;
```

 If you want to know more on REST Assured or Hamcrest matchers, check Appendix A.

Now execute the test with Maven or from your IDE. The test should pass and you should see similar logs as in Listing 22.

Listing 22. Tests Successful Output

```
[INFO] -------------------------------------------------
[INFO]  T E S T S
[INFO] -------------------------------------------------
[INFO] Running org.agoncal.fascicle.quarkus.number.NumberResourceTest

[INFO]   _    _                        _
[INFO]  | \  | |                 | |
[INFO]  |  \| |_    _ _ __ ___  | |__    ___ _ __
[INFO]  | . ` | | | | '_ ` _ \| '_ \ / _ \ '__|
[INFO]  | |\  | |_| | | | | | | | |_) |  __/ |
[INFO]  \_| \_/\__,_|_| |_| |_|_.__/ \___|_|
[INFO]                       Powered by Quarkus
[INFO] Quarkus started in 1.729s. Listening on: http://localhost:8081
[INFO] Profile test activated.
[INFO] Generating book numbers

[INFO] The application Number is stopping...
[INFO] Quarkus stopped in 0.027s

[INFO] Results:
[INFO] Tests run: 1, Failures: 0, Errors: 0, Skipped: 0
[INFO]
[INFO] -------------------------------------------------
[INFO] BUILD SUCCESS
[INFO] -------------------------------------------------
```

💻 Call to Action

(31)

To run the test with a Maven command, just execute `./mvnw test` from the root directory `rest-number`. Notice that Quarkus can still be running while the tests are getting executed. You don't have to stop Quarkus. That's because Quarkus listens on port 8701, while the tests execute on 8081.

There are a few interesting pieces of information on these logs. First of all, you notice that Quarkus starts and runs the application. Thanks to `@QuarkusTest` you get real integration tests with the Quarkus runtime. And when you look at the timestamps, you can see that starting and shutting down the application is quite quick. Quarkus makes your integration run quickly. While Quarkus will listen on port 8080 by default, when running tests it defaults to 8081. This allows you to run tests while having the application running in parallel.

Thanks to our `NumberApplicationLifeCycle` that displays the current active profile, the log is now *"The application Number is starting with profile test"* (*test* instead of *dev*).

Testing the OpenAPI

Let's add a few extra test methods that would make sure OpenAPI and Swagger UI are packaged in the application. In Listing 23 we just check that when accessing the URLs /q/openapi and /q/swagger-ui, a return code 200-OK is returned.

Listing 23. Testing the OpenAPI and SwaggerUI

```java
@Test
void shouldPingOpenAPI() {
  given()
    .header(ACCEPT, MediaType.APPLICATION_JSON).
  when()
    .get("/q/openapi").
  then()
    .statusCode(OK.getStatusCode());
}

@Test
void shouldPingSwaggerUI() {
  given().
  when()
    .get("/q/swagger-ui").
  then()
    .statusCode(OK.getStatusCode());
}
```

🖳 Call to Action

(32)

Edit the NumberResourceTest class, add the two methods as shown in Listing 23 that ping both OpenAPI and SwaggerUI URLs. Execute ./mvnw test again and make sure that all the tests pass.

Continuous Testing

Executing the tests with your IDE or Maven is great, but there is better when you are developing: Continuous Testing. Continuous testing means that tests are executed immediately after code changes have been saved. This allows you to get instant feedback on your code changes. Quarkus detects which tests cover which code, and uses this information to only run the relevant tests when code is changed.

When you start Quarkus with mvn quarkus:dev, you'll notice this message:

```
Tests paused
Press [r] to resume testing, [o] Toggle test output, [h] for more options>
```

This means that Quarkus is in continuous testing mode and has paused the tests. If you press `r`, the tests are executed and you will get the following:

```
All 3 tests are passing (0 skipped), 3 tests were run in 2307ms. Tests completed at
12:18:06.
Press [r] to resume testing, [o] Toggle test output, [h] for more options>
```

Now, break a test, save the file, and let Quarkus recompile the code and execute the tests. You'll get the following:

```
ERROR [i.q.test] ===================== TEST REPORT #2 =====================
ERROR [i.q.test] Test NumberResourceTest#shouldPingOpenAPI() failed
: java.lang.AssertionError: 1 expectation failed.
Expected status code <200> but was <404>.

    at ValidatableResponseImpl.statusCode(ValidatableResponseImpl.groovy)
    at NumberResourceTest.shouldPingOpenAPI(NumberResourceTest.java:39)

ERROR [i.q.test] >>>>>>>>>>>>>>>>>>>> 1 TEST FAILED <<<<<<<<<<<<<<<<<<<<

--
1 test failed (2 passing, 0 skipped), 3 tests were run in 576ms. Tests completed due
to changes to NumberResourceTest.class.
Press [r] to re-run, [o] Toggle test output, [h] for more options>
```

Fix the test, save the class, Quarkus reexecutes the tests again. Continuous testing is one of the numerous beauty of Quarkus.

4.8.4. Executing the Application

So far we've been running the *Number* microservice using `./mvnw quarkus:dev`. This development mode is really handy as it brings us live reload and continuous testing: we can execute the application, change some code, and Quarkus automatically restarts taking into account our changes. But this has a cost as the startup time is slower. In fact, if you check the banner displayed at startup in Listing 19 you will see "*Live Coding activated*" written as well as "*Profile dev activated*". So let's execute our microservice in production mode.

💻 Call to Action

(33)

Make sure to shutdown Quarkus that might be running in development mode. To execute our microservice in production mode, we first need to package. For that, execute the following Maven command:

```
rest-number$ ./mvnw package
```

That will result in an executable JAR under the target/quarkus-app directory. The executable JAR is called quarkus-run.jar. Having an executable JAR, we can execute it with:

```
rest-number$ java -jar target/quarkus-app/quarkus-run.jar
```

By doing so you will get traces that look like Listing 24.

If you get the following error, that's because you have several instances of Quarkus up and running, listening to the same port 8701. Shut them down, and start again.

```
ERROR [i.q.r.Application] Failed to start application (with profile prod)
Caused by: java.net.BindException: Address already in use
```

Listing 24. Startup Banner With Production Profile

```
INFO   _    _                       _
INFO  | \  | |                     | |
INFO  |  \| |_    _ _ __ ___  | |__    ___ _ __
INFO  | . ` | | | | | '_ ` _ \| '_ \ / _ \ '__|
INFO  | |\  | |_| | | | | | | | |_) | __/ |
INFO  \_| \_/\__,_|_| |_| |_|_.__/ \___|_|
INFO                      Powered by Quarkus
INFO  rest-number 2.0.0-SNAPSHOT on JVM started in 0.638s. Listening on:
http://0.0.0.0:8701
INFO  Profile prod activated.
INFO  Installed features: [cdi, resteasy, resteasy-jsonb, smallrye-openapi]
```

You'll notice a few things. First of all, the application has started slighter faster compared to development mode. Also, the logs show the message "*Profile prod activated*" and the message "*Live Coding activated*" has disappeared. By default, Quarkus disables Swagger UI in production mode. So, in the "*Installed features*" we no longer have the swagger-ui extension. Let's make sure our REST endpoint returns book numbers.

🖥️ Call to Action

Invoke a cURL command on the path `api/numbers` and you will get a JSON representation of book numbers:

```
$ curl -X GET -H "Accept: application/json" http://localhost:8701/api/numbers |
jq

{
  "asin": "B000A3PI3G",
  "ean_13": "7438504344437",
  "ean_8": "38833700",
  "isbn_10": "1-383-10381-X",
  "isbn_13": "978-0-929138-68-8"
}
```

Repeat the cURL command and you will see the numbers changing.

4.9. What You Have Built in This Chapter

After coding all the required artifacts, you should end up having the following directory structure for the *Number* microservice

```
.
└── rest-number
    ├── src
    │   ├── main
    │   │   ├── java
    │   │   │   └── org/agoncal/fascicle/quarkus/number
    │   │   │       ├── BookNumbers.java
    │   │   │       ├── NumberApplication.java
    │   │   │       ├── NumberApplicationLifeCycle.java
    │   │   │       └── NumberResource.java
    │   │   └── resources
    │   │       └── application.properties
    │   └── test
    │       └── java
    │           └── org/agoncal/fascicle/quarkus/number
    │               ├── NativeNumberResourceIT.java
    │               └── NumberResourceTest.java
    └── pom.xml
```

4.10. Summary

In this chapter, you developed a first microservice: the *Number* REST endpoint generates book numbers (ISBN, EAN and ASIN). In terms of business code, the endpoint is quite simple. What you focused on in this chapter was to develop a class with JAX-RS annotations and to execute it with Quarkus. Then, we used the Eclipse MicroProfile Configuration to inject a boolean value allowing the ISBN numbers to have separators, or not. This boolean is configurable externally in the `application.properties` file. Thanks to the JSON Binding we used a few annotations to customise the JSON output.

Quarkus comes with the `smallrye-openapi` extension that brings the OpenAPI and Swagger UI documentation for free in development mode. With a few Eclipse MicroProfile OpenAPI annotations, we managed to customise the documentation so that it's more explicit.

Testing a Quarkus application is quite easy: one annotation `@QuarkusTest` and we get the entire runtime environment for testing. We can even benefit from continuous testing will we develop. And when we finally need to execute an application in production, Quarkus can create an executable JAR suitable for production (no live reload and no Swagger UI).

In the next chapter, you will develop the *Book* microservice. It is a more complex microservice in terms of technology as it will access a relational database in a transactional way using object-relational mapping.

🖥 Call to Action

(35)

Now that you have your first microservice running and tested, you might want to commit your changes so you can come back to it later:

```
$ git add .
$ git commit -m "rest-number"
```

If in the next chapter, for some reason, you want to reset all your changes and come back to this commit, you can use the following commands:

```
$ git reset --hard
$ git clean -f -d
```

[37] **Quarkus Maven plugin** https://github.com/quarkusio/quarkus/tree/master/devtools/maven

[38] **JAX-RS** https://jcp.org/en/jsr/detail?id=370

[39] **JAX-RS GitHub** https://github.com/eclipse-ee4j/jaxrs-api

[40] **Java Faker** https://github.com/DiUS/java-faker

[41] **Ruby faker** https://github.com/faker-ruby

[42] **Configuration** https://microprofile.io/project/eclipse/microprofile-config

[43] **Configuration GitHub** https://github.com/eclipse/microprofile-config

[44] **JSON-B** https://jcp.org/en/jsr/detail?id=367

[45] **JSON-B GitHub** https://github.com/eclipse-ee4j/jsonb-api

[46] **OpenAPI Specification** https://github.com/OAI/OpenAPI-Specification

[47] **OpenAPI** https://microprofile.io/project/eclipse/microprofile-open-api

[48] **OpenAPI GitHub** https://github.com/eclipse/microprofile-open-api

[49] **Swagger UI** https://swagger.io/tools/swagger-ui

[50] **ASCII Art** https://en.wikipedia.org/wiki/ASCII_art

[51] **Observer Pattern** https://en.wikipedia.org/wiki/Observer_pattern

[52] **Configuring Logging** https://quarkus.io/guides/logging

[53] **REST Assured** http://rest-assured.io

Chapter 5. Developing the REST Book Microservice

So far the Vintage Store application is only made of one microservice: the *Number* REST endpoint. In this chapter, you will develop one extra microservice: a *Book* REST endpoint. The *Book* endpoint's role is to allow CRUD (*Create/Read/Update/Delete*) operations on books. In this chapter, you will create a Book entity and persist/update/delete/retrieve it from a PostgreSQL database in a transactional way.

 Remember that if you get stuck, you can get the entire code of the fascicle at https://github.com/agoncal/agoncal-fascicle-quarkus-pract/tree/2.0

5.1. What Will You Build in This Chapter?

In this chapter, you will:

- Bootstrap a new Quarkus application using its Maven plugin,
- Implement another REST API using JAX-RS,
- Constrain and validate business data with Bean Validation,
- Access the PostgreSQL database using Hibernate ORM with Panache,
- Use JTA transactions,
- Compose the application using CDI beans,
- Enable OpenAPI and Swagger UI on the *Book* endpoint,
- Display a banner at startup,
- Configure the datasource, logging and the HTTP port listening.

5.1.1. Overall Architecture

Figure 10 shows the architecture of what you will be building in this chapter. The *Number* REST API that we've built previously runs on Quarkus, on port 8701, and exposes an OpenAPI contract. As for the new *Book* REST API, it also runs on Quarkus (port 8702) and accesses a PostgreSQL database to store and retrieve books.

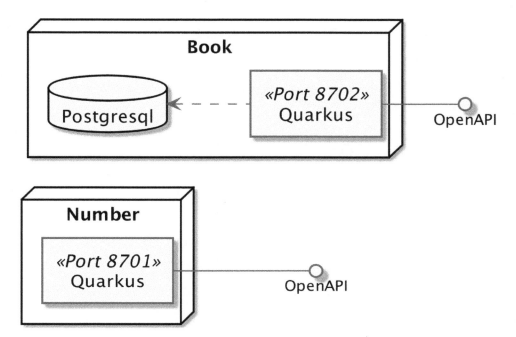

Figure 10. Overall architecture

5.2. Bootstrapping the REST Book Microservice

Like in the previous chapter, let's use the Quarkus Maven plugin to bootstrap the code of a new application to host the code of our *Book* microservice.

⌨ Call to Action

(36)

Bootstrap the *Book* microservice by using the Quarkus plugin and executing the following Maven command from the root directory:

```
mvn -U io.quarkus:quarkus-maven-plugin:2.5.0.Final:create \
    -DplatformVersion=2.5.0.Final \
    -DprojectGroupId=org.agoncal.fascicle.quarkus-practising \
    -DprojectArtifactId=rest-book \
    -DprojectVersion=2.0.0-SNAPSHOT \
    -DclassName="org.agoncal.fascicle.quarkus.book.BookResource" \
    -Dpath="/api/books" \
    -Dextensions="resteasy, resteasy-jsonb, hibernate-orm-panache, jdbc-
postgresql, hibernate-validator, smallrye-openapi"
```

Once the `rest-book` module created, you should see it declared in the Parent Maven POM with the other modules:

```
<modules>
  <module>first-step</module>
  <module>infrastructure</module>
  <module>load-vintagestore</module>
  <module>rest-book</module>
  <module>rest-number</module>
  <module>ui-vintagestore</module>
</modules>
```

5.2.1. Directory Structure

The Quarkus plugin command generates a new Maven module called `rest-book` with a REST endpoint called `BookResource` located at the `/api/books` path. Below the directory structure with all the generated artifacts:

```
.
└── rest-book
    ├── src
    │   ├── main
    │   │   ├── docker
    │   │   │   ├── Dockerfile.jvm
    │   │   │   ├── Dockerfile.legacy-jar
    │   │   │   ├── Dockerfile.native
    │   │   │   └── Dockerfile.native-distroless
    │   │   ├── java
    │   │   │   └── org/agoncal/fascicle/quarkus/book
    │   │   │       └── BookResource.java
    │   │   └── resources
    │   │       ├── META-INF
    │   │       │   └── resources
    │   │       │       └── index.html
    │   │       └── application.properties
    │   └── test
    │       └── java
    │           └── org/agoncal/fascicle/quarkus/book
    │               ├── BookResourceTest.java
    │               └── NativeBookResourceIT.java
    ├── mvnw
    ├── mvnw.cmd
    └── pom.xml
```

5.2.2. Maven Dependencies

Once generated, the pom.xml at the root of the rest-book looks like Listing 25. It has a header with
the same <groupId> as the *Number* microservice pom.xml but with a different <artifactId>. It defines
a set of properties and imports the Quarkus BOM (*Bill of Materials*).

Listing 25. Header of the pom.xml

```xml
<project xsi:schemaLocation="http://maven.apache.org/POM/4.0.0
https://maven.apache.org/xsd/maven-4.0.0.xsd" xmlns="
http://maven.apache.org/POM/4.0.0"
         xmlns:xsi="http://www.w3.org/2001/XMLSchema-instance">
  <modelVersion>4.0.0</modelVersion>

  <groupId>org.agoncal.fascicle.quarkus-practising</groupId>
  <artifactId>rest-book</artifactId>
  <version>2.0.0-SNAPSHOT</version>
  <name>Practising Quarkus :: Books REST Microservice</name>

  <properties>
    <compiler-plugin.version>3.8.1</compiler-plugin.version>
    <maven.compiler.parameters>true</maven.compiler.parameters>
    <maven.compiler.source>11</maven.compiler.source>
    <maven.compiler.target>11</maven.compiler.target>
    <project.build.sourceEncoding>UTF-8</project.build.sourceEncoding>
    <project.reporting.outputEncoding>UTF-8</project.reporting.outputEncoding>
    <quarkus.platform.artifact-id>quarkus-bom</quarkus.platform.artifact-id>
    <quarkus.platform.group-id>io.quarkus</quarkus.platform.group-id>
    <quarkus.platform.version>2.5.0.Final</quarkus.platform.version>
    <surefire-plugin.version>3.0.0-M5</surefire-plugin.version>
  </properties>
  <dependencyManagement>
    <dependencies>
      <dependency>
        <groupId>${quarkus.platform.group-id}</groupId>
        <artifactId>${quarkus.platform.artifact-id}</artifactId>
        <version>${quarkus.platform.version}</version>
        <type>pom</type>
        <scope>import</scope>
      </dependency>
    </dependencies>
  </dependencyManagement>
```

In the dependencies section in Listing 26 you find some of the same dependencies used in the previous chapter:

- quarkus-resteasy: REST framework implementing JAX-RS.

- quarkus-resteasy-jsonb: JSON-B serialisation support for RESTEasy.

- quarkus-smallrye-openapi: Documents the REST APIs with OpenAPI and comes with Swagger UI.

- quarkus-junit5: JUnit 5 support in Quarkus.

- rest-assured: Framework to easily test REST endpoints.

But with the *Book* microservice being more complex (database access, transactions, etc.), we need to add a few extra Maven dependencies:

- quarkus-hibernate-orm-panache: Hibernate ORM with Panache.

- quarkus-jdbc-postgresql: PostgreSQL JDBC driver.

- quarkus-hibernate-validator: Bean Validation to constrain our business model.

Listing 26. Maven Dependencies

```xml
<dependencies>
  <dependency>
    <groupId>io.quarkus</groupId>
    <artifactId>quarkus-hibernate-orm-panache</artifactId>
  </dependency>
  <dependency>
    <groupId>io.quarkus</groupId>
    <artifactId>quarkus-hibernate-validator</artifactId>
  </dependency>
  <dependency>
    <groupId>io.quarkus</groupId>
    <artifactId>quarkus-smallrye-openapi</artifactId>
  </dependency>
  <dependency>
    <groupId>io.quarkus</groupId>
    <artifactId>quarkus-resteasy-jsonb</artifactId>
  </dependency>
  <dependency>
    <groupId>io.quarkus</groupId>
    <artifactId>quarkus-jdbc-postgresql</artifactId>
  </dependency>
  <dependency>
    <groupId>io.quarkus</groupId>
    <artifactId>quarkus-resteasy</artifactId>
  </dependency>
  <dependency>
    <groupId>io.quarkus</groupId>
    <artifactId>quarkus-arc</artifactId>
  </dependency>
  <dependency>
    <groupId>io.quarkus</groupId>
    <artifactId>quarkus-junit5</artifactId>
    <scope>test</scope>
  </dependency>
  <dependency>
    <groupId>io.rest-assured</groupId>
    <artifactId>rest-assured</artifactId>
    <scope>test</scope>
  </dependency>
</dependencies>
```

As you saw in the previous chapter, testing a microservice with Quarkus is easy. As described in Listing 26 you just need a few test dependencies (quarkus-junit5 for JUnit support and rest-assured for testing REST endpoints).

The last part of the `pom.xml` in Listing 27 shows the required plugins to execute and test our code. The *Book* REST endpoint uses the same plugins as the *Number* REST endpoint that you saw in the previous chapter.

Listing 27. Building Steps

```xml
<build>
  <plugins>
    <plugin>
      <groupId>${quarkus.platform.group-id}</groupId>
      <artifactId>quarkus-maven-plugin</artifactId>
      <version>${quarkus.platform.version}</version>
      <extensions>true</extensions>
      <executions>
        <execution>
          <goals>
            <goal>build</goal>
            <goal>generate-code</goal>
            <goal>generate-code-tests</goal>
          </goals>
        </execution>
      </executions>
    </plugin>
    <plugin>
      <artifactId>maven-compiler-plugin</artifactId>
      <version>${compiler-plugin.version}</version>
      <configuration>
        <parameters>${maven.compiler.parameters}</parameters>
      </configuration>
    </plugin>
    <plugin>
      <artifactId>maven-surefire-plugin</artifactId>
      <version>${surefire-plugin.version}</version>
      <configuration>
        <systemPropertyVariables>
          <java.util.logging.manager>
org.jboss.logmanager.LogManager</java.util.logging.manager>
          <maven.home>${maven.home}</maven.home>
        </systemPropertyVariables>
      </configuration>
    </plugin>
  </plugins>
</build>
```

5.3. Mapping Objects to a Relational Database

The *Book* REST endpoint allows us to insert/update/delete and select books from the PostgreSQL relational database. When dealing with database access in Java, one can use JDBC (*Java DataBase*

Connectivity[54]). But this low-level API can be verbose and quite cumbersome for simple use cases. To ease the relational-database access, Quarkus implements the JPA specification.

Java Persistence API[55] (JPA) is a Java specification that manages objects stored in a relational database. JPA gives the developer an object-oriented view in order to transparently use entities instead of tables. It also comes with a query language (*Java Persistence Query Language*, or JPQL), allowing complex queries over objects.

The Java Persistence API APIs are all defined under the `javax.persistence` package. Table 10 lists the main subpackages defined in JPA 2.2 (under the root `javax.persistence` package[56]).

Table 10. Main javax.persistence Subpackages

Subpackage	Description
root	Root package of the JPA APIs
`criteria`	Java Persistence Criteria API, allowing the writing of queries in an object-oriented way
`metamodel`	Java Persistence Metamodel API, bringing type safety to the queries
`spi`	Internal SPIs (*Service Provider Interfaces*) implemented by the provider

 If you like the format of this fascicle and are interested in Java Persistence API, check out the references for my *Understanding JPA 2.2* fascicle in Appendix F.

Along with APIs, JPA comes with a set of annotations. Table 11 lists a subset of the most commonly used annotations.

Table 11. Main JPA Annotations

Annotation	Description
`@Entity`	POJOs become persistent objects when annotated with `@Entity`
`@Column`	Specifies the mapped column for a persistent property (name, length, unique, etc.)
`@GeneratedValue`	Defines the value generation policy of primary keys
`@Id`	Specifies the primary key of an entity
`@Table`	Specifies the primary table for the annotated entity
`@Transient`	Specifies that the property is not persistent
`@OneToOne, @OneToMany, @ManyToOne, @ManyToMany`	Relation multiplicity

To manipulate books in a relational database, we could create a `Book` entity using some of these JPA annotations. But with Quarkus, we can go further. Quarkus brings even more simplicity to JPA with a framework called *Hibernate ORM with Panache*.

Hibernate ORM is the Quarkus JPA implementation and offers you the full breadth of a JPA object-relational mapper. It makes complex mappings and queries possible, but it does not make simple and common mappings trivial. Hibernate ORM with Panache (pronounced *pa·nash*) focuses on simplifying your JPA entities as well as your repositories.

 Panache is about more than just making JPA easier. In fact, there is also a MongoDB with Panache extension and an experimental RESTful web service with Panache extension. MongoDB with Panache provides active record style entities (and repositories) and focuses on making entities trivial to map to a MongoDB database. To differentiate both technologies, we use the terms *Hibernate ORM with Panache* and *MongoDB with Panache*.

The Book entity in Listing 28 represents a book with a title, an author, ISBN numbers, a price and so on. Being a JPA entity it is annotated with @Entity and some attributes are annotated with @Column. And to define our Book JPA entity to be a Panache entity, we simply need to extend PanacheEntity.

Listing 28. Book Panache Entity with JPA Annotations

```
@Schema(description = "Book representation")
@Entity
public class Book extends PanacheEntity {

  @Schema(required = true)
  public String title;
  @Column(name = "isbn_13")
  public String isbn13;
  @Column(name = "isbn_10")
  public String isbn10;
  public String author;
  @Column(name = "year_of_publication")
  public Integer yearOfPublication;
  @Column(name = "nb_of_pages")
  public Integer nbOfPages;
  public Integer rank;
  public BigDecimal price;
  @Column(name = "small_image_url")
  public URL smallImageUrl;
  @Column(name = "medium_image_url")
  public URL mediumImageUrl;
  @Column(length = 10000)
  public String description;

}
```

💻 Call to Action

Create the new class `org.agoncal.fascicle.quarkus.book.Book` and add the code shown in Listing 28. The `Book` entity uses JPA annotations (eg. `@Entity`) and Panache APIs (eg. `PanacheEntity`). It is also annotated with the `@Schema` annotation from OpenAPI (this will be useful when we later check the documentation of the Book REST endpoint). Make sure to use the right imports:

```
import io.quarkus.hibernate.orm.panache.PanacheEntity;
import org.eclipse.microprofile.openapi.annotations.media.Schema;

import javax.persistence.Column;
import javax.persistence.Entity;
import java.net.URL;
```

Have you noticed that in Listing 28 we use public fields and got rid of getters and setters? Under the hood, Panache generates all getters and setters that are missing, and rewrites every access to these fields to use the accessor methods. This way you can still write useful accessors, but only when you need them. Did you also notice that we do not require to specify a default constructor anymore?

5.3.1. Adding Operations

`Book` needs to be stored, updated and retrieved from a database. Thanks to Panache, once `Book` extends `PanacheEntity`, it gets most of the common operations for free. Below are some operations you are able to do on a `Book` Panache entity:

```
// creating a book
Book book = new Book();
book.title = "H2G2";
book.rank = 9;

// persist it
book.persist();

// getting a list of all Book entities
List<Book> books = Book.listAll();

// finding a specific book by ID
book = Book.findById(id);

// counting all books
long countAll = Book.count();
```

But we are missing a business method. In our use case, we need to return a random book. For that, it's just a matter of adding the method findRandom() shown in Listing 29 to our Book entity.

Listing 29. Book Panache Entity with an Operation

```
public static Book findRandom() {
  long countBooks = Book.count();
  int randomBook = new Random().nextInt((int) countBooks);
  return Book.findAll().page(randomBook, 1).firstResult();
}
```

▣ Call to Action

(38)

Edit the Book class and add the findRandom() method with the code shown in Listing 29.

5.4. Accessing the Database in a Transactional Way

Thanks to JPA annotations, we are able to map our Book entity to a relational database. Panache brings CRUD operations so we can now persist or retrieve a book easily (e.g. book.persist() or Book.count()). What we are missing is a transactional layer so we can insert, update or delete a book in a transactional way. To manipulate the Book entity we need to develop a transactional BookService class. The idea is to wrap methods that modify the database (e.g. entity.persist()) within a transaction. For that, Quarkus implements the JTA specification.

In Java, transaction management is done through the *Java Transaction API* (JTA) specified by JSR 907[57]. JTA defines a set of interfaces for the application or the container in order to demarcate transaction boundaries, and it also defines APIs to deal with the transaction manager.

The Java Transaction API APIs are all defined under the javax.transaction package. Table 12 lists the main subpackages defined in JTA 1.2 (under the root javax.transaction package[58]).

Table 12. Main javax.transaction Subpackages

Subpackage	Description
root	Root package of the JTA APIs
xa	Interfaces and classes to accomplish distributed XA transactions[59]

Along with APIs, JTA comes with a set of annotations. Table 13 lists a subset of the most commonly used annotations.

Table 13. Main JTA Annotations

Annotation	Description
@Transactional	Gives the ability to declaratively control transaction boundaries
@TransactionScoped	Provides the ability to define bean instances whose life cycle is scoped to the currently active transaction

The BookService class in Listing 30 is a CDI bean with a life cycle bound to the life of the application (@ApplicationScoped). Then, to be transactional, it's just a matter of marking the entire class, or the methods we need with @Transactional.

Listing 30. Transactional Book Service

```java
@ApplicationScoped
@Transactional(Transactional.TxType.REQUIRED)
public class BookService {

  @Inject
  Logger LOGGER;

  @Inject
  EntityManager em;


  public Book persistBook(@Valid Book book) {
    Book.persist(book);
    return book;
  }

  @Transactional(Transactional.TxType.SUPPORTS)
  public List<Book> findAllBooks() {
    return Book.listAll();
  }

  @Transactional(Transactional.TxType.SUPPORTS)
  public Optional<Book> findBookById(Long id) {
    return Book.findByIdOptional(id);
  }

  @Transactional(Transactional.TxType.SUPPORTS)
  public Book findRandomBook() {
    Book randomBook = null;
    while (randomBook == null) {
      randomBook = Book.findRandom();
    }
    return randomBook;
  }

  public Book updateBook(@Valid Book book) {
    Book entity = em.merge(book);
    return entity;
  }

  public void deleteBook(Long id) {
    Book.deleteById(id);
  }
}
```

39

Create the new class org.agoncal.fascicle.quarkus.book.BookService class and add the code shown in Listing 30. BookService doesn't use any Panache APIs, but instead, CDI, JPA, JTA and Bean Validation. Make sure to import the right APIs:

```
import org.jboss.logging.Logger;
import javax.enterprise.context.ApplicationScoped;
import javax.inject.Inject;
import javax.persistence.EntityManager;
import javax.transaction.Transactional;
import javax.validation.Valid;
import java.util.List;
import java.util.Optional;
```

The @Transactional annotations can be used to control transaction boundaries at the method level or at the class level to ensure every method is transactional. That means that findAllBooks, findBookById and findRandomBook have a transaction of type SUPPORTS and persistBook, updateBook and deleteBook of type REQUIRED. These transaction types are explained in Table 14.

Table 14. Transaction Types

Attribute	Description
REQUIRED	This attribute (default value) means that a method must always be invoked within a transaction. The container creates a new transaction if the method is invoked from a non-transactional client. If the client (caller) has a transaction context, the business method runs within the client's transaction. You should use REQUIRED if you are making calls that should be managed in a transaction, but you can't assume that the client is calling the method from a transaction context.
REQUIRES_NEW	The container always creates a new transaction before executing a method, regardless of whether the client is executed within a transaction. If the client is running within a transaction, the container suspends that transaction temporarily, creates a second one, commits or rolls it back, and then resumes the first transaction. This means that the success or failure of the second transaction has no effect on the existing client transaction. You should use REQUIRES_NEW when you don't want a rollback to affect the client.
SUPPORTS	The transactional method inherits the client's transaction context. If a transaction context is available, it is used by the method; if not, the container invokes the method with no transaction context. You should use SUPPORTS when you have read-only access to the database table.
MANDATORY	The container requires a transaction before invoking the business method but should not create a new one. If the client has a transaction context, it is propagated; if not, a javax.transaction.TransactionalException is thrown.

Attribute	Description
NOT_SUPPORTED	The transactional method cannot be invoked in a transaction context. If the client has no transaction context, nothing happens; if it does, the container suspends the client's transaction, invokes the method, and then resumes the transaction when the method returns.
NEVER	The transactional method must not be invoked from a transactional client. If the client is running within a transaction context, the container throws a `javax.transaction.TransactionalException`.

5.5. Exposing the Book REST Endpoint

To expose a REST API of these transactional services, we need a REST endpoint. Like in the previous chapter, `BookResource` uses JAX-RS and OpenAPI annotations to expose a documented contract and a set of methods to allow CRUD operations.

💻 Call to Action

40

Edit the existing BookResource class (leave the generated method hello() we will need it later). This REST endpoint exposes a documented API (with OpenAPI) allowing users to create, read, update and delete book. Add to BookResource the code in Listing 31, Listing 32, Listing 33, Listing 34 and Listing 35. This code mostly uses JAX-RS and OpenAPI APIs:

```java
import org.eclipse.microprofile.openapi.annotations.Operation;
import org.eclipse.microprofile.openapi.annotations.enums.SchemaType;
import org.eclipse.microprofile.openapi.annotations.media.Content;
import org.eclipse.microprofile.openapi.annotations.media.Schema;
import org.eclipse.microprofile.openapi.annotations.parameters.Parameter;
import org.eclipse.microprofile.openapi.annotations.parameters.RequestBody;
import org.eclipse.microprofile.openapi.annotations.responses.APIResponse;
import org.eclipse.microprofile.openapi.annotations.tags.Tag;
import org.jboss.logging.Logger;

import javax.inject.Inject;
import javax.validation.Valid;
import javax.ws.rs.Consumes;
import javax.ws.rs.DELETE;
import javax.ws.rs.GET;
import javax.ws.rs.POST;
import javax.ws.rs.PUT;
import javax.ws.rs.Path;
import javax.ws.rs.PathParam;
import javax.ws.rs.Produces;
import javax.ws.rs.core.Context;
import javax.ws.rs.core.MediaType;
import javax.ws.rs.core.Response;
import javax.ws.rs.core.UriBuilder;
import javax.ws.rs.core.UriInfo;
import static javax.ws.rs.core.Response.Status.NOT_FOUND;
```

Listing 31 shows the header of the BookResource class. The @Path annotation tells us that the API will be accessible through the /api/books and will mostly produce and consume JSON. The getRandomBook() is accessible through an HTTP GET on /api/books/random and returns a random book from the database (invoking the BookService.findRandomBook() method). Both OpenAPI annotations @Operation and @APIResponse document the getRandomBook() method while @Tag gives a description to the entire endpoint. We will talk about @Inject and *Dependency Injection* in the next section.

Listing 31. Book REST Endpoint Retrieving a Random Book

```
@Path("/api/books")
@Produces(MediaType.APPLICATION_JSON)
@Consumes(MediaType.APPLICATION_JSON)
@Tag(name = "Book Endpoint")
public class BookResource {

  @Inject
  BookService service;

  @Inject
  Logger LOGGER;

  @Operation(summary = "Returns a random book")
  @APIResponse(responseCode = "200", content = @Content(mediaType = MediaType
.APPLICATION_JSON, schema = @Schema(implementation = Book.class)))
  @GET
  @Path("/random")
  public Response getRandomBook() {
    Book book = service.findRandomBook();
    LOGGER.debug("Found random book " + book);
    return Response.ok(book).build();
  }
}
```

The getAllBooks() method in Listing 32 returns the entire list of books from the database (notice the SchemaType.ARRAY type in the OpenAPI documentation). If the invocation returns at least one book, a 200-OK is returned by the response. If the list of books is empty, a 204-No Content is automatically sent as a response.

Listing 32. Retrieving All the Books

```
@Operation(summary = "Returns all the books from the database")
@APIResponse(responseCode = "200", content = @Content(mediaType = MediaType
.APPLICATION_JSON, schema = @Schema(implementation = Book.class, type = SchemaType
.ARRAY)))
@APIResponse(responseCode = "204", description = "No books")
@GET
public Response getAllBooks() {
  List<Book> books = service.findAllBooks();
  LOGGER.debug("Total number of books " + books);
  return Response.ok(books).build();
}
```

Listing 33 details the getBook() method that returns a book giving an identifier. To invoke this method you will need an HTTP GET on /api/books passing the book id (e.g. /api/books/1234). The binding of the parameter is made using the JAX-RS @PathParam annotation. The @Parameter annotation comes from OpenAPI and brings documentation to the REST contract.

Listing 33. Retrieving a Book By Identifier

```java
@Operation(summary = "Returns a book for a given identifier")
@APIResponse(responseCode = "200", content = @Content(mediaType = MediaType
.APPLICATION_JSON, schema = @Schema(implementation = Book.class)))
@APIResponse(responseCode = "404", description = "The book is not found for the given
identifier")
@GET
@Path("/{id}")
public Response getBook(@Parameter(description = "Book identifier", required = true)
@PathParam("id") Long id) {
  Optional<Book> book = service.findBookById(id);
  if (book.isPresent()) {
    LOGGER.debug("Found book " + book);
    return Response.ok(book).build();
  } else {
    LOGGER.debug("No book found with id " + id);
    return Response.status(NOT_FOUND).build();
  }
}
```

The createBook() method (see Listing 34) takes a JSON representation of a book from the HTTP request, and persists a book into the database thanks to the transactional method persistBook() from the BookService. Notice that once the book is persisted, createBook() returns the URI of the newly created book, not the book itself, and a return code 201-Created (thanks to the Response.created() method). With this URL, the consumer would be able to do an HTTP GET if needed. On the contrary, the updateBook() method returns the updated book. Both methods use the @Valid annotation from Bean Validation that we will see in the following section. Here we see the HTTP verbs in action: @POST to create a new book, @PUT to update an existing one.

Listing 34. Persisting and Updating a Book Into the Database

```
@Operation(summary = "Creates a valid book")
@APIResponse(responseCode = "201", description = "The URI of the created book",
content = @Content(mediaType = MediaType.APPLICATION_JSON, schema = @Schema
(implementation = URI.class)))
@POST
public Response createBook(@RequestBody(required = true, content = @Content(mediaType
= MediaType.APPLICATION_JSON, schema = @Schema(implementation = Book.class))) @Valid
Book book, @Context UriInfo uriInfo) {
  book = service.persistBook(book);
  UriBuilder builder = uriInfo.getAbsolutePathBuilder().path(Long.toString(book.id));
  LOGGER.debug("New book created with URI " + builder.build().toString());
  return Response.created(builder.build()).build();
}

@Operation(summary = "Updates an existing book")
@APIResponse(responseCode = "200", description = "The updated book", content =
@Content(mediaType = MediaType.APPLICATION_JSON, schema = @Schema(implementation =
Book.class)))
@PUT
public Response updateBook(@RequestBody(required = true, content = @Content(mediaType
= MediaType.APPLICATION_JSON, schema = @Schema(implementation = Book.class))) @Valid
Book book) {
  book = service.updateBook(book);
  LOGGER.debug("Book updated with new valued " + book);
  return Response.ok(book).build();
}
```

To delete a book, the deleteBook() method in Listing 35 takes a book identifier as a parameter and is accessible on an HTTP DELETE invocation. If the delete succeeds, a 204-NO CONTENT is sent back as a response.

Listing 35. Deleting a Book

```
@Operation(summary = "Deletes an existing book")
@APIResponse(responseCode = "204", description = "The book has been successfully
deleted")
@DELETE
@Path("/{id}")
public Response deleteBook(@Parameter(description = "Book identifier", required =
true) @PathParam("id") Long id) {
  service.deleteBook(id);
  LOGGER.debug("Book deleted with " + id);
  return Response.noContent().build();
}
```

All the methods of the BookResource have been annotated with OpenAPI annotations. Remember that @Operation informs us about the method, usually giving it a description, @APIResponse documents all the possible responses returned by the method, and @Parameter describes the parameters that each method takes. Thanks to these OpenAPI annotations, the OpenAPI v3 contract will be clearer and more documented.

5.5.1. Dependency Injection

The BookResource deals with all the REST concerns: it intercepts HTTP GET, POST, PUT, DELETE calls, deals with the JSON representation of a Book, sends back HTTP status codes, etc. But to actually insert, update or retrieve a book from the PostgreSQL database, it delegates all the calls to the transactional BookService. This separation of concerns[60] is good because it simplifies the development and maintenance of an application. But that means that BookResource depends on BookService. This dependence can be achieved with dependency injection and Quarkus, at its core, uses CDI to do dependency injection. Dependency injection in Quarkus is based on ArC[61] which is a CDI-lite dependency injection solution tailored for Quarkus' architecture.

Context and Dependency Injection[62] (CDI) is a central technology in Jakarta EE or in MicroProfile. Its programming model turns nearly every component into an injectable, interceptable and manageable bean. CDI is built on the concept of "*loose coupling, strong typing*", meaning that beans are loosely coupled, but in a strongly-typed way. Decoupling goes further by bringing interceptors, decorators and events to the entire platform. CDI homogenises scopes among beans, as well as context and life cycle management.

The Context and Dependency Injection APIs and annotations are defined under several root packages: javax.inject, javax.enterprise and javax.interceptor. Table 15 lists the main subpackages defined in CDI 2.0.

Table 15. Main CDI Subpackages

Subpackage	Description
javax.inject	Root package of the CDI APIs
javax.enterprise.inject	Core dependency injection APIs
javax.enterprise.context	Scope and contextual APIs
javax.enterprise.event	Event and observer APIs
javax.enterprise.util	Utility package
javax.interceptor	Interceptor APIs (JSR 318)

Along with APIs, CDI comes with a set of annotations. Table 16 lists a subset of the most commonly used annotations.

Table 16. Main CDI Annotations

Annotation	Description
@Inject	Identifies injectable constructors, methods, and fields
@Qualifier	Identifies qualifier annotations

Annotation	Description
@ApplicationScoped, @SessionScoped, @RequestScoped, @Singleton, @Dependent	Set of annotations defining the life cycle of a bean
@Observes	Identifies the event parameter of an observer method

 Not all the previous CDI annotations are supported by Quarkus. Quarkus does not fully implement CDI but, rather, a lighter version of it (a.k.a. CDI-lite). You can check the list of supported features and the list of limitations[63].

The way BookResource injects a reference of BookService is easy and straightforward. As shown in Listing 36, it's just a matter of using the @Inject annotation.

Listing 36. Dependency Injection

```
@Path("/api/books")
@Produces(MediaType.APPLICATION_JSON)
@Consumes(MediaType.APPLICATION_JSON)
@Tag(name = "Book Endpoint")
public class BookResource {

    @Inject
    BookService service;
```

5.6. Validating Data

Previously (see Listing 30), you've seen that the BookService uses the @Valid annotation on the parameters of a few methods. This is a way to validate data prior to entering a method: if the given parameters are not valid, then the method is not even invoked. This is possible because Quarkus implements Bean Validation.

Validating data is a common task that developers have to do and it is spread throughout all layers of an application (from client to database). This common practice is time-consuming, error prone, and hard to maintain in the long run. Besides, some of these constraints are so frequently used that they could be considered standard (checking for a null value, size, range, etc.). It would be good to be able to centralise these constraints in one place and share them across layers. That's where Bean Validation comes into play.

Bean Validation[64] allows you to write a constraint once and reuse it in different application layers. It is layer agnostic, meaning that the same constraint can be used from the presentation to the business model layer. Bean Validation is available for server-side applications as well as rich Java client graphical interfaces (Swing, Android, JavaFX etc.).

Bean Validation allows you to apply already-defined common constraints to your application, and also to write your own validation rules in order to validate beans, attributes, constructors, method return values and parameters. The API is very easy to use and flexible as it encourages you to define your constraints using annotations or XML descriptors.

 If you like the format of this fascicle and are interested in Bean Validation, check out the references for my *Understanding Bean Validation 2.0* fascicle in Appendix F.

The Bean Validation APIs and annotations are all defined under the `javax.validation` package. Table 17 lists the main subpackages defined in Bean Validation 2.0 (under the root `javax.validation` package[65]).

Table 17. Main javax.validation Subpackages

Subpackage	Description
root	Root package of the Bean Validation APIs
bootstrap	Classes used to bootstrap Bean Validation and to create a provider agnostic configuration
constraints	This package contains all the built-in constraints
constraintvalidation	Package containing constructs specific to constraint validators
executable	Package related to the control and execution of validation on constructors and methods
groups	Bean Validation groups for defining a subset of constraints
metadata	Metadata repository for all defined constraints and query API
spi	Internal SPIs (*Service Provider Interfaces*) implemented by the provider
valueextraction	Package dedicated to extracting values to validate container elements

Along with APIs, Bean Validation comes with a set of annotations. Table 18 lists a subset of the most commonly used annotations.

Table 18. Main Bean Validation Annotations

Annotation	Description
@Constraint	Marks an annotation as being a Bean Validation constraint
@Email	The string has to be a well-formed email address
@Max, @Min	The annotated element must be a number whose value is lower or equal, or higher or equal to the specified value
@Null, @NotNull	The annotated element must be null or not null
@Past, @Future	The annotated element must be an instant, date or time in the past or in the future
@Valid	Marks a property, method parameter or method return type for validation

But what does it mean to be valid? What makes a book valid and a book invalid? Well, it's just a matter of adding the right annotations on the Book class or attributes. As you can see in Listing 37, if you add a @NotNull annotation on the title attribute it will indicate to Bean Validation that the title of a book cannot be null. The rank attribute is annotated twice with @Min(1) and @Max(10) which indicates that the rank of a book should be between 1 and 10. The description of a book can be null, but if not, has to have a length between 1 and 10,000 characters.

Listing 37. Book Panache Entity with Bean Validation Annotations

```java
@Schema(description = "Book representation")
@Entity
public class Book extends PanacheEntity {

    @NotNull
    @Schema(required = true)
    public String title;
    @Column(name = "isbn_13")
    public String isbn13;
    @Column(name = "isbn_10")
    public String isbn10;
    public String author;
    @Column(name = "year_of_publication")
    public Integer yearOfPublication;
    @Column(name = "nb_of_pages")
    public Integer nbOfPages;
    @Min(1) @Max(10)
    public Integer rank;
    public BigDecimal price;
    @Column(name = "small_image_url")
    public URL smallImageUrl;
    @Column(name = "medium_image_url")
    public URL mediumImageUrl;
    @Column(length = 10000)
    @Size(min = 1, max = 10000)
    public String description;

}
```

Notice in Listing 37 that you can have JPA column annotations (e.g. @Column), Bean Validation constraint annotations (e.g. @Size) and OpenAPI annotations (e.g. @Schema) on the same attribute.

💻 Call to Action

(41)

Edit the Book class and add the Bean Validation annotations to the attributes as shown in Listing 37. These annotations are all under the javax.validation.constraints package:

```java
import javax.validation.constraints.Max;
import javax.validation.constraints.Min;
import javax.validation.constraints.NotNull;
import javax.validation.constraints.Size;
```

If you look at the code in Listing 38 you will see that both methods that persist and update a book, pass a Book object as a parameter. Thanks to the Bean Validation's @Valid annotation, the Book object will be checked to see if it's valid or not. If it's not, the method will not be invoked.

Listing 38. Book Service Validating the Book Parameter

```
public Book persistBook(@Valid Book book) {
  Book.persist(book);
  return book;
}

public Book updateBook(@Valid Book book) {
  Book entity = em.merge(book);
  return entity;
}
```

5.7. Documenting with OpenAPI

In Listing 28 we have added some OpenAPI annotations (e.g. @Schema) so the Book entity gets some extra information. We've also added some OpenAPI annotations to the BookResource class (see Listing 31). So we already have good documentation on the REST endpoint. Now it's just a matter of having documentation for the overall application.

5.7.1. Documenting the Application

The BookApplication class in Listing 39 is just there to customise the OpenAPI contract for the entire application. @OpenAPIDefinition provides metadata about the API such as the team to contact (@Contact) or the documentation to know more about the API (@ExternalDocumentation).

Listing 39. Custom OpenAPI Documentation for the Application

```
@ApplicationPath("/")
@OpenAPIDefinition(
  info = @Info(title = "Book API",
    description = "This API allows CRUD operations on books",
    version = "2.0",
    contact = @Contact(name = "@agoncal", url = "https://twitter.com/agoncal")),
  externalDocs = @ExternalDocumentation(url = "https://github.com/agoncal/agoncal-
fascicle-quarkus-pract", description = "All the Practising Quarkus code"),
  tags = {
    @Tag(name = "api", description = "Public API that can be used by anybody"),
    @Tag(name = "books", description = "Anybody interested in books")
  }
)
public class BookApplication extends Application {
}
```

Create a new class called `BookApplication` under the package `org.agoncal.fascicle.quarkus.book` with the code in Listing 39. Make sure you import the right annotations from the `org.eclipse.microprofile.openapi.annotations` package.

5.7.2. The Customised OpenAPI Contract

With all the added documentation that we've done on the `Book` entity, `BookResource` and `BookApplication`, the OpenAPI contract looks like the one in Listing 40.

Listing 40. Header of the Custom OpenAPI YAML Contract

```
openapi: 3.0.3
info:
  title: Book API
  description: This API allows CRUD operations on books
  contact:
    name: '@agoncal'
    url: https://twitter.com/agoncal
  version: "2.0"
externalDocs:
  description: All the Practising Quarkus code
  url: https://github.com/agoncal/agoncal-fascicle-quarkus-pract
tags:
  - name: api
    description: Public API that can be used by anybody
  - name: books
    description: Anybody interested in books
  - name: Book Endpoint
```

Listing 41 shows the documentation for the root path `/api/books`. You can see the GET, PUT, POST and DELETE methods being documented. Notice that most methods produce or consume a `Book` that is later documented (`$ref: '#/components/schemas/Book'`) in Listing 43.

Listing 41. Documentation for GET/POST/PUT/DELETE

```
paths:
  /api/books:
    get:
      summary: Returns all the books from the database
      responses:
        "200":
          description: OK
          content:
            application/json:
              schema:
```

```yaml
              type: array
              items:
                $ref: '#/components/schemas/Book'
      "204":
        description: No books
  put:
    summary: Updates an existing book
    requestBody:
      content:
        application/json:
          schema:
            $ref: '#/components/schemas/Book'
      required: true
    responses:
      "200":
        description: The updated book
        content:
          application/json:
            schema:
              $ref: '#/components/schemas/Book'
  post:
    summary: Creates a valid book
    requestBody:
      content:
        application/json:
          schema:
            $ref: '#/components/schemas/Book'
      required: true
    responses:
      "201":
        description: The URI of the created book
        content:
          application/json:
            schema:
              format: uri
              type: string
  delete:
    summary: Deletes an existing book
    parameters:
      - name: id
        in: path
        description: Book identifier
        required: true
        schema:
          format: int64
          type: integer
    responses:
      "204":
        description: The book has been successfully deleted
```

Listing 42 shows the documentation of the other paths: an HTTP GET on `/api/books/random` that returns a random book, and `/api/books/{id}` returning a book by identifier. Both endpoints return a Book.

Listing 42. Documentation for Other GET Invocations

```yaml
/api/books/random:
  get:
    summary: Returns a random book
    responses:
      "200":
        description: OK
        content:
          application/json:
            schema:
              $ref: '#/components/schemas/Book'

/api/books/{id}:
  get:
    summary: Returns a book for a given identifier
    parameters:
      - name: id
        in: path
        description: Book identifier
        required: true
        schema:
          format: int64
          type: integer
    responses:
      "200":
        description: OK
        content:
          application/json:
            schema:
              $ref: '#/components/schemas/Book'
      "404":
        description: The book is not found for the given identifier
```

At the end of the YAML documentation (see Listing 43) you'll find the description and documentation of our Book entity.

Listing 43. Documentation of the Book Component

```yaml
components:
  schemas:
    Book:
      description: Book representation
      required:
        - title
      type: object
      properties:
        id:
          format: int64
          type: integer
        author:
          type: string
        description:
          maxLength: 10000
          minLength: 1
          type: string
        isbn10:
          type: string
        isbn13:
          type: string
        mediumImageUrl:
          $ref: '#/components/schemas/URL'
        nbOfPages:
          format: int32
          type: integer
        price:
          $ref: '#/components/schemas/BigDecimal'
        rank:
          format: int32
          maximum: 10
          minimum: 1
          type: integer
        smallImageUrl:
          $ref: '#/components/schemas/URL'
        title:
          type: string
          nullable: false
        yearOfPublication:
          format: int32
          type: integer
```

5.7.3. Swagger UI

Having YAML or JSON OpenAPI documentation is very useful for other systems to interact with our API, but it can be difficult for a human to read if the contract is too long or complex. That's why you can go to the URL http://localhost:8080/q/swagger-ui and get the visual aspect of the contract thanks to Swagger UI. The Swagger UI web interface looks like the one in Figure 11. It gives you all the documentation we've just seen, plus you can interact with the *Book* REST endpoint by creating or deleting books from the database.

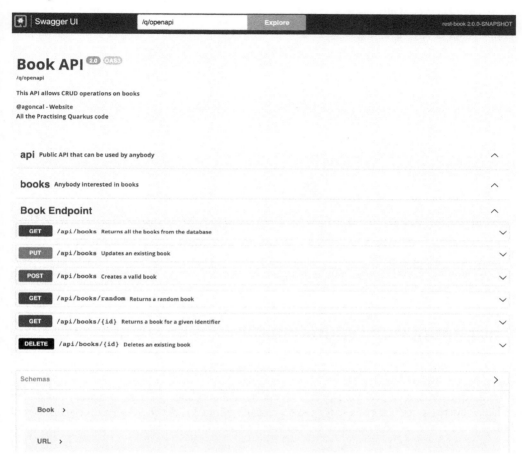

Figure 11. Swagger UI contract for the Book endpoint

⟨⟩ **Call to Action**

(43)

Make sure Quarkus is up and running and open your browser at http://localhost:8080/q/swagger-ui. For now, just use the Swagger UI interface to visualise the contract, not to interact with the APIs as they still don't work properly.

5.8. Displaying a Banner at Startup

In the last chapter, we added a nice banner to the *Number* microservice. Let's do the same for *Book*, but this time, using a different technique.

For the *Number* microservice_ we had to create a separate class (NumberApplicationLifeCycle) that would observe the StartupEvent and display the banner. This time let's just create the file src/main/resources/default_banner.txt and add some ASCII Art to it (see Listing 44).

Listing 44. Displaying a Banner at Startup

5.9. Running the Application

To run the *Number* microservice seen in the previous chapter was quite straightforward: some configuration and a ./mvnw quarkus:dev and that was it. The *Book* microservice is slightly more complex and needs a database to run and to test. But thanks to *Dev Services*, executing and testing the *Book* microservice will be as easy as executing and testing the *Number* microservice. But before testing and executing our microservice, let's first configure it.

5.9.1. Configuring the Application

Book microservice needs a bit more extra configuration than the *Number* microservice seen in the previous chapter. That's because it needs to access a database. So we need to configure Hibernate. But first let's configure the HTTP listening port.

Configuring the Quarkus Listening Port

Number microservice runs on port 8701, so let's change the port for our *Book* microservice so they listen on different ports.

💻 Call to Action

(45)

As we've seen in the previous chapter, add the `quarkus.http.port` property to the `src/main/resources/application.properties` file so Quarkus does not listen to the default 8080 port.

```
quarkus.http.port=8702
```

Configuring Hibernate

Quarkus development mode is really useful for applications that mix microservices and database access. When we use the property `quarkus.hibernate-orm.database.generation` set to `drop-and-create`, the database schema is automatically recreated by Quarkus each time the `Book` entity changes. And this is just a matter of changing a few properties in the `application.properties` file.

💻 Call to Action

(46)

To have Hibernate automatically dropping and creating a database, make sure you have the following configuration in the `application.properties`:

```
quarkus.hibernate-orm.database.generation=drop-and-create
quarkus.hibernate-orm.log.sql=true
quarkus.hibernate-orm.sql-load-script=import.sql
```

5.9.2. Adding Data

In development mode, for tests or demos, it is useful to have a data set ready. To load some SQL statements when Hibernate starts, we can add `INSERT` SQL statements to a file called `import.sql` (see Listing 45) located in the root of the `resources` directory. It contains SQL statements terminated by a semicolon. The `import.sql` file also works well with Quarkus live reload mode: our `Book` entity or the `import.sql` file changes, and this change is immediately picked up, the schema is updated and the data inserted without restarting the application!

Listing 45. import.sql File

```
INSERT INTO Book(id, isbn_13, title, rank, small_image_url, medium_image_url, price,
nb_of_pages, year_of_publication, author, description)
VALUES ( 997, '9781980399025', 'Understanding Bean Validation', 9, 'https://images-
na.ssl-images-amazon.com/images/I/31fHenHChZL._SL160_.jpg', 'https://images-na.ssl-
images-amazon.com/images/I/31fHenHChZL.jpg', 9.99, 129, 2018, 'Antonio Goncalves', 'In
this fascicle will you will learn Bean Validation and use its different APIs to apply
constraints on a bean, validate all sorts of constraints and write your own
constraints');

INSERT INTO Book(id, isbn_13, title, rank, small_image_url, medium_image_url, price,
nb_of_pages, year_of_publication, author, description)
VALUES ( 998, '9781093918977', 'Understanding JPA', 9, 'https://images-na.ssl-images-
amazon.com/images/I/3122s2sjOtL._SL160_.jpg', 'https://images-na.ssl-images-
amazon.com/images/I/3122s2sjOtL.jpg', 9.99, 246, 2019, 'Antonio Goncalves', 'In this
fascicle, you will learn Java Persistence API, its annotations for mapping entities,
as well as the Java Persistence Query Language and entity life cycle');
```

⌨ Call to Action

(47)

To add data to the database when Quarkus starts, you need to create the src/main/resources/import.sql file and add some INSERT statements such as in Listing 45. If you want to have more than just these two INSERT statements, you can download a bigger file from https://raw.githubusercontent.com/agoncal/agoncal-fascicle-quarkus-pract/2.0/rest-book/src/main/resources/import.sql.

5.9.3. Testing the Application

To test the BookResource endpoint, we will be using *Dev Services* to fire a PostgreSQL database and then test CRUD operations. As you will see, these tests are more complex testing all sorts of CRUD operations.

Dev Services

The *Book* microservice needs a database to run. We could use an in-memory database, such as H2 or Derby, for our tests, and a PostgreSQL database in production. But thanks to the integration between Quarkus and TestContainers, testing with a PostgreSQL database is as easy as testing with an in-memory database. This integration is called *Dev Services*.

Quarkus supports the automatic provisioning of unconfigured services in development and test mode. It is called *Dev Services*[66]. This means that if an extension is not configured, then Quarkus will automatically start the relevant service (using TestContainers), configure it with default properties and wire it up to the application.

TestContainers[67] is a Java library that supports JUnit tests, providing lightweight, throwaway instances of common Docker images. It allows us to use Docker containers within our tests.

The way Dev Services works is pretty simple. When you declare an extension in your `pom.xml`, Quarkus will check if it can add support for this extension. And as a matter of fact, Quarkus brings first-class support for PostgreSQL. For that, we just declare the PostgreSQL extension in our `pom.xml`, and Quarkus will use TestContainers to download, configure and start the database using all the defaults.

```
<dependency>
  <groupId>io.quarkus</groupId>
  <artifactId>quarkus-jdbc-postgresql</artifactId>
</dependency>
```

We will see this in action when we execute our test later on.

Testing the Business Logic

Let's test the business logic of our `BookResource` class.

▣ Call to Action

(48)

Under the src/test/java directory, edit the BookResourceTest class under the org.agoncal.fascicle.quarkus.book package. Get rid of the existing code and instead add the code shown in Listing 46, Listing 47, Listing 48, Listing 49, Listing 50 and Listing 51. This tests class is long and contains many import statements:

```
import io.quarkus.test.junit.DisabledOnNativeImage;
import io.quarkus.test.junit.QuarkusTest;
import io.restassured.common.mapper.TypeRef;
import org.hamcrest.core.Is;
import org.junit.jupiter.api.MethodOrderer;
import org.junit.jupiter.api.Order;
import org.junit.jupiter.api.Test;
import org.junit.jupiter.api.TestMethodOrder;
```

There is also many static imports to make the code easier to read:

```
import static io.restassured.RestAssured.given;
import static javax.ws.rs.core.HttpHeaders.ACCEPT;
import static javax.ws.rs.core.HttpHeaders.CONTENT_TYPE;
import static javax.ws.rs.core.MediaType.APPLICATION_JSON;
import static javax.ws.rs.core.Response.Status.BAD_REQUEST;
import static javax.ws.rs.core.Response.Status.CREATED;
import static javax.ws.rs.core.Response.Status.NOT_FOUND;
import static javax.ws.rs.core.Response.Status.NO_CONTENT;
import static javax.ws.rs.core.Response.Status.OK;
import static org.hamcrest.CoreMatchers.is;
import static org.hamcrest.Matchers.hasKey;
import static org.junit.jupiter.api.Assertions.assertEquals;
import static org.junit.jupiter.api.Assertions.assertNotNull;
import static org.junit.jupiter.api.Assertions.assertTrue;
```

Listing 46 shows the header of the BookResourceTest class. What's important to notice is the different annotations that annotate this class:

- @QuarkusTest: Annotates a Quarkus test

- @QuarkusTestResource: Used to define a test resource (e.g. a database, a tool, etc.)

- @TestMethodOrder: JUnit annotation used to configure the MethodOrderer for the test methods (e.g. @Order(1), @Order(2), etc.)

Then, the header is just a set of constants that will be used to create and update a book and check that the values are correct. nbBooks is the number of initial rows that are inserted in the database (coming from the import.sql file), and the bookId variable holds the current book that is being tested.

Listing 46. Test Case Header

```java
@QuarkusTest
@TestMethodOrder(MethodOrderer.OrderAnnotation.class)
public class BookResourceTest {

  private static final String DEFAULT_TITLE = "Title";
  private static final String UPDATED_TITLE = "Title (updated)";
  private static final String DEFAULT_AUTHOR = "Author";
  private static final String UPDATED_AUTHOR = "Author (updated)";
  private static final Integer DEFAULT_YEAR_OF_PUBLICATION = 1111;
  private static final Integer UPDATED_YEAR_OF_PUBLICATION = 2222;
  private static final Integer DEFAULT_NB_OF_PAGES = 111;
  private static final Integer UPDATED_NB_OF_PAGES = 222;
  private static final Integer DEFAULT_RANK = 1;
  private static final Integer UPDATED_RANK = 2;
  private static final BigDecimal DEFAULT_PRICE = new BigDecimal(11.0);
  private static final BigDecimal UPDATED_PRICE = new BigDecimal(22.0);
  private static final URL DEFAULT_SMALL_IMAGE_URL = makeUrl("http://www.url.com");
  private static final URL UPDATED_SMALL_IMAGE_URL = makeUrl(
"http://www.updatedurl.com");
  private static final URL DEFAULT_MEDIUM_IMAGE_URL = makeUrl("http://www.url.com");
  private static final URL UPDATED_MEDIUM_IMAGE_URL = makeUrl(
"http://www.updatedurl.com");
  private static final String DEFAULT_DESCRIPTION = "Description";
  private static final String UPDATED_DESCRIPTION = "Description (updated)";

  private static URL makeUrl(String urlString) {
    try {
      return new URL(urlString);
    } catch (MalformedURLException e) {
      return null;
    }
  }

  private static int nbBooks;
  private static String bookId;
```

The first test method that is executed (@Order(1)) in Listing 47 invokes an HTTP GET on /api/books.
With such a call, the method getAllBooks() of the BookResource in Listing 32 is executed and returns
the entire list of books from the database. The shouldGetInitialItems() method checks that the
invocation returns a 200-OK and stores the total number of books into the nbBooks variable (this
variable is then used in most of the following tests).

Listing 47. Returning All Books from the Database

```
@Test
@Order(1)
void shouldGetInitialBooks() {
  List<Book> books =
    given()
      .header(ACCEPT, APPLICATION_JSON).
    when()
      .get("/api/books").
    then()
      .statusCode(OK.getStatusCode())
      .header(CONTENT_TYPE, APPLICATION_JSON)
      .extract().body().as(getBookTypeRef());

  nbBooks = books.size();
}

private TypeRef<List<Book>> getBookTypeRef() {
  return new TypeRef<List<Book>>() {
  };
}
```

The second test in Listing 48 creates a new Book entity, sets some default values and invokes an HTTP POST on /api/books. If you check the createBook() method in Listing 34, you can see that once the book is persisted in the database, the URL of its location is returned. So, in this test case, we check that the method returns a Location HTTP header, extract the book identifier from it, and do an HTTP GET passing this identifier. The method then checks that the created book is the same as the one that we just got.

Listing 48. Test Case for Creating a New Book

```
@Test
@Order(2)
void shouldAddABook() {
  Book book = new Book();
  book.title = DEFAULT_TITLE;
  book.author = DEFAULT_AUTHOR;
  book.yearOfPublication = DEFAULT_YEAR_OF_PUBLICATION;
  book.nbOfPages = DEFAULT_NB_OF_PAGES;
  book.rank = DEFAULT_RANK;
  book.price = DEFAULT_PRICE;
  book.smallImageUrl = DEFAULT_SMALL_IMAGE_URL;
  book.mediumImageUrl = DEFAULT_MEDIUM_IMAGE_URL;
  book.description = DEFAULT_DESCRIPTION;

  // Persists a new book
  String location =
    given()
      .body(book)
```

```
    .header(CONTENT_TYPE, APPLICATION_JSON)
    .header(ACCEPT, APPLICATION_JSON).
  when()
    .post("/api/books").
  then()
    .statusCode(CREATED.getStatusCode())
    .extract().header("Location");

// Extracts the Location and stores the book id
assertTrue(location.contains("/api/books"));
String[] segments = location.split("/");
bookId = segments[segments.length - 1];
assertNotNull(bookId);

// Checks the book has been created
given()
  .header(ACCEPT, APPLICATION_JSON)
  .pathParam("id", bookId).
when()
  .get("/api/books/{id}").
then()
  .statusCode(OK.getStatusCode())
  .header(CONTENT_TYPE, APPLICATION_JSON)
  .body("title", Is.is(DEFAULT_TITLE))
  .body("author", Is.is(DEFAULT_AUTHOR))
  .body("yearOfPublication", Is.is(DEFAULT_YEAR_OF_PUBLICATION))
  .body("nbOfPages", Is.is(DEFAULT_NB_OF_PAGES))
  .body("rank", Is.is(DEFAULT_RANK))
  .body("smallImageUrl", Is.is(DEFAULT_SMALL_IMAGE_URL.toString()))
  .body("mediumImageUrl", Is.is(DEFAULT_MEDIUM_IMAGE_URL.toString()))
  .body("description", Is.is(DEFAULT_DESCRIPTION));

// Checks there is an extra book in the database
List<Book> books =
  given().
    header(ACCEPT, APPLICATION_JSON).
  when()
    .get("/api/books").
  then()
    .statusCode(OK.getStatusCode())
    .header(CONTENT_TYPE, APPLICATION_JSON)
    .extract().body().as(getBookTypeRef());

  assertEquals(nbBooks + 1, books.size());
}
```

The test case in Listing 49 checks that the BookResource endpoint updates the newly created book. It's just a matter of invoking an HTTP PUT with the updated book, and checking that the response is correct.

Listing 49. Test Case for Updating the Created Book

```java
@Test
@Order(3)
void shouldUpdateABook() {
  Book book = new Book();
  book.id = Long.valueOf(bookId);
  book.title = UPDATED_TITLE;
  book.author = UPDATED_AUTHOR;
  book.yearOfPublication = UPDATED_YEAR_OF_PUBLICATION;
  book.nbOfPages = UPDATED_NB_OF_PAGES;
  book.rank = UPDATED_RANK;
  book.price = UPDATED_PRICE;
  book.smallImageUrl = UPDATED_SMALL_IMAGE_URL;
  book.mediumImageUrl = UPDATED_MEDIUM_IMAGE_URL;
  book.description = UPDATED_DESCRIPTION;

  // Updates the previously created book
  given()
    .body(book)
    .header(CONTENT_TYPE, APPLICATION_JSON)
    .header(ACCEPT, APPLICATION_JSON).
  when()
    .put("/api/books").
  then()
    .statusCode(OK.getStatusCode())
    .header(CONTENT_TYPE, APPLICATION_JSON)
    .body("title", Is.is(UPDATED_TITLE))
    .body("author", Is.is(UPDATED_AUTHOR))
    .body("yearOfPublication", Is.is(UPDATED_YEAR_OF_PUBLICATION))
    .body("nbOfPages", Is.is(UPDATED_NB_OF_PAGES))
    .body("rank", Is.is(UPDATED_RANK))
    .body("price", Is.is(UPDATED_PRICE.intValue()))
    .body("smallImageUrl", Is.is(UPDATED_SMALL_IMAGE_URL.toString()))
    .body("mediumImageUrl", Is.is(UPDATED_MEDIUM_IMAGE_URL.toString()))
    .body("description", Is.is(UPDATED_DESCRIPTION));
}
```

Listing 50 checks that the BookResource endpoint deletes the book from the database. For that, not only does it test the HTTP status code (204 No Content) but also that a book has been removed from the database.

Listing 50. Test Case for Removing the Created Book

```
@Test
@Order(4)
void shouldRemoveABook() {
  // Deletes the previously created book
  given()
    .pathParam("id", bookId).
  when()
    .delete("/api/books/{id}").
  then()
    .statusCode(NO_CONTENT.getStatusCode());

  // Checks there is less a book in the database
  List<Book> books =
    given()
      .header(ACCEPT, APPLICATION_JSON).
    when()
      .get("/api/books").
    then()
      .statusCode(OK.getStatusCode())
      .header(CONTENT_TYPE, APPLICATION_JSON)
      .extract().body().as(getBookTypeRef());

  assertEquals(nbBooks, books.size());
}
```

Remember that we've annotated the Book entity with Bean Validation annotations (see Listing 37) to make sure the data is valid before persisting. In Listing 38 the BookService uses the @Valid annotation so the book passed as a parameter is first validated, and then persisted if valid. To test this behaviour, the test case in Listing 51 passes an invalid Book (with a null title) and checks that persisting it fails (HTTP status code 400 Bad Request).

Listing 51. Checking That Creating an Invalid Book Is Not Possible

```
@Test
void shouldNotAddInvalidBook() {
  Book book = new Book();
  book.title = null;

  given()
    .body(book)
    .header(CONTENT_TYPE, APPLICATION_JSON)
    .header(ACCEPT, APPLICATION_JSON).
  when()
    .post("/api/books").
  then()
    .statusCode(BAD_REQUEST.getStatusCode());
}
```

💬 Call to Action

From now on, to test the *Book* microservice we will need Docker to be up and running. Then, execute the test with ./mvnw test (or from your IDE). The first time you execute the tests, Dev Services will use TestContainers to download the PostgreSQL Docker image if it can't find it locally. This can take a while depending on your internet connection. Then, the tests are executed against a PostgreSQL database and should pass. During this moment, if you open the Docker dashboard you should see something similar to Figure 12: a TestContainers instance managing a PostgreSQL database.

Figure 12. Docker dashboard

Testing the OpenAPI

Like we did for the *Number* microservice, let's add a few extra tests to make sure OpenAPI and Swagger UI are packaged in the application. In Listing 52 we just check that when accessing the URLs /q/openapi and /q/swagger-ui, a return code 200-OK is returned.

Listing 52. Testing the OpenAPI and SwaggerUI

```
@Test
void shouldPingOpenAPI() {
  given()
    .header(ACCEPT, APPLICATION_JSON).
  when()
    .get("/q/openapi").
  then()
    .statusCode(OK.getStatusCode());
}

@Test
void shouldPingSwaggerUI() {
  given().
  when()
    .get("/q/swagger-ui").
  then()
    .statusCode(OK.getStatusCode());
}
```

🖳 Call to Action

(50)

Edit the BookResourceTest class, add the two methods as shown in Listing 52 that ping both OpenAPI and SwaggerUI URLs. Execute ./mvnw test again and make sure that all the tests pass.

5.9.4. Executing the Application

Now that the tests pass, we are ready to run our application. At this stage, you just run ./mvnw quarkus:dev in development mode and execute the application.

💻 Call to Action

Execute `./mvnw quarkus:dev` to start Quarkus.

Once started, check that there are books in the database with the following cURL command:

```
$ curl -X GET -H "Accept: application/json" http://localhost:8702/api/books/997 |
jq

{
  "id": 997,
  "author": "Antonio Goncalves",
  "description": "In this fascicle, you will learn Java Persistence API, its
annotations for mapping entities, as well as the Java Persistence Query Language
and entity life cycle",
  "isbn13": "9781980399025",
  "mediumImageUrl": "https://images-na.ssl-images-
amazon.com/images/I/31fHenHChZL.jpg",
  "nbOfPages": 129,
  "price": 9.99,
  "rank": 9,
  "smallImageUrl": "https://images-na.ssl-images-
amazon.com/images/I/31fHenHChZL._SL160_.jpg",
  "title": "Understanding Bean Validation",
  "yearOfPublication": 2018
}
```

You can also delete a book and check that it has been correctly deleted:

```
$ curl -X DELETE http://localhost:8702/api/books/997 -v
< HTTP/1.1 204 No Content

$ curl http://localhost:8702/api/books/997 -v
< HTTP/1.1 404 Not Found
< Content-Length: 0
```

And of course, you can invoke several times the `random` API and make sure that each time there is a different book returned:

```
$ curl http://localhost:8702/api/books/random | jq
$ curl http://localhost:8702/api/books/random | jq
$ curl http://localhost:8702/api/books/random | jq
```

Create a valid book with the following cURL command:

```
$ curl -X POST -d  '{"title":"Practising Quarkus", "author":"Antonio Goncalves",
"yearOfPublication":"2020"}'  -H "Content-Type: application/json"
http://localhost:8702/api/books -v

< HTTP/1.1 201 Created
< Location: http://localhost:8702/api/books/1
```

But also create an invalid book. Having a null title will violate the Bean Validation constraint
and will not insert any invalid data to the database:

```
$ curl -X POST -d  '{"author":"Antonio Goncalves", "yearOfPublication":"2020"}'
-H "Content-Type: application/json" http://localhost:8702/api/books -v

< HTTP/1.1 400 Bad Request
```

5.10. What You Have Built in This Chapter

After coding all the required artifacts, you should end up having the following directory structure
for the *Book* microservice

```
.
└── rest-book
    ├── src
    │   ├── main
    │   │   ├── java
    │   │   │   └── org/agoncal/fascicle/quarkus/book
    │   │   │       ├── Book.java
    │   │   │       ├── BookApplication.java
    │   │   │       ├── BookResource.java
    │   │   │       └── BookService.java
    │   │   └── resources
    │   │       ├── application.properties
    │   │       ├── default_banner.txt
    │   │       └── import.sql
    │   └── test
    │       └── java
    │           └── org/agoncal/fascicle/quarkus/number
    │               ├── BookResourceTest.java
    │               └── NativeBookResourceIT.java
    └── pom.xml
```

5.11. Summary

In this chapter, you've developed a second microservice: the *Book* microservice manipulates books
in the database. It is slightly more complex than the *Number* microservice because it stores and

retrieves data from a database. Because of that, we need to use some sort of persistence mechanism. JPA is a perfect technology when it comes to mapping objects to a relational database (Object-Relational Mapping tool). Panache is an extension of JPA allowing you to easily have access to common database operations (e.g. persisting an object, retrieving all the objects, retrieving by identifier, etc.). And if transaction management is needed, then it's just a matter of using a few annotations from JTA on a transactional service that can be injected thanks to CDI. Because manipulating valid information is crucial, you use Bean Validation constraint annotations to make sure the book object has valid data before persisting it.

But it's not because the *Book* microservice is more complex that testing or running it should be. Both *Book* and *Number* microservices are executed and tested the same way. The only difference is that in the *Book* microservice we use Dev Services to automatically start a PostgreSQL database container before testing our code, and shutting it down.

In the next chapter, you run an Angular application on Quarkus. The goal of the next chapter is not to teach you Angular as the application has already been coded. But, rather, understand how to make it available on Quarkus (and optionally build the Angular application if you want).

🖥 Call to Action

(52)

Now that you have your second microservice running and tested, you might want to commit your changes so you can come back to it later:

```
$ git add .
$ git commit -m "rest-book"
```

If in the next chapter, for some reason, you want to reset all your changes and come back to this commit, you can use the following commands:

```
$ git reset --hard
$ git clean -f -d
```

---

[54] JDBC https://en.wikipedia.org/wiki/Java_Database_Connectivity

[55] JPA https://jcp.org/en/jsr/detail?id=338

[56] JPA GitHub https://github.com/eclipse-ee4j/jpa-api

[57] JTA https://jcp.org/en/jsr/detail?id=907

[58] JTA GitHub https://github.com/eclipse-ee4j/jta-api

[59] Open XA https://en.wikipedia.org/wiki/X/Open_XA

[60] Separation of Concerns https://java-design-patterns.com/principles/#separation-of-concerns

[61] ArC https://github.com/quarkusio/quarkus/tree/master/independent-projects/arc

[62] CDI https://jcp.org/en/jsr/detail?id=365

[63] CDI limitations https://quarkus.io/guides/cdi-reference#limitations

[64] Bean Validation https://jcp.org/en/jsr/detail?id=380

[65] Bean Validation GitHub https://github.com/eclipse-ee4j/beanvalidation-api

[66] **Dev Services** https://quarkus.io/guides/dev-services

[67] **TestContainers** https://www.testcontainers.org

Chapter 6. Installing the Vintage Store User Interface

So far, the Vintage Store application is made up of two microservices: the *Number* REST endpoint and the *Book* REST endpoint. We've developed them, tested them and invoked a few URLs with cURL. So we know they work. In this chapter, you will execute and already-developed Angular user interface to interact with our microservices (optionally you can manually package and install the Angular application if you want).

6.1. What Will You Build in This Chapter?

The purpose of this chapter is not to develop a web interface and learn yet another web framework. This time you will just:

- How the Angular application is structured,
- Understand how the application communicates with the back end,
- Execute the application and see if it connects to the two microservices.
- Optionally package the Angular application on a Quarkus instance.

 When you've downloaded and unzipped the https://raw.githubusercontent.com/agoncal/agoncal-fascicle-quarkus-pract/2.0/dist/agoncal-fascicle-quarkus-practising-2.0.zip file, the Angular application is under the `ui-vintagestore` directory.

6.1.1. Overall Architecture

Figure 13 shows the architecture that you will have at the end of this chapter. The *Vintage Store* UI is exposed via Quarkus (port 8700) while the *Number* microservice listens on port 8701 and the *Book* microservice on port 8702. At this stage, the UI still does not communicate with the microservices (the communication will happen in the next chapter).

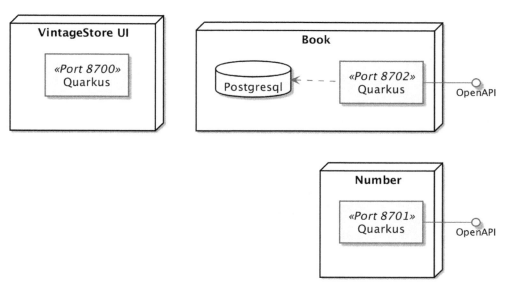

Figure 13. Overall architecture

6.1.2. Directory Structure

The directory structure of `ui-vintagestore` contains the TypeScript and HTML code of the graphical components to generate new book numbers as well as create/update/delete books from the database. It also contains the code to invoke the microservices through HTTP:

```
.
├── ui-vintagestore
│   ├── src
│   │   ├── main
│   │   │   └── resources
│   │   │       └── META-INF
│   │   │           └── resources
│   │   │               ├── ui-vintagestore
│   │   │               │   ├── xxxxx.ttf
│   │   │               │   ├── yyyyy.js
│   │   │               │   ├── zzzzz.css
│   │   │               │   └── index.html
│   │   │               └── index.html
│   │   ├── app
│   │   │   ├── book
│   │   │   │   ├── book-delete
│   │   │   │   │   ├── book-delete.component.html
│   │   │   │   │   └── book-delete.component.ts
│   │   │   │   ├── book-detail
│   │   │   │   ├── book-form
│   │   │   │   ├── book-list
│   │   │   │   ├── book-random
│   │   │   │   ├── book-routing.module.ts
│   │   │   │   └── book.module.ts
│   │   │   ├── number
│   │   │   │   ├── number-generate
│   │   │   │   ├── number-routing.module.ts
│   │   │   │   └── number.module.ts
│   │   │   ├── shared
│   │   │   │   ├── api
│   │   │   │   │   ├── bookEndpoint.service.ts
│   │   │   │   │   └── numberEndpoint.service.ts
│   │   │   │   └── model
│   │   │   │       ├── book.ts
│   │   │   │       └── bookNumbers.ts
│   │   │   ├── app-routing.module.ts
│   │   │   ├── app.component.html
│   │   │   ├── app.component.ts
│   │   │   └── app.module.ts
│   │   ├── index.html
│   │   ├── main.ts
│   │   └── styles.scss
│   ├── angular.json
│   ├── package.json
│   └── pom.xml
└── pom.xml
```

The `ui-vintagestore` project contains a mix of Angular and Quarkus:

- Under `src/main/resources` you will find the production ready Angular application packaged for

Quarkus.

- `src/main/resources/META-INF/resources/ui-vintagestore` contains all the HTML, CSS and JavaScript compiled for production.

- Under `src/app` you will find the code of the Angular application that you can optionally package for Quarkus.

- `src/app/book` contains the code of the Angular components for managing books, and `src/app/number` the graphical components to display generated book numbers.

- `src/app/shared` has all the Angular code to invoke our microservices.

6.2. Presenting the Angular Application

The main page of the Angular application in Figure 14 displays a random book which comes from the *Book* microservice. If you refresh this page, you will get a different book.

Vintage Store

You can buy Books for a cheap price. Browse our catalog and do not hesitate to shop online.

Understanding JPA
Antonio Goncalves

In this fascicle, you will learn Java Persistence API, its annotations for mapping entities, as well as the Java Persistence Query Language and entity life cycle

Figure 14. Main page displaying a random book

By clicking on the **Book** menu you get access to a list of all the books (see Figure 15) that has several buttons to allow CRUD operations on a specific book.

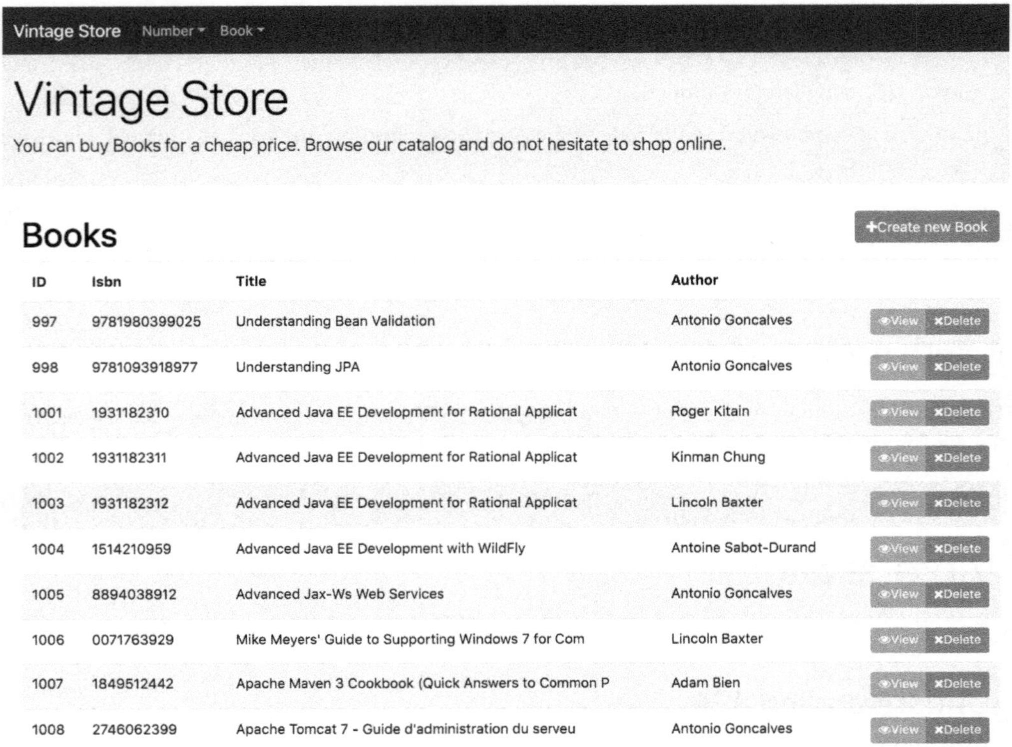

Vintage Store

You can buy Books for a cheap price. Browse our catalog and do not hesitate to shop online.

Books

+Create new Book

ID	Isbn	Title	Author		
997	9781980399025	Understanding Bean Validation	Antonio Goncalves	⊙View	✕Delete
998	9781093918977	Understanding JPA	Antonio Goncalves	⊙View	✕Delete
1001	1931182310	Advanced Java EE Development for Rational Applicat	Roger Kitain	⊙View	✕Delete
1002	1931182311	Advanced Java EE Development for Rational Applicat	Kinman Chung	⊙View	✕Delete
1003	1931182312	Advanced Java EE Development for Rational Applicat	Lincoln Baxter	⊙View	✕Delete
1004	1514210959	Advanced Java EE Development with WildFly	Antoine Sabot-Durand	⊙View	✕Delete
1005	8894038912	Advanced Jax-Ws Web Services	Antonio Goncalves	⊙View	✕Delete
1006	0071763929	Mike Meyers' Guide to Supporting Windows 7 for Com	Lincoln Baxter	⊙View	✕Delete
1007	1849512442	Apache Maven 3 Cookbook (Quick Answers to Common P	Adam Bien	⊙View	✕Delete
1008	2746062399	Apache Tomcat 7 - Guide d'administration du serveu	Antonio Goncalves	⊙View	✕Delete

Figure 15. Listing books

By clicking on "*Create new Book*" we go to a form (see Figure 16) allowing us to create a new book.

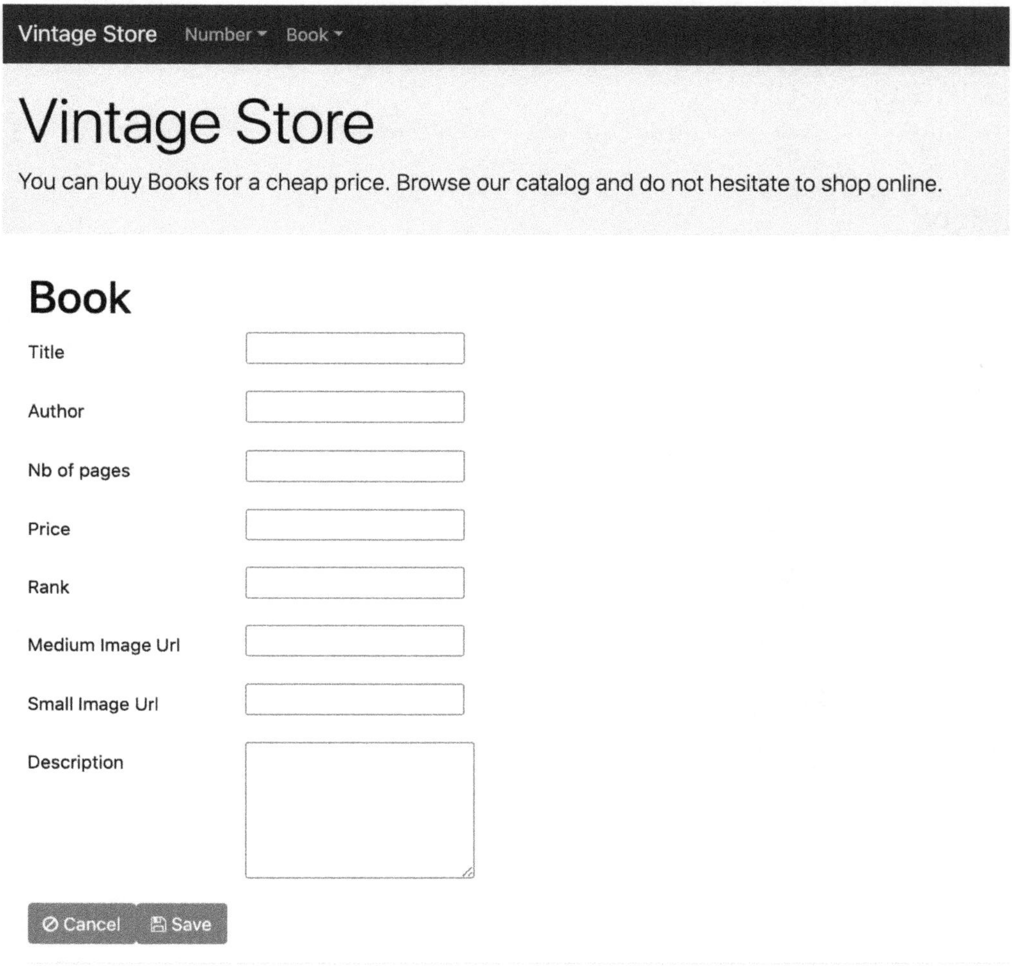
Vintage Store
Number
Book
Vintage Store
You can buy Books for a cheap price. Browse our catalog and do not hesitate to shop online.
Book
Title
Author
Nb of pages
Price
Rank
Medium Image Url
Small Image Url
Description
Cancel
Save

Figure 16. Creating a new book

On the list of books we have two buttons on each row:

- *View* which gives all the book details (see Figure 17),
- *Delete* to delete a book from the database (see Figure 18).

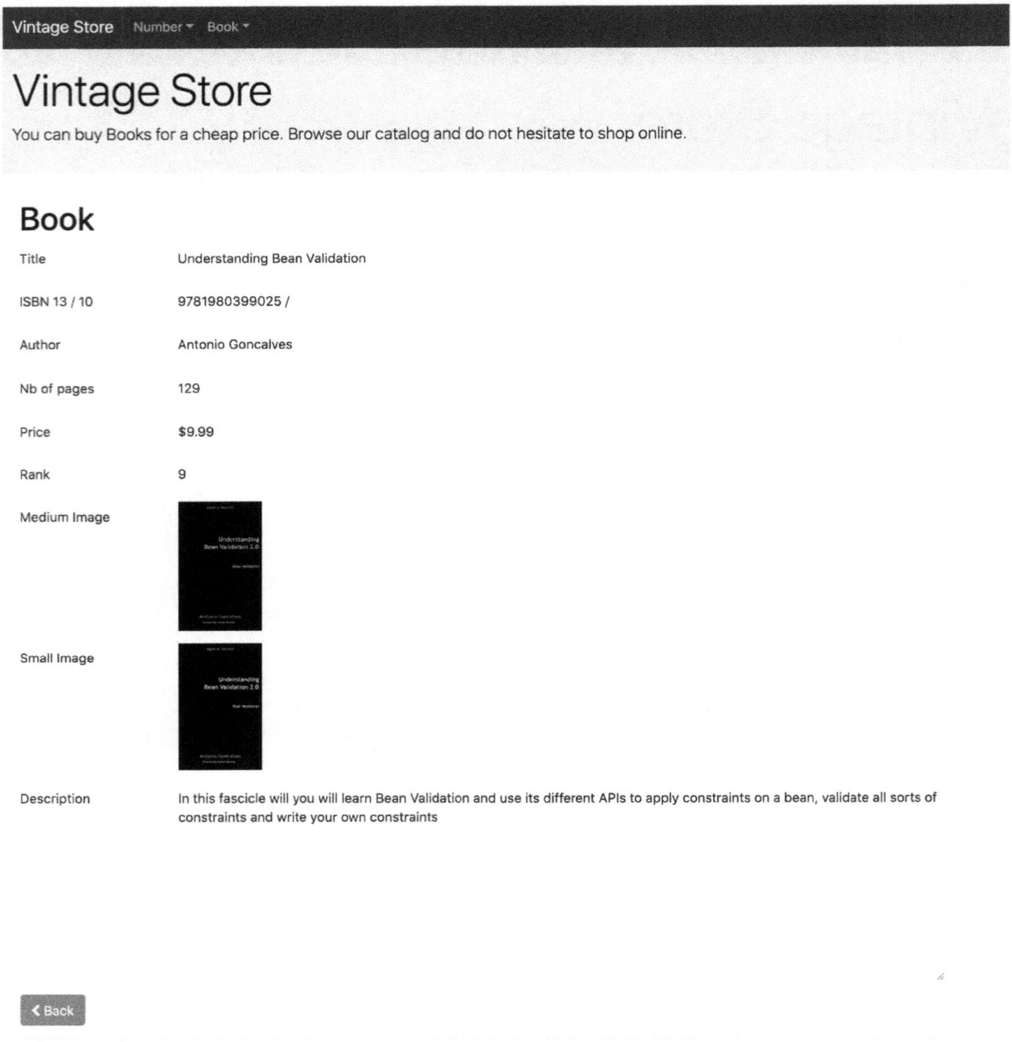
Vintage Store
Number
Book
Vintage Store
You can buy Books for a cheap price. Browse our catalog and do not hesitate to shop online.
Book
Title
Understanding Bean Validation
ISBN 13 / 10
9781980399025 /
Author
Antonio Goncalves
Nb of pages
129
Price
$9.99
Rank
9
Medium Image
Small Image
Description
In this fascicle will you will learn Bean Validation and use its different APIs to apply constraints on a bean, validate all sorts of constraints and write your own constraints
Back

Figure 17. Details of a book

Vintage Store   Number ▾   Book ▾

Vintage Store

You can buy Books for a cheap price. Browse our catalog and do not hesitate to shop online.

Understanding Bean Validation

Antonio Goncalves

In this fascicle will you will learn Bean Validation and use its different APIs to apply constraints on a bean, validate all sorts of constraints and write your own constraints

Figure 18. Deleting a book

Figure 19 shows the component that generates book numbers (ISBNs, ASIN and EAN numbers) by invoking the *Number* microservice.

Vintage Store   Number ▾   Book ▾

Vintage Store

You can buy Books for a cheap price. Browse our catalog and do not hesitate to shop online.

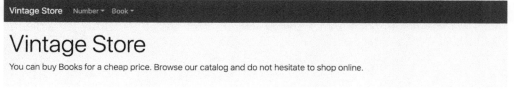

Book Numbers ⟳Generate

Asin	B000A143NO
EAN 8	12577842
EAN 13	8245028822117
ISBN 10	1-08-219071-3
ISBN 13	978-1-9760933-6-4

Figure 19. Generating book numbers

6.2.1. Services and Models

You don't need to be an Angular[68] expert, but there are some pieces of code that are worth looking at. If you look under the `src/app/shared` directory, you will find two sub-directories:

- `api`: Contains the two services (`NumberEndpointService` and `BookEndpointService`) accessing our two microservices.

- model: Contains the two interfaces (Book and BookNumbers) modelling the return types of our microservices.

For example, if you look at Listing 53 you'll see that it matches the BookNumbers Java class in Listing 10.

Listing 53. Book TypeScript Interface

```
export interface BookNumbers {
  asin?: string;
  ean_13?: string;
  ean_8?: string;
  isbn_10: string;
  isbn_13: string;
}
```

This interface allows a JSON book representation received from the *Number* REST endpoint to be mapped to an object structure. Then it's just a matter of using this structure in the NumberEndpointService defined in Listing 54. The NumberEndpointService is a TypeScript class that invokes the method generateBookNumbers of our remote JAX-RS NumberResource class. It just does an HTTP GET on the /api/numbers path.

Listing 54. TypeScript Service Invoking a Remote Microservice

```typescript
@Injectable()
export class NumberEndpointService {

  protected basePath = 'http://localhost:8701';

  constructor(protected httpClient: HttpClient) {
  }

  public generatesBookNumbers(observe: any = 'body', reportProgress: boolean = false):
Observable<any> {

    let headers = this.defaultHeaders;

    // to determine the Accept header
    let httpHeaderAccepts: string[] = [
      'application/json'
    ];
    headers = headers.set('Accept', httpHeaderAccepts);

    return this.httpClient.request<BookNumbers>('get', `${this.basePath}/api/numbers`,
      {
        headers: headers,
        observe: observe,
        reportProgress: reportProgress
      }
    );
  }
}
```

We see the same behaviour with the *Book* REST endpoint. The bookEndpoint.service.ts defines all the methods to access the *Book* REST endpoint through HTTP, and the book.ts represents our Book entity.

You didn't have to type this code... but neither did I. The code of the interface and the service was generated thanks to a tool called swagger-codegen[69].

Because both of our microservices expose an OpenAPI contract, swagger-codegen just swallows it, and generates the TypeScript code to access it. It's just a matter of running:

```
$ swagger-codegen generate -i http://localhost:8702/q/openapi -l typescript-angular -o
src/app/shared
```

Here, you see another advantage of exposing an OpenAPI contract: it documents the API which can be read by a human, or processed by tools.

6.2.2. UI Components

In Angular, a graphical component can be composed of a TypeScript class dealing with the behaviour, and an HTML and CSS file for the graphical representation. So the graphical component generating book numbers (shown in Figure 19) is called number-generate, and is made of two files (html and ts), both living in a number-generate subdirectory

```
.
└── ui-vintagestore
    └── src
        └── app
            └── number
                ├── number-generate
                │   ├── number-generate.component.html
                │   └── number-generate.component.ts
                ├── number-routing.module.ts
                └── number.module.ts
```

The TypeScript code of the graphical component generating book numbers is shown in Listing 55. When we click on the *Generate* button, the generateBookNumber() method is executed, and it then invokes the NumberEndpointService (which is the one doing the remote HTTP call). Notice that the templateUrl attribute references the HTML page dealing with the graphical representation of the component (see Listing 56).

Listing 55. TypeScript Code of the Generate Number Graphical Component

```
@Component({
  templateUrl: 'number-generate.component.html'
})
export class NumberGenerateComponent implements OnInit {

  bookNumbers?: BookNumbers;

  constructor(private numberEndpointService: NumberEndpointService) { }

  ngOnInit(): void {
    this.generateBookNumber();
  }

  generateBookNumber() {
    this.numberEndpointService.generatesBookNumbers().subscribe(bookNumbers => this
.bookNumbers = bookNumbers);
  }
}
```

The HTML side of the component generating book numbers is described in Listing 56. It is a classical HTML page using Bootstrap[70] for the graphical layout.

Listing 56. HTML Code of the Generate Number Graphical Component

```
<h1>
  <span>Book Numbers</span>
  <button class="btn btn-primary float-right create-book" (click)="generateBookNumber
()">
    <span class="fa fa-refresh"></span>
    <span>Generate</span>
  </button>
</h1>


<form>
  <div class="form-group row">
    <label for="asin" class="col-sm-2 col-form-label">Asin</label>
    <div class="col-sm-10">
      <input type="text" readonly class="form-control-plaintext" id="asin" value=
"{{bookNumbers?.asin}}">
    </div>
  </div>
  <div class="form-group row">
    <label for="ean_8" class="col-sm-2 col-form-label">EAN 8</label>
    <div class="col-sm-10">
      <input type="text" readonly class="form-control-plaintext" id="ean_8" value=
"{{bookNumbers?.ean_8}}">
    </div>
  </div>
  <div class="form-group row">
    <label for="ean_13" class="col-sm-2 col-form-label">EAN 13</label>
    <div class="col-sm-10">
      <input type="text" readonly class="form-control-plaintext" id="ean_13" value=
"{{bookNumbers?.ean_13}}">
    </div>
  </div>
  <div class="form-group row">
    <label for="isbn_10" class="col-sm-2 col-form-label">ISBN 10</label>
    <div class="col-sm-10">
      <input type="text" readonly class="form-control-plaintext" id="isbn_10" value=
"{{bookNumbers?.isbn_10}}">
    </div>
  </div>
  <div class="form-group row">
    <label for="isbn_13" class="col-sm-2 col-form-label">ISBN 13</label>
    <div class="col-sm-10">
      <input type="text" readonly class="form-control-plaintext" id="isbn_13" value=
"{{bookNumbers?.isbn_13}}">
    </div>
  </div>
</form>
```

All the other graphical components follow the same structure and pattern. You can browse through the rest of the code if you want to learn more about Angular.

6.3. Running the Application

Tha Angular application has already been built in production mode, installed in Quarkus, and configured. It runs inside Quarkus on port 8070 (configured in the `application.properties` file):

```
quarkus.http.port=8700
```

Quarkus manages all the Web resources under `resources/META-INF/resources` directory. That means that, by default, Quarkus will serve the `resources/META-INF/resources/index.html` first. We need to redirect the call to the `ui-vintagestore/index.html` page instead as shown in Listing 57.

Listing 57. Main index.html Page Redirecting to the Angular Application

```
<!DOCTYPE html>
<html lang="en">
<head>
  <meta http-equiv="refresh" content="0; url=ui-vintagestore/index.html"/>
</head>
</html>
```

We are all set. We just need to execute Quarkus in development mode.

💻 Call to Action

(53)

Make sure you have the *Number* and *Book* microservices running (as well as Docker, so Dev Services can run the PostgreSQL database). Then, under the `ui-vintagestore` directory, execute the following command to start Quarkus and the Angular application:

```
ui-vintagestore$ ./mvnw quarkus:dev
```

Once the application is started, go to http://localhost:8700. It should display the main Angular web page. Click on the menus, try to generate book numbers or display a random book: **Oops, not working!**

We must have forgotten something! Let's move on to the next chapter then and make the application work.

6.4. (Optional) Building the Web Application

If you want to build the Angular application your self, you can follow the steps described in this section. In fact, if you are familiar with Angular and have all the tools installed, you can install the dependencies with `npm install` or execute it with `ng serve`. But you can also use Maven to install all the needed tools.

6.4.1. NPM and Maven Dependencies

Being an Angular application, you will find a `package.json` file which defines all the dependencies that are required (see Listing 59). Notice that there is also a `pom.xml` file (Listing 58). This is just a convenient way to install NodeJS and npm so we can build the Angular application with Maven. The `pom.xml` also allows us to run the Angular application within Quarkus.

Listing 58. Installing NodeJS and NPM Using Maven

```xml
<profile>
  <id>install-node-and-npm</id>
  <build>
    <plugins>
      <plugin>
        <groupId>com.github.eirslett</groupId>
        <artifactId>frontend-maven-plugin</artifactId>
        <version>${frontend-maven-plugin.version}</version>
        <executions>
          <execution>
            <id>install node and npm</id>
            <goals>
              <goal>install-node-and-npm</goal>
            </goals>
            <phase>generate-resources</phase>
          </execution>
        </executions>
        <configuration>
          <nodeVersion>${node.version}</nodeVersion>
          <npmVersion>${npm.version}</npmVersion>
        </configuration>
      </plugin>
    </plugins>
  </build>
</profile>
<profile>
  <id>npm-install</id>
  <build>
    <plugins>
      <plugin>
        <groupId>com.github.eirslett</groupId>
        <artifactId>frontend-maven-plugin</artifactId>
        <version>${frontend-maven-plugin.version}</version>
        <executions>
          <execution>
            <id>npm install</id>
            <goals>
              <goal>npm</goal>
            </goals>
            <phase>generate-resources</phase>
          </execution>
        </executions>
        <configuration>
          <arguments>install</arguments>
        </configuration>
      </plugin>
    </plugins>
  </build>
</profile>
```

Listing 59. Angular Dependencies in package.json File

```json
    "@angular/animations": "~10.2.0",
    "@angular/common": "~10.2.0",
    "@angular/compiler": "~10.2.0",
    "@angular/core": "~10.2.0",
    "@angular/forms": "~10.2.0",
    "@angular/platform-browser": "~10.2.0",
    "@angular/platform-browser-dynamic": "~10.2.0",
    "@angular/router": "~10.2.0",
    "bootstrap": "^4.5.2",
    "font-awesome": "^4.7.0",
    "jquery": "^3.5.1",
    "ngx-bootstrap": "^5.6.2",
    "popper": "^1.0.1",
    "rxjs": "~6.6.0",
    "tslib": "^2.0.0",
    "zone.js": "~0.10.2"
  },
  "devDependencies": {
```

To build the Angular application, you don't need NodeJS nor npm installed globally in your machine. Thanks to the `frontend-maven-plugin` plugin declared on the `pom.xml` under `ui-vintagestore` (see Listing 58), we can use a good old Maven command to install locally NodeJS and npm.

🖥 Call to Action (Optional)

(54)

If you already have installed NodeJS and npm locally as explained in Chapter 3, *Getting Started*, you can skip this section. If you already have, then the following commands should work:

```
ui-vintagestore$ node/node -v
ui-vintagestore$ node/npm -version
```

If that's not the case, execute the following command to install NodeJS. The frontend-maven-plugin plugin will download NodeJS and npm from https://nodejs.org/dist and put it into a node folder (created under our ui-vintagestore directory). NodeJS and npm will only be installed locally to our project, it will not be installed globally on the whole system (and it will not interfere with any NodeJS/npm installations already present if any).

```
ui-vintagestore$ ./mvnw generate-resources -Pinstall-node-and-npm
```

Now that we know you have all the tools installed, we need to install the Angular dependencies of the application. For that, we could just run npm install if it was installed globally, but we don't have to. We can use the frontend-maven-plugin which will use the local NodeJS and npm:

```
ui-vintagestore$ ./mvnw generate-resources -Pnpm-install
```

You should now see a node_modules directory under ui-vintagestore.

6.4.2. Installing the Web Application on Quarkus

Time to package and install the Angular application on Quarkus. To install the Angular application into a Quarkus instance, we need to build the application in production mode and copy the JavaScript bundles under the resources/META-INF/resources directory. Look at the package.sh in Listing 60, that's exactly what it does. ng build will compile all the TypeScript code and package all the code and HTML resources into a few bundles. Then, these bundles are copied to the right location under resources/META-INF/resources/ui-vintagestore.

Listing 60. Script Building the Angular Application in Production Mode

```
export DEST=src/main/resources/META-INF/resources
./node_modules/.bin/ng build --prod --base-href "."
rm -Rf ${DEST}/ui-vintagestore
mkdir -p ${DEST}/ui-vintagestore
cp -R dist/* ${DEST}
```

🖥 Call to Action (Optional)

(55)

Execute the `package.sh` script shown in Listing 60:

```
ui-vintagestore$ ./package.sh
```

You will see all the JavaScript and HTML files under `resources/META-INF/resources/ui-vintagestore` directory.

6.5. Summary

In this chapter, you've packaged an Angular application and installed it on Quarkus. The idea of this chapter is not for you to learn Angular, but instead package it with NodeJS and npm and install it on Quarkus. The Angular framework is made for Single Page Applications (SPA), meaning that all necessary HTML, JavaScript, and CSS code is retrieved by the browser with a single page load. But these resources have to be available on an HTTP Server so they can be rendered to the browser. Quarkus can also be used as an HTTP server to render the HTML resources.

What's missing now is the communication between the Angular application and the microservices. In the next chapter, you will solve this communication problem, as well as develop the communication between the *Book* and *Number* microservices in a reliable way.

[68] **Angular** https://angular.io

[69] **Swagger-Codegen** https://github.com/swagger-api/swagger-codegen

[70] **Bootstrap** https://getbootstrap.com

Chapter 7. Adding Communication and Fault Tolerance

So far, we've built one *Book* microservice and one *Number* microservice. Both are totally isolated and do not communicate with each other. We've also deployed an Angular application that is supposed to access both microservices, but the communication is not working. In this chapter, you will make each component communicate with each other.

 Any problems, don't hesitate to get the code for the fascicle at https://github.com/ agoncal/agoncal-fascicle-quarkus-pract/tree/2.0

7.1. What Will You Build in This Chapter?

In this chapter, you will:

- Configure CORS so the Angular application can communicate with the microservices,
- Implement the communication between the *Book* and *Number* microservices, thanks to the Eclipse MicroProfile REST Client,
- Deal with fault tolerance thanks to timeouts and fallbacks.

7.1.1. Overall Architecture

Figure 20 shows the architecture of what you will be building in this chapter. The user interface will communicate with both microservices, and the *Book* microservice will invoke the *Number* microservice to get ISBN numbers when creating a new book.

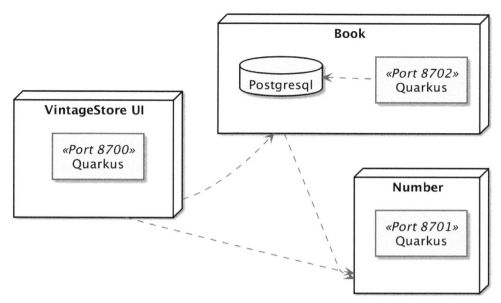

Figure 20. Overall architecture

7.1.2. Maven Dependencies

To deal with fault-tolerance and for the *Book* microservice to communicate with the *Number* microservice, we will need a few extra Maven dependencies as shown in Listing 61:

- `quarkus-rest-client`: REST Client in order to interact with REST APIs.

- `quarkus-smallrye-fault-tolerance`: Communication with external systems being inherently unreliable, we need the Fault Tolerance dependency.

Listing 61. REST Client and Fault Tolerance Maven Dependencies

```xml
<dependency>
  <groupId>io.quarkus</groupId>
  <artifactId>quarkus-rest-client</artifactId>
</dependency>
<dependency>
  <groupId>io.quarkus</groupId>
  <artifactId>quarkus-smallrye-fault-tolerance</artifactId>
</dependency>
```

You can either edit the pom.xml files of both the *Number* and *Book* microservices and add manually the dependencies in Listing 61, or you can use the Quarkus Maven plugin. For that, go to the rest-number directory and execute:

```
./mvnw quarkus:add-extension -Dextensions="smallrye-fault-tolerance"
```

For the *Book* microservice, go to the rest-book directory and execute:

```
./mvnw quarkus:add-extension -Dextensions="rest-client, smallrye-fault-tolerance"
```

7.2. Fixing CORS

But first, let's solve the communication problem between the Angular application and our microservices. So when the Angular application wants to access the *Book* and *Number* microservices, we actually cross several *origins*: we go from localhost:8700 (port in which the Angular application is running) to localhost:8701 (the *Number* REST endpoint) and localhost:8702 (the *Book* REST endpoint).

Make sure the two microservices are up and running as well as the Angular application. Open up the development tools of your browser and go to http://localhost:8700. If you look at the console of your browser, you should see something similar to Figure 21.

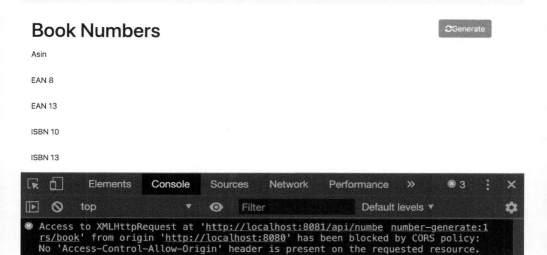

Book Store

You can buy Books for a cheap price. Browse our catalog and do not hesitate to shop online.

Book Numbers

⟳ Generate

Asin

EAN 8

EAN 13

ISBN 10

ISBN 13

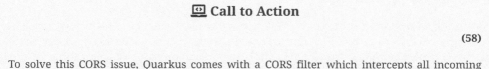

Figure 21. Cross origin issues when generating book numbers

We have a CORS issue. *Cross-origin Resource Sharing*[71] (CORS) is a mechanism that allows restricted resources on a web page to be requested from another domain outside the domain from which the first resource was served.

💻 Call to Action

(58)

To solve this CORS issue, Quarkus comes with a CORS filter which intercepts all incoming HTTP requests. It can be enabled in the Quarkus configuration file `application.properties`:

```
quarkus.http.cors=true
```

Make sure you set the `quarkus.http.cors` property to `true` on both the *Number* and *Book* microservice `application.properties` files. If you access the Angular application again at http://localhost:8700 you should finally see the welcome page displaying a random book as in Figure 22.

Vintage Store

You can buy Books for a cheap price. Browse our catalog and do not hesitate to shop online.

Understanding JPA

Antonio Goncalves

In this fascicle, you will learn Java Persistence API, its annotations for mapping entities, as well as the Java Persistence Query Language and entity life cycle

Figure 22. Main page displaying a random book

7.3. Microservices Communicating

Now that the Angular application works, let's create the communication link between the Book and *Number* REST endpoints. When we create a new book, we want the *Book* microservice to invoke the *Number* microservice in order to get the ISBN numbers. You can do so using the Eclipse MicroProfile REST Client in order to interact with REST APIs with very little effort.

Eclipse MicroProfile REST Client[72] provides a type safe approach using proxies and annotations for invoking RESTful services over HTTP. The Eclipse MicroProfile REST Client builds upon the JAX-RS 2.1 APIs for consistency and ease-of-use.

The Eclipse MicroProfile REST Client APIs and annotations are all defined under the main `org.eclipse.microprofile.rest.client` package, either at the root, or under the other subpackages. Table 19 lists the main subpackages defined in Eclipse MicroProfile REST Client version 2.0 (under the root `org.eclipse.microprofile.rest.client` package[73]).

Table 19. Main org.eclipse.microprofile.rest.client Subpackages

Subpackage	Description
root	Root package of the REST Client APIs
annotation	APIs for annotating client interfaces
ext	APIs for extending REST Client functionality
inject	APIs to aid in CDI-based injection
spi	Internal SPIs (*Service Provider Interfaces*) implemented by the provider

Along with APIs, REST Client comes with a set of annotations. Table 20 lists a subset of the most commonly used annotations.

Table 20. Main REST Client Annotations

Annotation	Description
@RegisterRestClient	A marker annotation to register a rest client at runtime
@RestClient	CDI qualifier used to indicate that this injection point is meant to use an instance of a type safe REST Client

Let's see how to use Eclipse MicroProfile REST Client in the *Book* microservice to invoke the *Number* microservice.

7.3.1. Book Microservice Invoking the Number Microservice

Remember that in the previous chapters we created a transactional BookService.persistBook() method to insert a book into the database. At that moment, we would like to insert the book with its ISBN numbers. That's when we want the *Book* microservice to invoke the *Number* microservice so that it gets the ISBN numbers and then persists the book in the database.

💻 Call to Action

(59)

To have the *Book* microservice invoking the remote *Number* microserviceFor, we'll use a proxy. For that, edit the BookService and update the persistBook() method as shown in Listing 62. It invokes a remote method that generates numbers and returns a IsbnNumbers class.

Listing 62. BookService Injecting the Proxy

```
public Book persistBook(@Valid Book book) {
    // The Book microservice invokes the Number microservice
    IsbnNumbers isbnNumbers = numberProxy.generateNumbers();
    book.isbn13 = isbnNumbers.isbn13;
    book.isbn10 = isbnNumbers.isbn10;

    Book.persist(book);
    return book;
}
```

🖵 Call to Action

(60)

The code does not compile yet, so let's go step by step. To use the proxy, we need to inject it. In the BookService, declare the variable numberProxy and use injection as follow:

```
@Inject
@RestClient
NumberProxy numberProxy;
```

We use the standard CDI @Inject annotation in conjunction with the MicroProfile @RestClient annotation to inject the NumberProxy interface:

```
import org.eclipse.microprofile.rest.client.inject.RestClient;
```

This NumberProxy interface acts like a proxy and allows us to remotely invoke the *Number* microservice through HTTP and return ISBNs with both 10 and 13 digits.

The sequence of invocation is better described in the sequence diagram shown in Figure 23. The JAX-RS resource invokes the persist() method on the service. The service needs to generate ISBN numbers, therefore, it invokes the remote *Number* microservice.

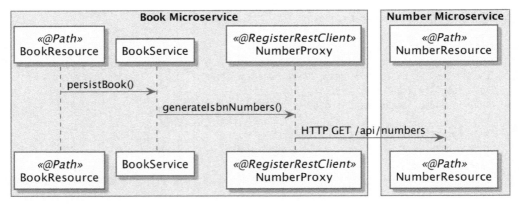

Figure 23. Book microservice invoking the Number microservice

7.3.2. The Remote Number Microservice Interface

Using the Eclipse MicroProfile REST Client is as simple as creating a NumbersProxy interface (under the client subpackage) using the proper JAX-RS and MicroProfile annotations (see Listing 63):

- @RegisterRestClient allows Quarkus to know that this interface is meant to be available for CDI injection as a REST Client,

- @Path and @GET are the standard JAX-RS annotations used to define how to access the remote service,

- @Produces defines the expected content-type.

🖳 Call to Action

(61)

Create the client subpackage and a new interface called NumberProxy under org.agoncal.fascicle.quarkus.book.client. Add the code shown in Listing 63. Make sure to fix the import statements (careful with the @Produces annotation):

```
import org.eclipse.microprofile.rest.client.inject.RegisterRestClient;

import javax.ws.rs.GET;
import javax.ws.rs.Path;
import javax.ws.rs.Produces;
import javax.ws.rs.core.MediaType;
```

Listing 63. The Proxy Interface

```
@Path("/api/numbers")
@Produces(MediaType.APPLICATION_JSON)
@RegisterRestClient
public interface NumberProxy {

  @GET
  IsbnNumbers generateNumbers();
}
```

The generateNumbers() method gives our code the ability to get ISBN numbers from the remote *Number* REST endpoint. The Eclipse MicroProfile REST Client will handle all the networking and marshalling, leaving our code clean of such technical details.

Notice in Listing 63 that the proxy returns a POJO with ISBN numbers of 10 and 13 digits (see Listing 64). This class contains JSON-B annotations to customise the binding from/to JSON.

Listing 64. The POJO Returned by the Proxy

```
public class IsbnNumbers {

  @JsonbProperty("isbn_10")
  public String isbn10;
  @JsonbProperty("isbn_13")
  public String isbn13;
}
```

7.3.3. Configuring the REST Client Invocation

But where is the *Number* microservice located? In order to determine the base URL to which REST calls will be made, the REST Client uses configuration from the `application.properties` file.

Having this configuration means that all requests performed using the `NumberProxy` interface will use http://localhost:8701 as the base URL. Using this configuration and the code in Listing 63, calling the `generateNumbers()` method of `NumberProxy` would result in an HTTP GET request being made to http://localhost:8701/api/numbers.

7.3.4. Executing the REST Client Invocation

Let's quickly see if this code works. For that, it's just a matter of starting both Quarkus instances and executing a few cURL commands.

⌨ Call to Action

First, start both Quarkus instances, one for the *Book* microservice, and the other one for the *Number* microservice:

```
rest-book$ ./mvnw quarkus:dev
rest-number$ ./mvnw quarkus:dev
```

Then, make sure both microservices are up and running by executing a few HTTP GET cURL commands:

```
$ curl -X GET -H "Accept: application/json" http://localhost:8701/api/numbers
$ curl -X GET -H "Accept: application/json" http://localhost:8702/api/books
```

Then create a new book with an HTTP POST cURL command just passing the title, author, and the year of publication of the book:

```
$ curl -X POST -d '{"title":"Practising Quarkus", "author":"Antonio Goncalves",
"yearOfPublication":"2020"}'  -H "Content-Type: application/json"
http://localhost:8702/api/books -v

< HTTP/1.1 201 Created
< Location: http://localhost:8702/api/books/1
```

Once the book is created, the cURL command returns its URI (in the Location HTTP header). Then, it's just a matter of invoking an HTTP GET on this URI, and checking that the ISBN numbers are set:

```
$ curl -X GET -H "Accept: application/json" http://localhost:8702/api/books/1 |
jq
{
  "id": 1,
  "author": "Antonio Goncalves",
  "isbn10": "1-361-87642-5",
  "isbn13": "978-0-85541-146-6",
  "title": "Practising Quarkus",
  "yearOfPublication": 2020
}
```

If the ISBN numbers are set on the newly created book, that means the *Book* microservice has managed to invoke the *Number* microservices. If you check the console of both microservices, you should also see some logs going on.

7.4. Dealing with Communication Failure

So now you've been creating books for a few hours... and you kill the *Number* microservice. What happens? Well, the *Book* microservice cannot invoke the *Number* microservice anymore and breaks with a ConnectException:

💻 Call to Action

(65)

Stop the *Number* microservice and execute the following cURL command to create a book:

```
$ curl -X POST -d  '{"title":"Practising Quarkus", "author":"Antonio Goncalves",
"yearOfPublication":"2020"}'  -H "Content-Type: application/json"
http://localhost:8702/api/books -v

ERROR [io.qua.ver.htt.run.QuarkusErrorHandler] HTTP Request to /api/books failed
org.jboss.resteasy.spi.UnhandledException: javax.ws.rs.ProcessingException:
RESTEASY004655: Unable to invoke request: java.net.ConnectException: Connection
refused (Connection refused)
```

One of the challenges brought by the distributed nature of microservices is that communication with external systems is inherently unreliable. This increases the demand on the resiliency of applications. To simplify making more resilient applications, Quarkus contains an implementation of the Eclipse MicroProfile Fault Tolerance specification.

As the number of services grows, the odds of any service failing also grows. If one of the involved services does not respond as expected, e.g. because of fragile network communication, we have to compensate for this exceptional situation. *Eclipse MicroProfile Fault Tolerance*[74] allows us to build up our microservice architecture to be resilient and fault tolerant by design. This means we must not only be able to detect any issue but also to handle it automatically.

The Eclipse MicroProfile Fault Tolerance APIs and annotations are all defined under the main org.eclipse.microprofile.faulttolerance package, either at the root, or under the other subpackages. Table 21 lists the main subpackages defined in Eclipse MicroProfile Fault Tolerance version 3.0 (under the root org.eclipse.microprofile.faulttolerance package[75]).

Table 21. Main org.eclipse.microprofile.faulttolerance Subpackages

Subpackage	Description
root	Root package of the Fault Tolerance APIs
exceptions	Exceptions for Fault Tolerance

Along with APIs, Fault Tolerance comes with a set of annotations. Table 22 lists a subset of the most commonly used annotations.

Table 22. Main Fault Tolerance Annotations

Annotation	Description
@Timeout	Defines a duration for timeout
@Retry	Defines a criteria on when to retry
@Fallback	Provides an alternative solution for a failed execution
@Bulkhead	Isolates failures in part of the system while the rest of the system can still function
@CircuitBreaker	Offers a way to fail fast by automatically failing the execution to prevent the system overloading and an indefinite wait or timeout by the clients
@Asynchronous	Invokes the operation asynchronously

7.4.1. Fallbacks

Let's provide a fallback for persisting a book in case of failure. For example, we could serialise the JSON representation of a book into a file so it can be processed later.

🖳 Call to Action

(66)

Edit the BookService class and add one fallback method to the BookService called fallbackPersistBook() with the code in the code in Listing 65. Then, add a @Fallback annotation to the persistBook() method pointing to the newly created fallbackPersistBook() method:

```
import org.eclipse.microprofile.faulttolerance.Fallback;
```

Listing 65. Falling Back on Persisting a Book

```
@Fallback(fallbackMethod = "fallbackPersistBook")
public Book persistBook(@Valid Book book) {
  // The Book microservice invokes the Number microservice
  IsbnNumbers isbnNumbers = numberProxy.generateNumbers();
  book.isbn13 = isbnNumbers.isbn13;
  book.isbn10 = isbnNumbers.isbn10;

  Book.persist(book);
  return book;
}

private Book fallbackPersistBook(Book book) throws FileNotFoundException {
  LOGGER.warn("Falling back on persisting a book");
  book.id = 0L;
  book.isbn13 = "to be fixed";
  book.isbn10 = "to be fixed";
  String bookJson = JsonbBuilder.create().toJson(book);
  try (PrintWriter out = new PrintWriter("book-" + Instant.now().toEpochMilli() +
".json")) {
    out.println(bookJson);
  }
  throw new IllegalStateException();
}
```

The fallbackPersistBook() method must have the same method signature as persistBook() (in our case, it takes and returns a Book object). In case the *Book* microservice cannot invoke the *Number* microservice, the fallbackPersistBook() is invoked and the JSON representation of the book is written on the disk.

Let's run our application and test the fallbacks. If both microservices are still up and running, kill the *Number* microservice and start creating new books again with the following cURL command:

```
$ curl -X POST -d  '{"title":"Practising Quarkus", "author":"Antonio Goncalves",
"yearOfPublication":"2020"}'  -H "Content-Type: application/json"
http://localhost:8702/api/books -v

< HTTP/1.1 500 Internal Server Error
```

You will get a very long stacktrace but you should see JSON files being created on your disk (under the `target` folder). This means the fallback is working. Open one of these JSON files and you should have something like that:

```
{
  "id": 0,
  "author": "Antonio Goncalves",
  "isbn10": "to be fixed",
  "isbn13": "to be fixed",
  "title": "Practising Quarkus",
  "yearOfPublication": 2020
}
```

Restart the *Number* microservice and keep on creating books: the books are not stored on your disk anymore but yes getting persisted on the database with their ISBN numbers.

7.4.2. Timeout

Sometimes invoking a REST API can take a long time. In fact, the more microservices invoke other microservices, the more network latency you can have. And what happens when an HTTP request takes a long time? Well, it hangs. Figure 24 shows the dev tools of a browser where you can see the request pending.

Figure 24. HTTP request hanging

Let's say that getting ISBN numbers actually takes longer than expected. What happens to the *Book*

147

microservice invoking a long-running *Number* microservice to get the ISBN numbers? It hangs too, and we don't want that to happen.

🖵 Call to Action

(68)

Let's simulate a long-running process by adding a sleep. Edit the NumberResource class and add an attribute that gets injected a number of seconds to sleep. Thanks to the configuration capabilities of Quarkus it's just a matter of having:

```
@ConfigProperty(name = "seconds.sleep", defaultValue = "0")
int secondsToSleep = 0;
```

Then, add this sleep time in the generateBookNumbers() method as shown in Listing 66. Now that we can simulate a long-running process of generating ISBN numbers, we would rather time it out than leave it just hanging. For that, add the @Timeout annotation to the method. @Timeout waits a number of milliseconds before timing out:

```
import org.eclipse.microprofile.faulttolerance.Timeout;
```

Listing 66. The Number Microservice Timing Out

```
@Timeout(250)
@GET
@Produces(MediaType.APPLICATION_JSON)
public Response generateBookNumbers() throws InterruptedException {
  LOGGER.info("Waiting for " + secondsToSleep + " seconds");
  TimeUnit.SECONDS.sleep(secondsToSleep);
  LOGGER.info("Generating book numbers");
  Faker faker = new Faker();
  BookNumbers bookNumbers = new BookNumbers();
  bookNumbers.isbn10 = faker.code().isbn10(separator);
  bookNumbers.isbn13 = faker.code().isbn13(separator);
  bookNumbers.asin = faker.code().asin();
  bookNumbers.ean8 = faker.code().ean8();
  bookNumbers.ean13 = faker.code().ean13();
  bookNumbers.generationDate = Instant.now();
  return Response.ok(bookNumbers).build();
}
```

Note that the timeout is configured to 250 ms, and a `Thread.sleep` was introduced and can be configured, let's update it. Edit the `rest-number/src/main/resources/application.properties` file add the following property with a value or 10 seconds:

```
seconds.sleep=10
```

Let's start the *Number* microservice and invoke a number generation with the following command:

```
$ curl -X GET -H "Accept: application/json" http://localhost:8701/api/numbers
```

The timeout is at 250ms and we are sleeping for 10 seconds, thereforen, the request should be interrupted and you should see the following:

```
INFO [o.a.f.q.n.NumberResource] Waiting for 10 seconds
ERROR [i.q.v.h.r.QuarkusErrorHandler] HTTP Request to /api/numbers failed
org.jboss.resteasy.spi.UnhandledException:
org.eclipse.microprofile.faulttolerance.exceptions.TimeoutException:
Timeout[org.agoncal.fascicle.quarkus.number.NumberResource#generateBookNumbers]
timed out
```

Now that you've seen timeout in action, you can set the `seconds.sleep` property to 0.

7.5. Running the Application

To run the entire application now we need to start three Quarkus instances:

- The User Interface on port 8700,
- The *Number* microservice on port 8701,
- And the *Book* microservice on port 8702.

Then it's just a matter of using cURL commands to either generate book numbers or persist new books. We can also use the Angular application to ease the creation or deletion of a book. But what about testing?

7.5.1. Testing the Application

So now we have a problem: to run the tests of the *Book* microservice we need the *Number* microservice to be up and running.

🖥 Call to Action

(70)

Shutdown all the processes and execute the tests of the *Book* microservice. They should fail and you should see a BUILD FAILURE:

```
rest-book$ ./mvnw test
(...)
[ERROR] Tests run: 5, Failures: 1, Errors: 2
[INFO]
[INFO] -------------
[INFO] BUILD FAILURE
[INFO] -------------
```

Now, if you start the *Number* microservice and execute the tests again, they succeed. The *Book* tests depend on *Number* being up and running.

The tests of the *Book* microservice don't work anymore, let's fix that. We need to Mock the *Number* REST API interface. Quarkus supports the use of mock objects using the CDI @Alternative mechanism[76]. To use this, simply override the bean you wish to mock with a class in the src/test/java directory, and put the @io.quarkus.test.Mock annotation on the bean. This built-in Mock stereotype declares @Alternative, @Priority(1) and @Dependent.

🖥 Call to Action

(71)

To mock the NumberProxy interface, create a new class called MockNumberProxy under the src/test/java directory. The MockNumberProxy class (under the org.agoncal.fascicle.quarkus.book.client package with the code in Listing 67) implements NumberProxy interface and returns mocked data. Don't worry, the code doesn't compile yet but we will fix it soon.

Listing 67. Class Mocking the Proxy Invocation

```
@Mock
@ApplicationScoped
@RestClient
public class MockNumberProxy implements NumberProxy {

  @Override
  public IsbnNumbers generateNumbers() {
    IsbnNumbers isbnNumbers = new IsbnNumbers();
    isbnNumbers.isbn13 = "Dummy Isbn 13";
    isbnNumbers.isbn10 = "Dummy Isbn 10";
    return isbnNumbers;
  }
}
```

So instead of invoking the NumberProxy, the alternative MockNumberProxy is automatically called during the test phase as shown in Figure 25. The *Number* microservice is never invoked and is not needed when testing the *Book* microservice.

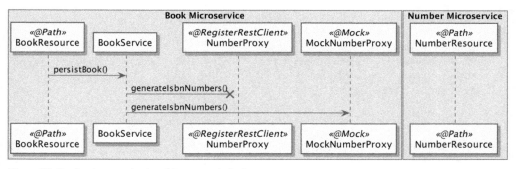

Figure 25. Book microservice invoking a mock during a test

Let's see if our mock works. For that we can add another test that makes sure we get the mocked data when we create a new book.

🖥 Call to Action

(72)

Edit the BookResourceTest and add the new test method defined in Listing 68. Execute the *Book* microservice tests again (./mvnw test), they should all pass.

Listing 68. Testing the Mocked Invocation

```
@Test
@Order(5)
void shouldAddABookUsingProxy() {
  Book book = new Book();
```

```java
book.title = DEFAULT_TITLE;
book.author = DEFAULT_AUTHOR;
book.yearOfPublication = DEFAULT_YEAR_OF_PUBLICATION;
book.nbOfPages = DEFAULT_NB_OF_PAGES;
book.rank = DEFAULT_RANK;
book.price = DEFAULT_PRICE;
book.smallImageUrl = DEFAULT_SMALL_IMAGE_URL;
book.mediumImageUrl = DEFAULT_MEDIUM_IMAGE_URL;
book.description = DEFAULT_DESCRIPTION;

// Persists a new book
String location =
  given()
    .body(book)
    .header(CONTENT_TYPE, APPLICATION_JSON)
    .header(ACCEPT, APPLICATION_JSON).
  when()
    .post("/api/books").
    then()
    .statusCode(CREATED.getStatusCode())
    .extract().header("Location");

// Extracts the Location and stores the book id
assertTrue(location.contains("/api/books"));
String[] segments = location.split("/");
bookId = segments[segments.length - 1];
assertNotNull(bookId);

// Checks the book has been created
given()
  .header(ACCEPT, APPLICATION_JSON)
  .pathParam("id", bookId).
when()
  .get("/api/books/{id}").
then()
  .statusCode(OK.getStatusCode())
  .header(CONTENT_TYPE, APPLICATION_JSON)
  .body("title", Is.is(DEFAULT_TITLE))
  .body("$", hasKey("isbn13"))
  .body("$", hasKey("isbn10"))
  .body("author", Is.is(DEFAULT_AUTHOR))
  .body("yearOfPublication", Is.is(DEFAULT_YEAR_OF_PUBLICATION))
  .body("nbOfPages", Is.is(DEFAULT_NB_OF_PAGES))
  .body("rank", Is.is(DEFAULT_RANK))
  .body("smallImageUrl", Is.is(DEFAULT_SMALL_IMAGE_URL.toString()))
  .body("mediumImageUrl", Is.is(DEFAULT_MEDIUM_IMAGE_URL.toString()))
  .body("description", Is.is(DEFAULT_DESCRIPTION));

// Checks there is an extra book in the database
List<Book> books =
  given()
```

```
      .header(ACCEPT, APPLICATION_JSON).
    when()
      .get("/api/books").
    then()
      .statusCode(OK.getStatusCode())
      .header(CONTENT_TYPE, APPLICATION_JSON)
      .extract().body().as(getBookTypeRef());

  assertEquals(nbBooks + 1, books.size());
}
```

This new test as well as all the tests that we created in Chapter 5, *Developing the REST Book Microservice* should pass.

7.5.2. Executing the Application

Let's make sure we have our two microservices started as well as the user interface.

🖳 Call to Action

(73)

Before starting our instances of Quarkus you might want to check if you have already started some of these instances. If you are lost in all your running processes, remember that you can check the listening ports:

```
$ lsof -i tcp:8700
$ lsof -i tcp:8701
$ lsof -i tcp:8702
```

Start the three Quarkus instances if they are not already started:

```
rest-book$ ./mvnw quarkus:dev
rest-number$ ./mvnw quarkus:dev
ui-vintagestore$ ./mvnw quarkus:dev
```

With all the Quarkus instances up and running, open your browser at http://localhost:8700 and start generating ISBN numbers and creating books.

7.5.3. Breaking the Communication

Time to see if our architecture is tolerant to failure.

To check that our fallback is working, kill the *Number* microservice Quarkus instance. In the browser, try to generate some numbers and ake sure it fails. Now, create a book using the user interface. It should fail and a JSON file should have been created under the rest-book/target directory.

7.6. What You Have Built in This Chapter

Most of the changes in the code took place under the client subpackage of the *Book* microservice. That's where we've added the code to invoke the *Number* microservice, and also, from a test point of view, that's where we'll add a mocked service:

```
.
└── rest-book
    ├── src
    │   ├── main
    │   │   ├── java
    │   │   │   └── org/agoncal/fascicle/quarkus/book
    │   │   │       ├── client
    │   │   │       │   ├── IsbnNumbers.java
    │   │   │       │   └── NumberProxy.java
    │   │   │       ├── Book.java
    │   │   │       ├── BookApplication.java
    │   │   │       ├── BookResource.java
    │   │   │       └── BookService.java
    │   │   └── resources
    │   │       ├── application.properties
    │   │       ├── default_banner.txt
    │   │       └── import.sql
    │   └── test
    │       └── java
    │           └── org/agoncal/fascicle/quarkus/book
    │               ├── client
    │               │   └── MockNumberProxy.java
    │               ├── BookResourceTest.java
    │               └── NativeBookResourceIT.java
    └── pom.xml
```

7.7. Summary

In this chapter, you've solved the communication issue between the components that make our architecture. First of all, you've solved the common CORS problem, which happens frequently with single page applications and, of course, microservices: changing origins is by default forbidden, so you need to configure Quarkus to let invocations span throughout several origins.

The communication between microservices is very challenging. In a distributed architecture, you rely on an unreliable network: the network can slow down, can be cut, a microservice can hang and have a domino effect on other microservices, and so on. Thanks to Quarkus and its Eclipse MicroProfile Fault Tolerance implementation, you can develop a fallback mechanism as well as timeout a long-running request.

In the next chapter, you will add health checks to the microservices so you know when they are up or down. You will also add some metrics and use Prometheus so you know if your microservices are correctly responding.

🖥 Call to Action

(75)

Now that you have your microservices talking to each other, you might want to commit your changes so you can come back to it later:

```
$ git add .
$ git commit -m "fault-tolerance"
```

If in the next chapter, for some reason, you want to reset all your changes and come back to this commit, you can use the following commands:

```
$ git reset --hard
$ git clean -f -d
```

---

[71] **CORS** https://en.wikipedia.org/wiki/Cross-origin_resource_sharing

[72] **REST Client** https://microprofile.io/project/eclipse/microprofile-rest-client

[73] **REST Client GitHub** https://github.com/eclipse/microprofile-rest-client

[74] **Fault Tolerance** https://microprofile.io/project/eclipse/microprofile-fault-tolerance

[75] **Fault Tolerance GitHub** https://github.com/eclipse/microprofile-fault-tolerance

[76] **CDI Alternatives** https://docs.jboss.org/weld/reference/latest/en-US/html/specialization.html

Chapter 8. Monitoring the Microservices

Now that we have several microservices, observing them starts to be a bit tricky: we can't just look at the logs of all the microservices to see if they are up and running or behaving correctly. In this chapter, you will add health checks and several metrics to the *Number* and *Book* microservices and gather them within Prometheus.

8.1. What Will You Build in This Chapter?

In this chapter, you will:

- Add health checks to our microservices so we know they are up and running,
- Add metrics to all the REST endpoints methods so we can measure the execution time and the number of calls,
- Configure Prometheus so we can visualise all the metrics.

8.1.1. Overall Architecture

Figure 26 shows the architecture that you will have at the end of this chapter. Prometheus sits in the middle of the *Number* and *Book* microservices to gather some metrics and displays them graphically.

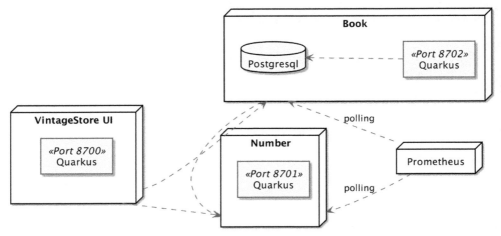

Figure 26. Overall architecture

8.1.2. Directory Structure

In this module, you will add the extra subpackage health with the classes needed to handle the health checks. The load-vintagestore module contains the code to stress the application, simulating users using the microservices. You will end-up with the following directory structure:

```
.
├── load-vintagestore
│   └── pom.xml
├── rest-book
│   ├── src
│   │   └── main
│   │       └── java
│   │           └── org/agoncal/fascicle/quarkus/book
│   │               └── health
│   │                   ├── DatabaseConnectionHealthCheck.java
│   │                   └── PingBookResourceHealthCheck.java
│   └── pom.xml
├── rest-number
│   ├── src
│   │   └── main
│   │       └── java
│   │           └── org/agoncal/fascicle/quarkus/number
│   │               └── health
│   │                   └── PingNumberResourceHealthCheck.java
│   └── pom.xml
└── pom.xml
```

8.1.3. Maven Dependencies

To expose the metrics and health for the *Number* and *Book* microservices, we will need a few extra Maven dependencies as shown in Listing 69 in both `rest-book/pom.xml` and `rest-number/pom.xml`:

- `quarkus-smallrye-health`: Eclipse MicroProfile Health dependency so we know our microservices are up and running.

- `quarkus-smallrye-metrics`: Eclipse MicroProfile Metrics dependency to gather metrics relating to the time it takes to process a request.

Listing 69. Observability Maven Dependencies

```xml
<dependency>
  <groupId>io.quarkus</groupId>
  <artifactId>quarkus-smallrye-health</artifactId>
</dependency>
<dependency>
  <groupId>io.quarkus</groupId>
  <artifactId>quarkus-smallrye-metrics</artifactId>
</dependency>
```

You can either edit the `pom.xml` files of both the *Number* and *Book* microservices and add manually the dependencies in Listing 69, or you can use the Quarkus Maven plugin. For that, go to the `rest-number` and `rest-book` directory and execute:

```
./mvnw quarkus:add-extension -Dextensions="smallrye-health, smallrye-metrics"
```

8.2. Checking Health

When using several microservices, it's important to be able to automatically check if they are up and running. A way to do this is to expose some sort of endpoint for each microservice so we can check its state. That's the purpose of *Eclipse MicroProfile Health*, and it is easily integrated with Quarkus.

Eclipse MicroProfile Health[77] provides the ability to probe the state of a computing node from another machine. The Eclipse MicroProfile Health APIs allow applications to provide information about their state to external viewers which is typically useful in cloud environments where automated processes must be able to determine whether the application should be discarded or restarted.

The Eclipse MicroProfile Health APIs and annotations are all defined under the `org.eclipse.microprofile.health` package. Table 23 lists the main subpackages defined in Eclipse MicroProfile Health version 3.1 (under the root `org.eclipse.microprofile.health` package[78]).

Table 23. Main org.eclipse.microprofile.health Subpackages

Subpackage	Description
root	Root package of the Health APIs
spi	Internal SPIs (*Service Provider Interfaces*) implemented by the provider

Along with APIs, Health comes with a set of annotations. Table 24 lists a subset of the most commonly used annotations.

Table 24. Main Health Annotations

Annotation	Description
@Startup	Defines a Startup Health Check procedure mapped to the Startup Kubernetes
@Liveness	Used to define a liveness health check procedure
@Readiness	Used to define a readiness health check procedure

8.2.1. Running the Default Health Check

Importing the `smallrye-health` extension directly exposes three REST endpoints:

Eclipse MicroProfile Health allows services to report their health, and it publishes the overall health status to defined endpoints:

- `/health/started`: Returns the result of all startup checks and determines whether or not your application is started.
- `/health/live`: Returns the result of all liveness checks and determines whether or not your application is up and running.
- `/health/ready`: Returns the result of all readiness checks and determines whether or not your application can process requests.
- `/health`: Accumulates the result of all health check types.

These endpoints are linked to health check procedures annotated respectively with `@Startup`, `@Liveness` and `@Readiness` annotations.

💻 Call to Action

(77)

To check that the health extension is working as expected, make sure both microservices are up and running. For example, access the *Number* microservice using your browser or cURL at:

- http://localhost:8701/q/health/live
- http://localhost:8701/q/health/ready
- http://localhost:8701/q/health

No health checks are defined, you should get an empty JSON array as follow:

```
{
  "status": "UP",
  "checks": []
}
```

For now, the checks array is empty as we have not specified any health check procedure yet so let's define some.

8.2.2. Adding a Liveness Health Check

To add a liveness health check to our *Number* microservice, we can check that our `hello()` method returns the `hello` string. If it does, we know the REST endpoint responds and is alive.

📺 Call to Action

(78)

Edit the NumberResource class, find the hello() method (the one generated at the very beginning) and add a specific @Path annotation as shown in Listing 70. Do exactly the same for the hello() method in BookResource.

Listing 70. The Number REST Endpoint Returning a Ping

```
@GET
@Produces(MediaType.TEXT_PLAIN)
@Path("/ping")
public String hello() {
  return "hello";
}
```

Then, we need to create a liveness health check that invokes this hello() method.

📺 Call to Action

(79)

Create a new class called PingNumberResourceHealthCheck (under the health subpackage in rest-number module) that invokes this hello() method. The class in Listing 71 extends HealthCheck and overrides the call() method. That's where we invoke the endpoint's hello() method. If the call succeeds, we return an up response (meaning the REST endpoint is live). Make sure you use the import statements of Eclipse MicroProfile Health:

```
import org.eclipse.microprofile.health.HealthCheck;
import org.eclipse.microprofile.health.HealthCheckResponse;
import org.eclipse.microprofile.health.Liveness;
```

Do the same for the *Book* microservice. Create a PingBookResourceHealthCheck class (under the org.agoncal.fascicle.quarkus.book.health package) that also invokes the hello() method.

Listing 71. Checks the Liveness of the Number Microservice

```java
@Liveness
@ApplicationScoped
public class PingNumberResourceHealthCheck implements HealthCheck {

  @Inject
  NumberResource numberResource;

  @Override
  public HealthCheckResponse call() {
    numberResource.hello();
    return HealthCheckResponse.named("Ping Number REST Endpoint").up().build();
  }
}
```

As you can see, health check procedures are defined as implementations of the HealthCheck interface which are defined as CDI beans with the CDI qualifier @Liveness. HealthCheck is a functional interface whose single method call() returns a HealthCheckResponse object which can be easily constructed by the fluent builder API shown in the example. Because we defined our health check as being a liveness procedure (with @Liveness qualifier) the new health check procedure will be present in the checks array in Listing 72.

Listing 72. Liveness JSON Result of the Number Microservice

```json
{
  "status": "UP",
  "checks": [
    {
      "name": "Ping Number REST Endpoint",
      "status": "UP"
    }
  ]
}
```

💻 Call to Action

(80)

Make sure Quarkus is started in dev mode (./mvnw quarkus:dev) and simply repeat the request to http://localhost:8701/q/health/live by refreshing your browser window or by using cURL. You should see the JSON result as in Listing 72 showing that our microservice is live. If you have written the same health check for the *Book* microservice, you should get something similar at http://localhost:8702/q/health.

8.2.3. Adding a Readiness Health Check

We've just created a simple liveness health check procedure which states whether our application is running or not. But it's not because the application is live that it's ready. So let's create a readiness health check in the rest-book module which will be able to state whether our application is able to process requests.

🖳 Call to Action

(81)

To create a readiness health check that accesses the database of the *Book* microservice, create a new class DatabaseConnectionHealthCheck under the subpackage health. If the database can be accessed, then we return the response indicating that the application is ready. As you can see in Listing 73 this time we use a @Readiness qualifier instead of @Liveness.

Listing 73. Checks the Readiness of the Book Microservice

```java
@Readiness
@ApplicationScoped
public class DatabaseConnectionHealthCheck implements HealthCheck {

  @Inject
  BookService bookService;

  @Override
  public HealthCheckResponse call() {
    HealthCheckResponseBuilder responseBuilder = HealthCheckResponse
      .named("Book Datasource connection health check");

    try {
      List<Book> books = bookService.findAllBooks();
      responseBuilder.withData("Number of books in the database", books.size()).up();
    } catch (IllegalStateException e) {
      responseBuilder.down();
    }

    return responseBuilder.build();
  }
}
```

If you now re-run the health check at http://localhost:8702/q/health/live the checks array contains only the previously defined PingBookResourceHealthCheck as it is the only check defined with the @Liveness qualifier. However, if you access http://localhost:8702/q/health/ready you only see the Database connection health check. That's because it's the only health check defined with the @Readiness qualifier as being the readiness health check procedure. If you access http://localhost:8702/q/health you will get back both checks as shown in Listing 74.

Listing 74. Array of All Health Checks

```
{
  "status": "UP",
  "checks": [
    {
      "name": "Ping Book REST Endpoint",
      "status": "UP"
    },
    {
      "name": "Book Datasource connection health check",
      "status": "UP",
      "data": {
        "Number of books in the database": 102
      }
    }
  ]
}
```

8.3. Gathering Metrics

Having health checks on our microservices is very important: it quickly indicates if an instance is live and ready to process requests. But health checks do not indicate if the microservice is running at its full speed or slowing down. It doesn't indicate either if it's performing faster or slower than yesterday, for example. That's when metrics come in handy. To know if your entire microservice architecture is performing at its right speed, you need to gather metrics and be able to visualise them.

Eclipse MicroProfile Metrics[79] provides a unified way for MicroProfile servers to export monitoring data to management agents. Metrics will also provide a common Java API for exposing their telemetry data. MicroProfile Metrics allows applications to gather various metrics and statistics that provide insights into what is happening inside the application. The metrics can be read remotely using a JSON or OpenMetrics format to be processed by additional tools such as Prometheus, and stored for analysis and visualisation.

The Eclipse MicroProfile Metrics APIs and annotations are all defined under the main `org.eclipse.microprofile.metrics` package, either at the root, or under the other subpackages. Table 25 lists the main subpackages defined in Eclipse MicroProfile Metrics version 3.0 (under the root `org.eclipse.microprofile.metrics` package[80]).

Table 25. Main org.eclipse.microprofile.metrics Subpackages

Subpackage	Description
root	Root package of the Metrics APIs
annotation	APIs for annotating methods and classes to get metrics from

Along with APIs, Metrics comes with a set of annotations. Table 26 lists a subset of the most commonly used annotations.

Table 26. Main Metrics Annotations

Annotation	Description
@Counted	Marks a method, constructor, or class invocation as counted
@Gauge	Simplest metric type that just returns a value
@Metered	Measures the rate at which a set of events occur
@Timed	Aggregates timing durations and provides duration statistics, plus throughput statistics
@SimplyTimed	Tracks elapsed time duration and count

Importing the `smallrye-metrics` extension directly exposes a few endpoints with default metrics:

The Eclipse MicroProfile Metrics architecture consists of four endpoints:

- `/metrics/base`: Set of metrics that all MicroProfile-compliant servers have to provide.
- `/metrics/vendor`: Vendor-specific metrics on top of the basic set of required metrics.
- `/metrics/application`: Metrics provided by the application at runtime.
- `/metrics`: Aggregates all the metrics.

Now let's have metrics on all the methods of all our microservices. For that, we need a few annotations to make sure that our desired metrics are calculated over time and can be exported for manual analysis or processing by additional tooling. The metrics that we will gather are these:

- @Counted: A counter which is increased by one each time the user makes a request.
- @Timed: This is a timer, therefore a compound metric that benchmarks how much time the request takes.

Methods in Listing 75 are annotated with Eclipse MicroProfile Metrics annotations (@Counted and @Timed) so metrics can be gathered.

Listing 75. Metrics on Methods to Create and Update a Book

```
@Counted(name = "countCreateBook", description = "Counts how many times the createBook
method has been invoked")
@Timed(name = "timeCreateBook", description = "Times how long it takes to invoke the
createBook method", unit = MetricUnits.MILLISECONDS)
@POST
public Response createBook(@RequestBody(required = true, content = @Content(mediaType
= MediaType.APPLICATION_JSON, schema = @Schema(implementation = Book.class))) @Valid
Book book, @Context UriInfo uriInfo) {
  book = service.persistBook(book);
  UriBuilder builder = uriInfo.getAbsolutePathBuilder().path(Long.toString(book.id));
  LOGGER.debug("New book created with URI " + builder.build().toString());
  return Response.created(builder.build()).build();
}

@Counted(name = "countUpdateBook", description = "Counts how many times the updateBook
method has been invoked")
@Timed(name = "timeUpdateBook", description = "Times how long it takes to invoke the
updateBook method", unit = MetricUnits.MILLISECONDS)
@PUT
public Response updateBook(@RequestBody(required = true, content = @Content(mediaType
= MediaType.APPLICATION_JSON, schema = @Schema(implementation = Book.class))) @Valid
Book book) {
  book = service.updateBook(book);
  LOGGER.debug("Book updated with new valued " + book);
  return Response.ok(book).build();
}
```

🖥 Call to Action

(83)

Edit the class BookResource and add the Metrics annotations on all the methods of all the
microservices as shown in Listing 75. Listing 75 just shows the code of the methods to create
and update a book (but make sure to add metrics on all methods of all microservices). You
need to use a unique name for each metric, such as name = "countCreateBook", countDeleteBook
or countGenerateBookNumber.

8.4. Running the Application

This time, we don't need the user interface to run. We need to run our infrastructure, the *Number*
and *Book* microservices (which have health checks and metrics) and add some load. But first, a few
tests.

8.4.1. Testing the Application

We could leave the test suite as it is. We have a nice suite of tests that make sure our business logic works, and that is the most important thing. However, we can add a few extra tests just to check that our health check and metrics endpoints are accessible.

Testing Health Check

Listing 76 adds a few extra test methods that make sure both health check endpoints are available. They just invoke an HTTP GET on both /q/health/live and /q/health/ready URIs and make sure they return a 200-OK response. Add these tests to both the NumberResourceTest and BookResourceTest classes.

Listing 76. Testing Health Check Endpoints Availability

```
@Test
void shouldPingLiveness() {
  given()
    .header(ACCEPT, APPLICATION_JSON).
  when()
    .get("/q/health/live").
  then()
    .statusCode(OK.getStatusCode());
}

@Test
void shouldPingReadiness() {
  given()
    .header(ACCEPT, APPLICATION_JSON).
  when()
    .get("/q/health/ready").
  then()
    .statusCode(OK.getStatusCode());
}
```

💻 Call to Action

(84)

Edit the NumberResourceTest and BookResourceTest classes and add the health checks defined in Listing 76. Now execute the tests on both microservices (either with the following Maven commands, or using Continuous Testing):

```
rest-book$ ./mvnw test
rest-number$ ./mvnw test
```

Testing Metrics

We use the same testing approach in Listing 77 to make sure the Metrics endpoint is available. We just ping a few internal Quarkus URLs (under the /q/metrics path) and make sure we have a return code 200.

Listing 77. Testing Metrics Endpoint Availability

```
@Test
void shouldPingMetrics() {
  given()
    .header(ACCEPT, MediaType.APPLICATION_JSON).
  when()
    .get("/q/metrics/application").
  then()
    .statusCode(OK.getStatusCode());
}
```

💻 Call to Action

(85)

Edit the NumberResourceTest and BookResourceTest classes and add the Metrics test in Listing 77. Now execute the tests on both microservices:

```
rest-book$ ./mvnw test
rest-number$ ./mvnw test
```

8.4.2. Running the Infrastructure

To execute the application and get some metrics, we now need Prometheus. As usual, let's use Docker and Docker Compose to ease the installation of this tool.

Listing 78. Docker Compose File With a Prometheus

```
services:
  monitoring:
    image: "prom/prometheus:v2.31.1"
    container_name: "vintage_store_monitoring"
    ports:
      - 9090:9090
    volumes:
      - ./monitoring/prometheus.yml:/etc/prometheus/prometheus.yml
```

8.4.3. Executing the Application

Now that the tests pass and that our infrastructure is up and running, let's start our two microservices, add some load and get some metrics.

8.4.4. Adding Load to the Application

Now that we have the microservices exposing health checks and metrics, time to add some load to our application and have a decent user interface to monitor how the system behaves. In the load-vintagestore directory, there is an application that is NOT a Quarkus application. It's a simple Java application that simulates users interacting with the system so it generates some load.

The VintageStoreLoad class in Listing 79 is just a main that executes several scenarios in different threads.

Listing 79. Main Class Executing the Load Scenarios

```
public class VintageStoreLoad {

  public static void main(String[] args) {
    Thread bookScenario = new Thread(new ScenarioBook());
    bookScenario.start();
    Thread numberScenario = new Thread(new ScenarioNumber());
    numberScenario.start();
  }
}
```

For example, if you look at the ScenarioBook in Listing 80, you will see that it's just a suite of HTTP calls on the Book API.

Listing 80. Book Load Scenario

```
protected List<Endpoint> getEndpoints() {
  return Stream.of(
    endpoint(contextRoot, "GET"),
    endpoint(contextRoot + "/ping", "GET"),
    endpoint(contextRoot + "/random", "GET"),
    endpointWithTemplates(contextRoot + "/{id}", "GET", this::idParam),
    endpointWithTemplates(contextRoot + "/{id}", "DELETE", this::idParam),
    endpointWithEntity(contextRoot, "POST", this::createBook)
  )
    .collect(collectingAndThen(toList(), Collections::unmodifiableList));
}
```

💻 Call to Action

(88)

To add some load, you need to compile and start the *Load* application using the following commands:

```
load-vintagestore$ ./mvnw compile
load-vintagestore$ ./mvnw exec:java
```

You will see the following logs on the load-vintagestore project:

```
INFO: GET     - http://localhost:8702/api/books/ping    - 200
INFO: GET     - http://localhost:8701/api/numbers        - 200
INFO: GET     - http://localhost:8702/api/books/random   - 200
INFO: GET     - http://localhost:8701/api/numbers        - 200
INFO: GET     - http://localhost:8702/api/books/1077     - 200
INFO: GET     - http://localhost:8701/api/numbers        - 200
INFO: POST    - http://localhost:8702/api/books          - 201
INFO: DELETE  - http://localhost:8702/api/books/1055     - 204
INFO: GET     - http://localhost:8702/api/books/random   - 200
INFO: GET     - http://localhost:8701/api/numbers        - 200
```

You should also see some logs appearing on the *Number* and *Book* microservices. Leave it running for a while so we have enough data to monitor.

8.4.5. Monitoring the Application

Before collecting the metrics with Prometheus, let's just check them with cURL.

🖳 Call to Action

(89)

To view the metrics of the *Number* and *Book* microservices in JSON format, execute the following commands:

```
$ curl -H "Accept: application/json" http://localhost:8701/q/metrics
$ curl -H "Accept: application/json" http://localhost:8701/q/metrics/application
$ curl -H "Accept: application/json" http://localhost:8701/q/metrics/base
$ curl -H "Accept: application/json" http://localhost:8701/q/metrics/vendor
$ curl -H "Accept: application/json" http://localhost:8702/q/metrics
$ curl -H "Accept: application/json" http://localhost:8702/q/metrics/application
$ curl -H "Accept: application/json" http://localhost:8702/q/metrics/base
$ curl -H "Accept: application/json" http://localhost:8702/q/metrics/vendor
```

You will receive a response similar to the one in Listing 81.

Listing 81. Metrics Class

```json
{
  "NumberResource.countGenerateBookNumber": 23,
  "NumberResource.timeGenerateBookNumber": {
    "p99": 2.552359,
    "min": 2.351004,
    "max": 4.142853,
    "mean": 2.4475338218611054,
    "p50": 2.459645,
    "p999": 2.552359,
    "stddev": 0.059644582615724376,
    "p95": 2.552359,
    "p98": 2.552359,
    "p75": 2.475044,
    "fiveMinRate": 0.0427305308960399,
    "fifteenMinRate": 0.018611613176138856,
    "meanRate": 0.005087646702440494,
    "count": 23,
    "oneMinRate": 0.1733913276585504
  }
}
```

Let's explain the meaning of each metric:

- countGenerateBookNumber: A counter which is increased by one each time the user asks for a book number.

- timeGenerateBookNumber: This is a timer, therefore a compound metric that benchmarks how much time the request takes. All durations are measured in milliseconds. It consists of these values:

  - min: The shortest duration it took to perform a request.

  - max: The longest duration.

  - mean: The mean value of the measured durations.

  - stddev: The standard deviation.

  - count: The number of observations (so it will be the same value as countGenerateBookNumber).

  - p50, p75, p95, p99, p999: Percentiles of the durations. For example the value in p95 means that 95% of the measurements were faster than this duration.

  - meanRate, oneMinRate, fiveMinRate, fifteenMinRate: Mean throughput and one-, five-, and fifteen-minute exponentially-weighted moving average throughput.

If you prefer an OpenMetrics[81] export rather than the JSON format, remove the -H "Accept: application/json" argument from your command line.

8.4.6. Collecting Metrics on Prometheus

Having a JSON representation of the metrics is ok, but we will have to have a graphical interface.

That's when Prometheus comes in to play. *Prometheus*[82] is an open source systems monitoring and alerting toolkit.

Configuring Prometheus

Prometheus needs to be configured to poll data from our microservices. This is made under our infrastructure/monitoring directory, in the prometheus.yml file as shown in Listing 82. This file contains a basic Prometheus configuration, plus a specific configuration which instructs Prometheus to look for application metrics from our Quarkus microservices.

Listing 82. Prometheus YAML Configuration

```
scrape_configs:
  - job_name: 'prometheus'
    static_configs:
      - targets: ['host.docker.internal:9090']
  - job_name: 'number'
    metrics_path: '/q/metrics'
    static_configs:
      - targets: ['host.docker.internal:8701']
  - job_name: 'book'
    metrics_path: '/q/metrics'
    static_configs:
      - targets: ['host.docker.internal:8702']
```

Adding Graphs to Prometheus

Now is the time to add some graphs to Prometheus. Figure 27 shows the Prometheus console that is accessible at http://localhost:9090.

Figure 27. Prometheus admin console

Out of the box, you get a lot of basic JVM metrics or even metrics of Prometheus itself, which are useful. But let's create new graphs with the metrics of our microservices.

💻 Call to Action

We have added a few health checks and metrics to our application, so let's display them. First, go to http://localhost:9090/targets so you can see our microservices state (up or down as shown in Figure 27). Because we still have the *Load* application running and adding load to our microservices, let's check the metrics. In the combobox shown in Figure 28, type `timeCreateBook`, select `application_org_agoncal_fascicle_quarkus_book_BookResource_timeCreateBook_five_min_rate_per_second`, and click *Execute*. Do the same for `countGenerateBookNumber` and other metrics you wish to visualise.

Figure 28. Looking for available metrics

This will fetch the values from our metric showing the average throughput as shown in Figure 29.

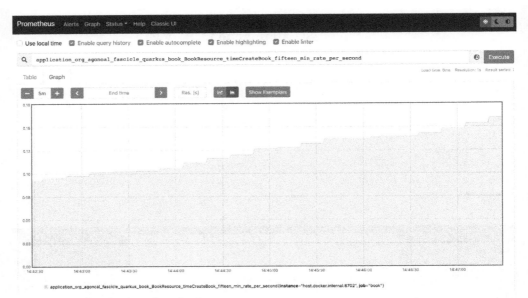

Figure 29. Metrics when creating a book

8.5. Summary

In this chapter, you've managed to monitor the microservices of our architecture. Health checks are a way to know if a microservice is started, alive and/or ready. This is very important in a distributed architecture where each microservice relies on others. Knowing that a process is dead or not ready allows other distributed services to adapt to the broken communication. You've implemented several health checks thanks to Eclipse MicroProfile Health.

Once a microservice is up and running, it is important to know if it responds to the incoming requests within a certain amount of time. Thanks to the Eclipse MicroProfile Metrics, you were able to add metrics to each of our microservices and monitor them with Prometheus.

In the next chapter, you will use Quarkus and GraalVM to build native executables. These executables will then be packaged as Docker images so they can be portable and executed on any server or cloud provider.

⌨ Call to Action

(91)

Now that your microservices have health check and metrics, you might want to commit your changes so you can come back to it later:

```
$ git add .
$ git commit -m "observability"
```

If in the next chapter, for some reason, you want to reset all your changes and come back to this commit, you can use the following commands:

```
$ git reset --hard
$ git clean -f -d
```

[77] **Health** https://microprofile.io/project/eclipse/microprofile-health

[78] **Health GitHub** https://github.com/eclipse/microprofile-health

[79] **Metrics** https://microprofile.io/project/eclipse/microprofile-metrics

[80] **Metrics GitHub** https://github.com/eclipse/microprofile-metrics

[81] **OpenMetrics** https://openmetrics.io

[82] **Prometheus** https://prometheus.io

Chapter 9. Deploying the Application

Our application is finally complete: we have several microservices communicating with each other so we can create/read/update/delete books from a database using a user interface. And all of that running on several Quarkus instances, in development mode. Time to go to production! Quarkus makes it possible to easily build native executables as well as executable JARs and package them within containers. In this chapter, you will use Quarkus to package our microservices into executables, and Docker to package them into containers and execute them.

 Make sure your development environment is set up to execute the code in this chapter. You can go to Appendix A to check that you have all the required tools installed, in particular Docker and GraalVM 21.3.0 working with JDK 11.0.13.

9.1. What Will You Build in This Chapter?

In this chapter, you will:

- Build executables and executable JARs out of our microservices,
- Package the executables into Docker images,
- Execute the entire application (our microservices, the PostgreSQL database and Prometheus) thanks to Docker Compose.

9.1.1. Overall Architecture

Figure 30 shows the architecture that you will have at the end of this chapter. The *Number* will get packaged into an executable JAR. Both, the *Book* microservice and the Angular application, will get packaged into executable binaries. Each of these executables will get packaged and executed inside a Docker container.

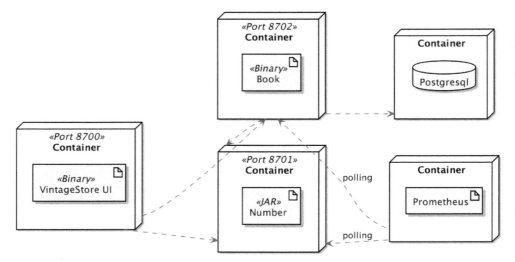

Figure 30. Overall architecture

9.1.2. Maven Dependencies

We don't need any Quarkus extension to package our microservices into executable JAR files or native binaries. This is taken care of by the Quarkus plugin. But to have Quarkus generate Docker images based on Dockerfiles, we need to add the Docker extension to our pom.xml (see Listing 83).

Listing 83. Docker Extension

```xml
<dependency>
  <groupId>io.quarkus</groupId>
  <artifactId>quarkus-container-image-docker</artifactId>
</dependency>
```

🖳 Call to Action

(92)

Add the Docker extension to your microservices (it's already in the user interface pom.xml). You can either edit the pom.xml files and add the extension shown in Listing 83 or execute the following commands on each microservice:

```
./mvnw quarkus:add-extension -Dextensions="container-image-docker"
```

Listing 84 shows the Maven profile that execute the test on the native executable. It configures the maven-failsafe-plugin so it runs the integration tests against the native executable.

Listing 84. Maven Profile to Test Native Images

```xml
<profiles>
  <profile>
    <id>native</id>
    <activation>
      <property>
        <name>native</name>
      </property>
    </activation>
    <build>
      <plugins>
        <plugin>
          <artifactId>maven-failsafe-plugin</artifactId>
          <version>${surefire-plugin.version}</version>
          <executions>
            <execution>
              <goals>
                <goal>integration-test</goal>
                <goal>verify</goal>
              </goals>
              <configuration>
                <systemPropertyVariables>

<native.image.path>${project.build.directory}/${project.build.finalName}-
runner</native.image.path>
                  <java.util.logging.manager>
org.jboss.logmanager.LogManager</java.util.logging.manager>
                  <maven.home>${maven.home}</maven.home>
                </systemPropertyVariables>
              </configuration>
            </execution>
          </executions>
        </plugin>
      </plugins>
    </build>
    <properties>
      <quarkus.package.type>native</quarkus.package.type>
    </properties>
  </profile>
</profiles>
```

9.2. Building and Executing Executables

Quarkus can package our code in different ways. In *JVM mode* Quarkus packages the code within JARs that need to be executed with a JVM. In *Native mode*, using GraalVM, Quarkus creates executables. The different formats are:

- JVM mode: JAR, Legacy-JAR, Uber-JAR.

- Native mode: Native Executable (OS dependent), Linux Native Executable.

Native mode being more performant, let's try to produce native executables for our application. Thanks to GraalVM, Quarkus is able to generate native executables. Just like Go, native executables don't need a Virtual Machine (VM) to run, they contain the whole application, like an .exe file on Windows. Native executables improve the startup time of the application, memory consumption, and produce a minimal disk footprint. The executable has everything to run the application including the JVM (shrunk to be just enough to run the application), and the application itself.

9.2.1. Testing the Native Executable

Producing a native executable can lead to a few issues, so it's also a good idea to run some tests against the native executables. This is quite easy. Listing 85 shows the NativeBookResourceIT test class. As you can see, instead of being annotated with @QuarkusTest, it uses the @NativeImageTest test runner. We can leave it empty (or add specific tests for native code) and we just extend from our previous test.

Listing 85. Native Test

```
package org.agoncal.fascicle.quarkus.book;

import io.quarkus.test.junit.NativeImageTest;

@NativeImageTest
public class NativeBookResourceIT extends BookResourceTest {

  // Execute the same tests but in native mode.
}
```

⌨ Call to Action

(93)

Let's start by testing the native executable of the *Book* microservice. When executing native tests, Quarkus uses the prod profile. This means that our *Book* microservice, in production, relies on the *Number* microservice, not the mock. Therefore, to execute the native tests, we first need to start the *Number* microservice, and then execute the tests of the *Book* microservice with the native profile. We need the following commands:

```
rest-number$ ./mvnw quarkus:dev
rest-book$ ./mvnw verify -Pnative
```

Running native tests will first execute the JVM mode tests, and then, the native tests. So the workflow is:

- The Surefire plugin executes the JVM mode tests (Quarkus is started in JVM mode);

- GraalVM compiles the code into a binary;
- The Failsafe plugin executes the binary (Quarkus is started in native mode);
- The Failsafe plugin runs the native tests.

But unfortunatelly, the native tests will not pass! Remember that we have created a test that pings the URL for SwaggerUI. But SwaggerUI is not available in production, so the shouldPingSwaggerUI() in Listing 86 only makes sense in development and test, not in production. To exclude certain tests when running as a native executable we can mark them with the @DisabledOnNativeImage annotation in order to only run them on the JVM.

Listing 86. Excluding a Test When Running as a Native Executable

```
@DisabledOnNativeImage
@Test
void shouldPingSwaggerUI() {
  given().
  when()
    .get("/q/swagger-ui").
  then()
    .statusCode(OK.getStatusCode());
}
```

🖥 Call to Action

(94)

Edit the BookResourceTest class and annotate the shouldPingSwaggerUI() method with @DisabledOnNativeImage as shown in Listing 86. Do the same for the NumberResourceTest.

Start again your native tests by running the *Number* microservice and testing the *Book* microservice with:

```
rest-number$ ./mvnw quarkus:dev
rest-book$ ./mvnw verify -Pnative
```

You should see similar traces:

```
[INFO] ------------------
[INFO] Building rest-book
[INFO] ------------------
[INFO]
[INFO] --- maven-surefire-plugin:test
[INFO]
[INFO] ----------
[INFO]  T E S T S
[INFO] ----------
[INFO] Running BookResourceTest
[INFO] [io.quarkus] Quarkus on JVM started in 1.772s
[INFO] [io.quarkus] Profile test activated.
[INFO] Tests run: 10, Failures: 0, Errors: 0, Skipped: 0, Time elapsed: 9.689 s - in
BookResourceTest
[INFO] [io.quarkus] Quarkus stopped in 0.029s
[INFO]
[INFO] Results:
[INFO]
[INFO] Tests run: 10, Failures: 0, Errors: 0, Skipped: 0
[INFO]
[INFO] --- quarkus-maven-plugin:build
[INFO] Building native image from rest-book/target/rest-book-2.0.0-SNAPSHOT-native-
image-source-jar/rest-book-2.0.0-SNAPSHOT-runner.jar
[INFO] Running Quarkus native-image plugin on GraalVM
[rest-number]    classlist:   3,955.96 ms,  1.19 GB
[rest-number]       setup:   2,928.73 ms,  1.19 GB
[rest-number]     (clinit):    947.39 ms,  5.11 GB
[rest-number]   (features):    657.81 ms,  5.11 GB
[rest-number]      (parse):  1,091.40 ms,  5.11 GB
[rest-number]     (inline):  2,587.20 ms,  6.05 GB
[rest-number]       image:   3,208.63 ms,  6.05 GB
[rest-number]     [total]:  59,936.70 ms,  6.01 GB
[INFO]
[INFO] --- maven-failsafe-plugin:integration-test
[INFO]
[INFO] ----------
[INFO]  T E S T S
[INFO] ----------
[INFO] Running NativeBookResourceIT
Executing target/rest-book-2.0.0-SNAPSHOT-runner
14:01:26 INFO [i.quarkus] rest-book native
14:01:26 INFO [i.quarkus] Profile prod activated.
[INFO]
[INFO] Results:
[INFO]
[WARNING] Tests run: 10, Failures: 0, Errors: 0, Skipped: 1
[INFO]
[INFO] -------------
[INFO] BUILD SUCCESS
[INFO] -------------
```

Great! The native tests have all passed on the the *Book* microservice, let's do the same for the *Number* microservice.

But the native tests of the *Number* microservice fail. That's because our microservices use Java Faker. And Java Faker uses a lot of introspection, which GraalVM can't cope with. GraalVM will eliminate code from Java Faker during the dead-code elimination phase and the tests won't pass. We can't compile *Number* withe GraalVM! Let's forget about creating a native executable for the *Number* microservice and package it as an executable JAR.

 A real life project has many dependencies on external frameworks. To be able to build a native executable with GraalVM, all these frameworks have to be compatible with the GraalVM dead-code elimination phase. You won't be able to always produce binaries out of your projects.

9.2.2. Building Executable JARs

Up to now, we've mostly used Maven to execute Quarkus in development mode with the `./mvnw quarkus:dev` command. But we can also build package an application using a common `./mvnw package`. That's the way we will package the *Number* microservice.

The Maven command produces different artifacts under the `target` directory:

- `rest-number-2.0.0-SNAPSHOT.jar`: Contains just the classes and resources of the projects, it's the regular artifact produced by the Maven build.

- `quarkus-app/`: Is the directory that contains the executable application.

```
rest-number$ ls -lh target

drwxr-xr-x    192B   quarkus-app/
-rw-r--r--     10K   rest-number-2.0.0-SNAPSHOT.jar
```

What we are interested in, is what's packaged under the `target/quarkus-app` directory. The `quarkus-app` directory contains the following:

- `app/`: Contains the code of our *Number* microservice.
- `lib/`: Contains all the external librairies.
- `quarkus/`: Quarkus specific directory with generated bytecode and classpath index.
- `quarkus-run.jar`: Executable JAR.

```
rest-number$ ls -lh target/quarkus-app

drwxr-xr-x     96B   app/
drwxr-xr-x    128B   lib/
drwxr-xr-x    160B   quarkus/
-rw-r--r--    598B   quarkus-run.jar
```

Quarkus packages the application and the dependencies under `target/quarkus-app`. Then, it's just a matter of executing the `quarkus-run.jar` file and our microservice is executed with the production profile.

🖥 Call to Action

(97)

With an executable JAR, you can run the application using the following command:

```
rest-number$ java -jar target/quarkus-app/quarkus-run.jar
```

Notice that Quarkus starts much quicker than when we were using the `mvn quarkus:dev` command. That's because in development mode, Quarkus watches our code for changes and live reload, as well as continuous testing. In production mode you don't get all these services but instead, you get fast startup time.

But be aware that `quarkus-run.jar` is an executable JAR, not an Uber-JAR. An Uber-JAR contains both the code of our application and all its dependencies in one single JAR file. This is not the case here. Quarkus copies all the dependencies into the `target/quarkus-app/lib` directory and `quarkus-run.jar` depends on this `target/quarkus-app/lib` directory. If you remove the `target/quarkus-app/lib` and re-run the application with `java -jar target/quarkus-app/quarkus-run.jar` it won't work (you will get a `ClassNotFoundException`).

9.2.3. Configuring the Production Datasource

So far we've been using Dev Services with our *Book* microservice to interact with a PostgreSQL database. But Dev Services is not available in production. We now need a real PostgreSQL database and connect our microservice to it. The way to obtain connections to a database is to use a *datasource*[83]. In Quarkus, the datasource and connection pooling implementation is called *Agroal*[84].

🖵 Call to Action

(98)

Configure the datasource for production by adding the following configuration in the application.properties:

```
%prod.quarkus.datasource.db-kind=postgresql
%prod.quarkus.datasource.username=book
%prod.quarkus.datasource.password=book
%prod.quarkus.datasource.jdbc.url=jdbc:postgresql://localhost:5432/books_database
%prod.quarkus.datasource.jdbc.min-size=2
%prod.quarkus.datasource.jdbc.max-size=8
```

9.2.4. Building Native Executables

As we've seen during the test phase, Quarkus, with the help of GraalVM, can build a native executable. Thanks to the built-in Maven native profile again, you can easily create a native executable.

🖵 Call to Action

(99)

Because of Java Faker we can't build a native executable for the *Number* microservice, but we can for *Book* as well as for the user interface. Execute the following commands so GraalVM can compile our code into binaries:

```
rest-book$ ./mvnw package -Pnative
ui-vintagestore$ ./mvnw package -Pnative
```

By executing these command, you should have a similar output (the following log is for the *Book* microservice, but you will have a similar one for the user interface):

```
[rest-book-2.0.0-SNAPSHOT-runner]    (typeflow):   12,887.14 ms
[rest-book-2.0.0-SNAPSHOT-runner]     (objects):   22,387.32 ms
[rest-book-2.0.0-SNAPSHOT-runner]    (features):      767.28 ms
[rest-book-2.0.0-SNAPSHOT-runner]     analysis:    38,747.95 ms
[rest-book-2.0.0-SNAPSHOT-runner]      (clinit):    1,216.40 ms
[rest-book-2.0.0-SNAPSHOT-runner]     universe:     2,525.15 ms
[rest-book-2.0.0-SNAPSHOT-runner]       (parse):    1,330.51 ms
[rest-book-2.0.0-SNAPSHOT-runner]      (inline):    2,863.40 ms
[rest-book-2.0.0-SNAPSHOT-runner]    (compile):    12,952.72 ms
[rest-book-2.0.0-SNAPSHOT-runner]      compile:    19,802.63 ms
[rest-book-2.0.0-SNAPSHOT-runner]        image:     3,567.13 ms
[rest-book-2.0.0-SNAPSHOT-runner]        write:     1,090.45 ms
[rest-book-2.0.0-SNAPSHOT-runner]      [total]:    77,137.84 ms
[INFO] Quarkus augmentation completed in 80641ms
```

 Creating a native executable requires a lot of memory and CPU. It also takes a few minutes, even for a simple application like the *Number* microservice. Most of the time is spent during the dead-code elimination, as it traverses the whole closed-world[85].

In addition to the regular files, the build also produces the rest-book-2.0.0-SNAPSHOT-runner (notice that there is no .jar file extension). And if you check the permissions of the files, you'll notice that rest-book-2.0.0-SNAPSHOT-runner is an executable (x allowing executable permissions).

```
rest-book$ ls -lh target/rest-book*

-rwxr-xr-x   73M   rest-book-2.0.0-SNAPSHOT-runner*
-rw-r--r--   61K   rest-book-2.0.0-SNAPSHOT.jar
```

9.2.5. Running the Infrastructure

To execute our application, we first need to make sure the infrastructure is up and running.

Call to Action

Check if the PostgreSQL database and Prometheus are running by executing the following Docker command:

```
$ docker container ls
CONTAINER ID    IMAGE                    PORTS                      NAMES
938b0bbd2e91    prom/prometheus:v2.31.1  0.0.0.0:9090->9090/tcp     
vintage_store_monitoring
7e6da3145e29    postgres:14.1            0.0.0.0:5432->5432/tcp     
vintage_store_books_data
```

If the infrastructure is not running, go to the root of the infrastructure directory and execute the following docker compose commands:

```
infrastructure$ docker compose -f postgresql.yaml up -d
infrastructure$ docker compose -f prometheus.yaml up -d
Creating network "infrastructure_default" with the default driver
Creating vintage_store_books_database ... done
Creating vintage_store_monitoring     ... done
```

9.2.6. Running the Application in Production Mode

Before building Docker containers out of our executables, let's execute the entire application first.

Call to Action

(101)

We have our infrastructure up and running, time to start application by executing the native executables for *Book* and *UI Vintage Store* and the executable JAR of *Number*. And to get some load, we can also execute our *Load Vintage Store* project. For that, execute the following commands:

```
rest-number$ java -jar target/quarkus-app/quarkus-run.jar
rest-book$ ./target/rest-book-2.0.0-SNAPSHOT-runner
ui-vintagestore$ ./target/ui-vintagestore-2.0.0-SNAPSHOT-runner
load-vintagestore$ ./mvnw exec:java
```

You can check the UI Vintage Store at http://localhost:8700 and Prometheus at http://localhost:9090.

One thing to notice when starting the native executables, is the startup time. Depending on your machine, starting the native executable can be 4 to 6 times faster that executing the executable JAR. The memory footprint is also smaller.

9.3. Building and Executing Containers

To run the entire application, we need to start several artifacts (native executables, executable JARs) as well as external tools, such as a PostgreSQL database or Prometheus. We already use Docker compose to startup and shutdown PostgreSQL and Prometheus. Wouldn't it be nice to do the same for our microservices and user interface? Let's build Docker images out of our code and execute these images into Docker containers.

9.3.1. Building Linux Native Executables

But first, let's build Linux executables. We managed to create native executables for the *Book* microservice as well as the user interface. But these executables are OS dependent: for example, if you've built them on Windows, they will only work on Windows!

So, the idea is to produce Linux 64-bit native executables to be able to run them in a Docker container. The native compilation uses the OS and architecture of the host system. So, before being able to build a container with Linux native executables, we need to produce compatible native executables. If you are using a Linux 64-bit machine, you are good to go with the executables that we just built. If not, Quarkus comes with a trick to produce these executables: The -Dquarkus.native.container-build parameter allows running the native compilation inside a container (provided by Quarkus). The result is a Linux 64-bit executable.

💻 Call to Action

(102)

Execute the following commands to produce Linux native executables on the *Book* microservice and the user interface:

```
rest-book$ ./mvnw package -Pnative -Dquarkus.native.container-build=true
-DskipTests
ui-vintagestore$ ./mvnw package -Pnative -Dquarkus.native.container-build=true
-DskipTests
```

The *Number* microservice cannot be packaged into a native executable (because of Java Faker). Let's leave it as an executable JAR.

```
rest-number$ ./mvnw package -DskipTests
```

Like before, the 64-bit Linux executable is generated under the target directory:

```
rest-book$ ls -lh target/rest-book*

-rwxr-xr-x    73M  target/rest-book-2.0.0-SNAPSHOT-runner*
-rw-r--r--    61K  target/rest-book-2.0.0-SNAPSHOT.jar
```

But, depending on your operating system, it may no longer be runnable. For example, if you are running on macOS and execute this file, you will get the following error:

```
$ ./target/rest-book-2.0.0-SNAPSHOT-runner
Failed to execute process './target/rest-book-2.0.0-SNAPSHOT-runner'. Reason:
exec: Exec format error
The file './target/rest-book-2.0.0-SNAPSHOT-runner' is marked as an executable but
could not be run by the operating system.
```

9.3.2. Packaging Linux Native Executables into Containers

Now that we have all our native executables and executable JARs under the target folders, we can build the containers. For that, Quarkus uses several Dock *Dockerfiles*:

- src/main/docker/Dockerfile.native: Packages Linux native executables (see Listing 87).

- src/main/docker/Dockerfile.jvm: Packages executable JARs (see Listing 89).

Listing 87. Dockerfile to Package the Linux Native Image

```
FROM registry.access.redhat.com/ubi8/ubi-minimal:8.4
WORKDIR /work/
RUN chown 1001 /work \
    && chmod "g+rwX" /work \
    && chown 1001:root /work
COPY --chown=1001:root target/*-runner /work/application

EXPOSE 8702
USER 1001

CMD ["./application", "-Dquarkus.http.host=0.0.0.0"]
```

Each of our microservices have a similar *Dockerfile*. The only thing that changes is the exposed port. We expose the port 8700 for the user interface, port 8701 for the *Number* microservice and port 8702 for the *Book* microservice. If you look at Listing 87 and Listing 88, only the port number changes.

Listing 88. Dockerfile for the User Interface

```
FROM registry.access.redhat.com/ubi8/ubi-minimal:8.4
WORKDIR /work/
RUN chown 1001 /work \
    && chmod "g+rwX" /work \
    && chown 1001:root /work
COPY --chown=1001:root target/*-runner /work/application

EXPOSE 8700
USER 1001

CMD ["./application", "-Dquarkus.http.host=0.0.0.0"]
```

To have Quarkus build Docker images based on the Dockerfiles located under src/main/docker we need to set the configuration property quarkus.container-image.build to true.

🖥 Call to Action

(103)

Let's create our Docker images based on the Dockerfile.native files for the *Book* microservice and the Angular application. Execute the following commands to let Quarkus automatically build the images:

```
rest-book$ ./mvnw package -Dquarkus.container-image.build=true
-Dquarkus.package.type=native -Dquarkus.native.container-build=true
ui-vintagestore$ ./mvnw package -Dquarkus.container-image.build=true
-Dquarkus.package.type=native -Dquarkus.native.container-build=true
```

Then you can check the built images with a docker image ls command:

```
$ docker image ls | grep agoncal

REPOSITORY                    TAG                  SIZE
agoncal/ui-vintagestore       2.0.0-SNAPSHOT       145MB
agoncal/rest-book             2.0.0-SNAPSHOT       179MB
```

9.3.3. Packaging Executable JARs into Containers

The Docker file in Listing 89 shows how to build a Docker image with our executable JAR. This Dockerfile is pretty straightforward as it takes a minimal base image (ubi-minimal) and copies the generated executable JAR and its dependencies (target/quarkus-app) to the /deployments directory.

Listing 89. Dockerfile to Package the Executable JAR

```
FROM registry.access.redhat.com/ubi8/ubi-minimal:8.4

ARG JAVA_PACKAGE=java-11-openjdk-headless
ARG RUN_JAVA_VERSION=1.3.8
ENV LANG='en_US.UTF-8' LANGUAGE='en_US:en'
# Install java and the run-java script
# Also set up permissions for user `1001`
RUN microdnf install curl ca-certificates ${JAVA_PACKAGE} \
    && microdnf update \
    && microdnf clean all \
    && mkdir /deployments \
    && chown 1001 /deployments \
    && chmod "g+rwX" /deployments \
    && chown 1001:root /deployments \
    && curl https://repo1.maven.org/maven2/io/fabric8/run-java-
sh/${RUN_JAVA_VERSION}/run-java-sh-${RUN_JAVA_VERSION}-sh.sh -o /deployments/run-
java.sh \
    && chown 1001 /deployments/run-java.sh \
    && chmod 540 /deployments/run-java.sh \
    && echo "securerandom.source=file:/dev/urandom" >>
/etc/alternatives/jre/conf/security/java.security

# Configure the JAVA_OPTIONS, you can add -XshowSettings:vm to also display the heap
size.
ENV JAVA_OPTIONS="-Dquarkus.http.host=0.0.0.0
-Djava.util.logging.manager=org.jboss.logmanager.LogManager"
# We make four distinct layers so if there are application changes the library layers
can be re-used
COPY --chown=1001 target/quarkus-app/lib/ /deployments/lib/
COPY --chown=1001 target/quarkus-app/*.jar /deployments/
COPY --chown=1001 target/quarkus-app/app/ /deployments/app/
COPY --chown=1001 target/quarkus-app/quarkus/ /deployments/quarkus/

EXPOSE 8701
USER 1001

ENTRYPOINT [ "/deployments/run-java.sh" ]
```

 **Call to Action**

(104)

Let's create the Docker image based on the `Dockerfile.jvm` file for the *Number* microservice. To build the container, use the following command:

```
rest-number$ ./mvnw package -Dquarkus.container-image.build=true
-Dquarkus.package.type=jar
```

Then you can check the built images with a `docker image ls` command. Notice the size of the images. `rest-number` is much bigger as it contains the JAR file with a JVM:

```
$ docker image ls | grep agoncal

REPOSITORY                  TAG               SIZE
agoncal/rest-number         2.0.0-SNAPSHOT    393MB
agoncal/ui-vintagestore     2.0.0-SNAPSHOT    145MB
agoncal/rest-book           2.0.0-SNAPSHOT    179MB
```

9.3.4. Running the Application

You could then start each image with a `docker container run` command. But this would be cumbersome as each microservice needs some configuration. The easiest is to use the Docker compose file `vintage-store-app.yaml` in Listing 90, located under the `infrastructure` directory.

Listing 90. Docker Compose File Defining the Entire Application

```
services:
  ui-vintagestore:
    image: "agoncal/ui-vintagestore:2.0.0-SNAPSHOT"
    container_name: "vintage_store_ui"
    ports:
      - "8700:8700"
    depends_on:
      - rest-number
      - rest-book
  rest-number:
    image: "agoncal/rest-number:2.0.0-SNAPSHOT"
    container_name: "vintage_store_rest_number"
    ports:
      - "8701:8701"
  rest-book:
    image: "agoncal/rest-book:2.0.0-SNAPSHOT"
    container_name: "vintage_store_rest_book"
    ports:
      - "8702:8702"
    depends_on:
      database:
        condition: service_healthy
    environment:
      - QUARKUS_DATASOURCE_JDBC_URL=jdbc:postgresql://database:5432/books_database
      - ORG_AGONCAL_FASCICLE_QUARKUS_BOOK_CLIENT_NUMBERPROXY_MP_REST_URL=http://rest-
number:8701
  database:
    image: "postgres:14.1"
    container_name: "vintage_store_books_database"
    ports:
      - "5432:5432"
    environment:
      - POSTGRES_DB=books_database
      - POSTGRES_USER=book
      - POSTGRES_PASSWORD=book
    healthcheck:
      test: ["CMD-SHELL", "pg_isready -U postgres"]
      interval: 5s
      timeout: 5s
      retries: 5
  monitoring:
    image: "prom/prometheus:v2.31.1"
    container_name: "vintage_store_monitoring"
    ports:
      - 9090:9090
    volumes:
      - ./monitoring/prometheus.yml:/etc/prometheus/prometheus.yml
```

The Docker compose defines the following services:

- `ui-vintagestore` is our user interface, packaged as a native executable, listening on port 8700 and depending on both *Number* and *Book* microservices.

- `rest-number` is our *Number* microservice, packaged as an executable JAR, listening on port 8701.

- `rest-book` is our *Book* microservice, packaged as a native executable, listening on port 8702, and needs the PostgreSQL database up and running before it starts. Also notice that we override the URL of the database (using the URI `database:5432` instead of the default `localhost:5432` defined in the `application.properties`). We also override the URL of the *Number* microservice.

- `database` is our PostgreSQL database.

- `monitoring` is Prometheus listening on port 9090.

🖥 Call to Action

(105)

Before executing the application, checkout if you have the infrastructure up and running with the `docker container ls` command. If you see the Prometheus or PostgreSQL container running, stop them with:

```
infrastructure$ docker compose -f postgresql.yaml down
infrastructure$ docker compose -f prometheus.yaml down
```

Then, to run all the components of our application, it's just a matter of executing the following command:

```
infrastructure$ docker compose -f vintage-store-app.yaml up -d

Creating network "infrastructure_default" with the default driver
Creating vintage_store_rest_number    ... done
Creating vintage_store_monitoring     ... done
Creating vintage_store_books_database ... done
Creating vintage_store_rest_book      ... done
Creating vintage_store_ui             ... done
```

You can now access the different URLs that we have seen so far:

- Open your browser at http://localhost:8700 to access the user interface

- Generate some ISBN numbers invoking the *Number* microservice with `curl -X GET -H "Accept: application/json"` http://localhost:8701/api/numbers | jq

- Get the list of all the books from the database invoking the *Book* microservice at `curl -X GET -H "Accept: application/json"` http://localhost:8702/api/books | jq

- You can create a new book with `curl -X POST -d '{"title":"Practising Quarkus", "author":"Antonio Goncalves", "yearOfPublication":"2020"}'  -H  "Content-Type:`

```
application/json" http://localhost:8702/api/books -v
```

- Remember to check Prometheus at http://localhost:9090/graph

While you are browsing the user interface and Prometheus, remember to add some load to our application with the following command:

```
load-vintagestore$ ./mvnw exec:java

INFO: GET    - http://localhost:8702/api/books/1077   - 200
INFO: GET    - http://localhost:8701/api/numbers      - 200
INFO: POST   - http://localhost:8702/api/books        - 201
INFO: DELETE - http://localhost:8702/api/books/1055   - 204
INFO: GET    - http://localhost:8702/api/books/random - 200
INFO: GET    - http://localhost:8701/api/numbers - 200
```

Once you are finished and you want to shutdown the entire system, you can do it with a single Docker compose command:

```
infrastructure$ docker compose -f vintage-store-app.yaml down

Stopping ui-vintagestore    ... done
Stopping rest-book          ... done
Stopping books-database     ... done
Stopping books-monitoring   ... done
Stopping rest-number        ... done
Removing ui-vintagestore    ... done
Removing rest-book          ... done
Removing books-database     ... done
Removing books-monitoring   ... done
Removing rest-number        ... done
Removing network infrastructure_default
```

9.4. Summary

In this chapter, you didn't develop any new component for our distributed architecture. Instead, you used the Quarkus Maven plugin to package each microservice into executables and containerise them. The *Book* microservices became an executable binary, as well as the Angular application. The *Number* microservice couldn't be compiled with GraalVM (due to agressive code elimination) so we packaged it into an executable JAR. These executables start way faster than when developing with Quarkus in development mode.

Thanks to Docker, it is easy to package these executables into container images and execute them. This enhances the portability of the components of our architecture which can now be deployed in any in-house or cloud server supporting containers. Thanks to Docker Compose, with just a one line command, we fired a PostgreSQL database, Prometheus, and executed our microservices.

💻 Call to Action

(106)

Now that the application is deployed and running, you might want to commit your changes:

```
$ git add .
$ git commit -m "container"
```

[83] **DataSource** https://docs.oracle.com/en/java/javase/11/docs/api/java.sql/javax/sql/DataSource.html

[84] **Agroal** https://agroal.github.io

[85] **Closed-World Assumption** https://www.graalvm.org/community/opensource

Chapter 10. Summary

Chapter 2, *Understanding Quarkus* started with some very brief terminology to help you in understanding some concepts around Quarkus. If you find it was too short and need more details on Quarkus, Microservices, MicroProfile, Cloud Native, or GraalVM, make sure your read my other Quarkus book entitled *Understanding Quarkus 2.x* (see Appendix F for references).

Then, thanks to Chapter 3, *Getting Started*, you made sure your environment was ready to develop the application.

Chapter 4, *Developing the REST Number Microservice* and Chapter 5, *Developing the REST Book Microservice* focused on developing two isolated JAX-RS microservices. The *Number* microservice returns a few book numbers in JSON, while the *Book* microservice stores, deletes and retrieves books from a relational database with the help of JPA, Panache and JTA.

In Chapter 6, *Installing the Vintage Store User Interface* you installed an already coded Angular application on another instance of Quarkus. At this stage, the Angular application couldn't access the microservices because of CORS issues that we quickly fixed.

In Chapter 7, *Adding Communication and Fault Tolerance* we made the two microservices communicate with each other thanks to Eclipse MicroProfile REST Client. But HTTP-related technologies usually use synchronous communication and therefore need to deal with invocation failure. With Eclipse MicroProfile Fault Tolerance, it was just a matter of using a few annotations and we can get some fallback when the communication fails.

When there are many microservices, observability becomes mandatory. In Chapter 8, *Monitoring the Microservices* we added some health checks and metrics to our microservices.

Then, comes production time. In Chapter 9, *Deploying the Application*, we built executable JARs and binaries, and packaged our microservices into Docker containers.

This is the end of the *Practising Quarkus 2.x* fascicle. I hope you liked it, learnt a few things, and more importantly, will be able to take this knowledge back to your projects.

Remember that you can find all the code for this fascicle at https://github.com/agoncal/agoncal-fascicle-quarkus-pract/tree/2.0. If some parts were not clear enough, or if you found something missing, a bug, or you just want to leave a note or suggestion, please use the GitHub issue tracker at https://github.com/agoncal/agoncal-fascicle-quarkus-pract/issues.

If you liked the format of this fascicle, you might want to read others that I have written. Check out Appendix F for the full list of fascicles.

Thanks for reading!

Antonio

Appendix A: Setting up the Development Environment on macOS

This appendix focuses on setting up your development environment so you can do the hands-on work by following the code snippets listed in the previous chapters. Being a *Practising* fascicle, each chapter asks you to develop, build or package the components of our microservice architecture. You need to install the required software in order to develop, compile, deploy, execute and test the components.

Bear in mind that I run all of these tools on macOS. So, this appendix gives you all of the installation guidelines for the macOS operating system. If your machine runs on Linux or Windows, check online to know how to install the following tools on your platform.

A.1. Homebrew

One of the pre-requisites is that you have *Homebrew* installed. *Homebrew*[86] is a package manager for macOS.

A.1.1. A Brief History of Homebrew

The name *Homebrew* is intended to suggest the idea of building software on the Mac depending on the user's taste. It was written by Max Howell in 2009 in Ruby[87]. On September 2016, Homebrew version 1.0.0 was released. In January 2019, Linuxbrew was merged back into Homebrew, adding beta support for Linux and the Windows Subsystem for Linux to Homebrew's feature set.

A.1.2. Installing Homebrew on macOS

To install Homebrew, just execute the following command:

```
$ /bin/bash -c "$(curl -fsSL
https://raw.githubusercontent.com/Homebrew/install/master/install.sh)"
```

You also need *Homebrew Cask*[88] which extends Homebrew and brings installation and management of GUI macOS applications. Install it by running:

```
$ brew tap homebrew/cask
```

A.1.3. Checking for Homebrew Installation

Now you should be able to execute a few Homebrew commands:

```
$ brew --version

Homebrew 3.3.2
Homebrew/homebrew-core
Homebrew/homebrew-cask
```

A.1.4. Some Homebrew Commands

- brew commands: Lists the built-in and external commands.
- brew help: Displays help.
- brew doctor: Checks for potential problems.
- brew install: Installs a formula.
- brew uninstall: Uninstalls a formula.
- brew list: Lists all installed formulae.
- brew upgrade: Upgrades outdated casks and formulae.
- brew update: Fetches the newest version of Homebrew.
- brew cask help: Displays Homebrew Cask help.
- brew cask install: Installs a cask.
- brew cask uninstall: Uninstalls a cask.
- brew cask list: Lists installed casks.
- brew cask upgrade: Upgrades all outdated casks (or the specified casks).

A.2. Java 11

Essential for the development and execution of the examples in the fascicle is the *Java Development Kit*[89] (JDK). The JDK includes several tools such as a compiler (javac), a virtual machine, a documentation generator (javadoc), monitoring tools (Visual VM[90]) and so on. The code in this fascicle uses Java 11 (JDK 11.0.13).

A.2.1. Architecture

One design goal of Java is portability, which means that programs written for the Java platform must run similarly on any combination of hardware and operating system with adequate runtime support. This is achieved by compiling the Java language code to an intermediate representation called *bytecode*, instead of directly to a specific machine code. This bytecode is then analysed, interpreted and executed on the *Java Virtual Machine* (JVM).

The *Interpreter* is the one interpreting the bytecode. It does it quickly, but executes slowly. The disadvantage of the interpreter is that, when one method is called multiple times, a new interpretation is required every time. That's when the *Just In Time* (JIT) compiler kicks in. JIT is basically the component that translates the JVM bytecode (generated by your javac command) into machine code which is the language that your underlying execution environment (i.e. your processor) can understand—and all that happens dynamically at runtime! When the JIT finds repeated code, it compiles the bytecode and changes it to native code. This native code will then be used directly for repeated method calls, which improves the performance of the system. This JIT is also called the *Java HotSpot*[91] (a.k.a. Java HotSpot Performance Engine, or HotSpot VM). Then, the *Garbage Collector* will collect and remove unreferenced objects.

When using GraalVM you have the choice of doing just-in-time or ahead-of-time compilation. GraalVM includes a high performance Java compiler, itself called Graal, which can be used in the HotSpot VM.

A.2.2. A Brief History of Java

James Gosling, Mike Sheridan, and Patrick Naughton initiated the Java language project in June 1991. Java was originally designed for interactive television, but it was too advanced for the digital cable television industry at the time. The language was initially called Oak after an oak tree that stood outside Gosling's office. Later, the project went by the name Green and was finally renamed Java, from Java coffee. Gosling designed Java with a C/C++-style syntax that system and application programmers would find familiar. Sun Microsystems released the first public implementation as Java 1.0 in 1996. Following Oracle Corporation's acquisition of Sun Microsystems in 2009–10, Oracle has described itself as the "*steward of Java technology*" since then[92].

A.2.3. Installing the JDK on macOS

To install the JDK 11.0.13, go to the official website, select the appropriate platform and language, and download[93] the distribution. For example, on macOS, download the file jdk-11.0.13_osx-x64_bin.dmg shown in Figure 31 (you should check out the *Accept License Agreement* check box before hitting the download link to let the download start). If you are not on Mac, the download steps are still pretty similar.

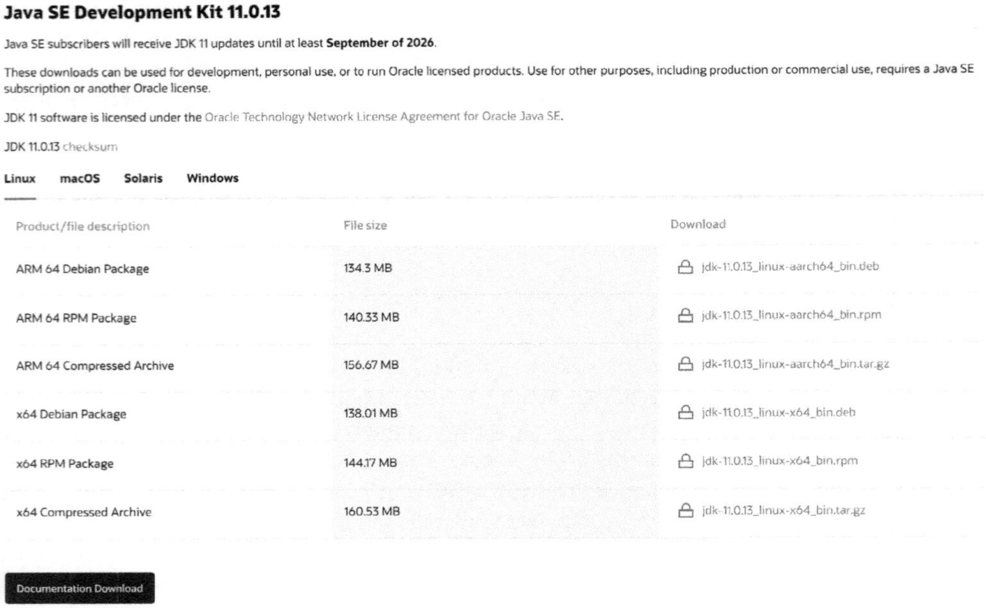

Java SE Development Kit 11.0.13

Java SE subscribers will receive JDK 11 updates until at least **September of 2026**.

These downloads can be used for development, personal use, or to run Oracle licensed products. Use for other purposes, including production or commercial use, requires a Java SE subscription or another Oracle license.

JDK 11 software is licensed under the Oracle Technology Network License Agreement for Oracle Java SE.

JDK 11.0.13 checksum

Linux   macOS   Solaris   Windows

Product/file description	File size	Download
ARM 64 Debian Package	134.3 MB	jdk-11.0.13_linux-aarch64_bin.deb
ARM 64 RPM Package	140.33 MB	jdk-11.0.13_linux-aarch64_bin.rpm
ARM 64 Compressed Archive	156.67 MB	jdk-11.0.13_linux-aarch64_bin.tar.gz
x64 Debian Package	138.01 MB	jdk-11.0.13_linux-x64_bin.deb
x64 RPM Package	144.17 MB	jdk-11.0.13_linux-x64_bin.rpm
x64 Compressed Archive	160.53 MB	jdk-11.0.13_linux-x64_bin.tar.gz

Documentation Download

Figure 31. Downloading the JDK distribution

Double-click on the file `jdk-11.0.13_osx-x64_bin.dmg`. This will bring up a pop-up screen (see Figure 32), asking you to start the installation.

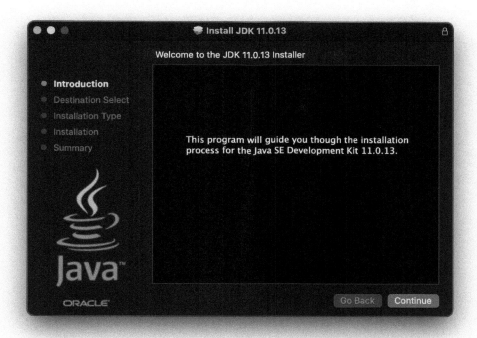

Figure 32. Installation pop-up screen

The wizard invites you to accept the licence for the software and install the JDK successfully (see Figure 33).

Figure 33. Successful JDK installation

There is also an easier way to install Java using Homebrew. First of all, check if you already have the Java formula installed on your machine:

```
$ brew cask list java11
Error: Cask 'java11' is not installed.
```

If the Java formula is not installed, execute the following Homebrew commands to install it:

```
$ brew tap homebrew/cask-versions
$ brew cask install java11
...
java11 was successfully installed!
```

A.2.4. Checking for Java Installation

Once the installation is complete, it is necessary to set the JAVA_HOME variable and the $JAVA_HOME/bin directory to the PATH variable. Check that your system recognises Java by entering java -version as well as the Java compiler with javac -version.

```
$ java -version
java version "11.0.13" LTS
Java(TM) SE Runtime Environment 18.9 (build 11.0.13-LTS)
Java HotSpot(TM) 64-Bit Server VM 18.9 (build 11.0.13-LTS, mixed mode)

$ javac -version
javac 11.0.13
```

Notice that, in the previous output, the HotSpot build is displayed. This is one easy way to know that you are using the HotSpot VM instead of the Graal VM.

A.3. GraalVM 21.3.0

GraalVM[94] is an extension of the *Java Virtual Machine* (JVM) to support more languages and several execution modes. It is itself implemented in Java. GraalVM supports a large set of languages: Java, of course, other JVM-based languages (such as Groovy, Kotlin etc.) but also JavaScript, Ruby, Python, R and C/C++.

But it also includes a new high performance Java compiler, itself called *Graal*. Running your application inside a JVM comes with startup and footprint costs. GraalVM has a feature to create *native images* for existing JVM-based applications. The image generation process employs static analysis to find any code reachable from the main Java method and then performs full *Ahead-Of-Time* (AOT) compilation on the *Substrate VM*[95]. The resulting native binary contains the whole program in machine code form for its immediate execution. This improves the performance of Java to match the performance of native languages for fast startup and low memory footprint.

A.3.1. Architecture

Figure 34 depicts a high-level view of the GraalVM stack. The *Graal Compiler* is a high performance JIT compiler written in Java. It accepts the JVM bytecode and produces the machine code. It uses the new *JVM Compiler Interface* (JVMCI) to communicate with the *Java HotSpot VM*. On top of all that, you will find the *Truffle* framework that enables you to build interpreters and implementations for other languages except JVM-based languages (such as Java, Groovy or Scala). If you want to run a new programming language, you will just have to integrate it with Truffle and the framework will produce the optimised machine code for you. As you can see, there are already language implementations for R, Ruby, or JavaScript. For LLVM-based languages (e.g. C/C++, Fortran), *Sulong* guarantees memory safety.

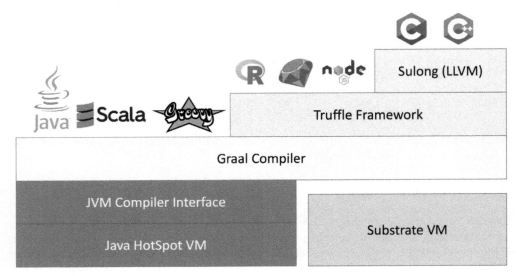

Figure 34. GraalVM architecture

The major differentiators of GraalVM compared to the base JDK are:

- *Sulong*[96]: Guarantees memory safety for C/C++ and other LLVM-based languages (e.g. Fortran).

- *Truffle*[97]: A language implementation framework for creating languages and instrumentations for GraalVM (e.g. R, Ruby, Python, NodeJS, etc.).

- *Graal Compiler*[98]: Written in Java and supports both dynamic and static compilation.

- *JVM Compiler Interface*[99] (JVMCI): Is part of the regular JDK and allows us to plug-in additional Java compilers (such as Graal) to the JVM.

- *Java HotSpot VM*: Runtime with the GraalVM compiler enabled as the top tier JIT compiler for JVM-based languages.

- *Substrate VM*[100]: Allows AOT compilation for applications written in various languages.

GraalVM allows you to ahead-of-time compile Java code to a standalone executable, called a *native image*. This executable includes the application classes, classes from its dependencies, runtime library classes from the JDK and statically linked native code from the JDK. It does not run on the Java VM, but includes necessary components like memory management and thread scheduling from a different virtual machine, called *Substrate VM*. Substrate VM is the name for the runtime components.

A.3.2. A Brief History of GraalVM

The history of Graal dates back to the research works on *MaxineVM*[101] in 2013, also known as a *meta-circular virtual machine* because this JVM is actually written in Java itself. Oracle invested in this research project and then released it under the name of GraalVM. GraalVM is a production-ready software and is available as a *Community Edition* (open source license) and as an *Enterprise Edition* (OTN License[102]). Oracle Corporation announced the release of Oracle GraalVM Enterprise Edition in May 2019.

A.3.3. Installing GraalVM on macOS

GraalVM can be installed from the GraalVM web site[103]. As shown in Figure 35, it shows two versions of GraalVM:

- *Community Edition*: Available for free for any use and built from the GraalVM sources available on GitHub.

- *Enterprise Edition*: Provides additional performance, security, and scalability relevant for running applications in production.

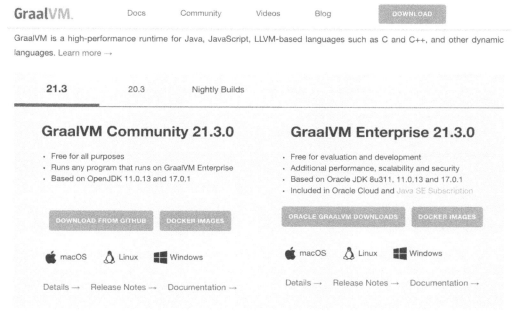

Figure 35. Community and enterprise edition of GraalVM

Using the community edition is enough. So you will be redirected to the GitHub account of GraalVM [104] (see Figure 36) where you can download the latest versions. Make sure you pick up version 21.3.0 and download the GraalVM file specific to your OS platform. For example, on macOS, download the file `graalvm-ce-java11-darwin-amd64-21.3.0.tar.gz` shown in Figure 36. If you are not on Mac, the download steps are still pretty similar.

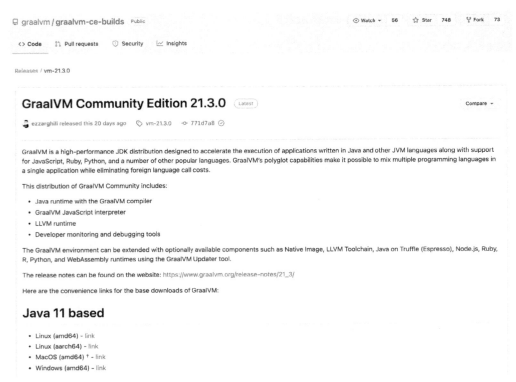

Figure 36. Download GraalVM

Double-click on the file `graalvm-ce-java11-darwin-amd64-21.3.0.tar.gz` and this will install GraalVM. Once installed, configure the `GRAALVM_HOME` environment variable to point to the directory where GraalVM is installed (e.g. on macOS it will be `/Library/Java/JavaVirtualMachines/graalvm-ce-java11-21.3.0/Contents/Home`).

A.3.4. Installing the Native Image Generator

The *Native Image Generator*[105], or `native-image`, is a utility that processes all the classes of your application and their dependencies, including those from the JDK. It statically analyses these classes to determine which classes and methods are reachable and used during application execution (a.k.a. *closed-world*). Then it passes all this reachable code as the input to the GraalVM compiler which ahead-of-time compiles it to the native binary.

So we need to install the `native-image` tool. This can be done by running the following command from your GraalVM directory (inside the `bin` directory).

```
$GRAALVM_HOME/bin $ ./gu install native-image
```

When installing Native Image, if you have a popup showing an error message such as "*21.3.0 is damaged and can't be opened. You should move it to the Bin.*", then you can get around this by executing:

```
$ xattr -d com.apple.quarantine /Library/Java/JavaVirtualMachines/graalvm-ce-java11-
21.3.0
```

A.3.5. Checking for GraalVM Installation

Once installed and setup, you should be able to run the following command and get the following output.

```
$ $GRAALVM_HOME/bin/native-image --version
GraalVM 21.3.0 Java 11 CE (Java Version 11.0.13)
```

A.4. Maven 3.8.x

All the examples of this fascicle are built and tested using Maven[106]. Maven offers a building solution, shared libraries, and a plugin platform for your projects, allowing you to do quality control, documentation, teamwork and so forth. Based on the *"convention over configuration"* principle, Maven brings a standard project description and a number of conventions such as a standard directory structure. With an extensible architecture based on plugins, Maven can offer many different services.

A.4.1. A Brief History of Maven

Maven, created by Jason van Zyl, began as a subproject of Apache Turbine in 2002. In 2003, it was voted on and accepted as a top-level Apache Software Foundation project. In July 2004, Maven's release was the critical first milestone, v1.0. Maven 2 was declared v2.0 in October 2005 after about six months in beta cycles. Maven 3.0 was released in October 2010, being mostly backwards compatible with Maven 2[107].

A.4.2. Project Descriptor

Maven is based on the fact that a majority of Java projects face similar requirements when building applications. A Maven project needs to follow some standards as well as define specific features in a project descriptor, or *Project Object Model* (POM). The POM is an XML file (pom.xml) placed at the root of the project and contains all the metadata of the project. As shown in Listing 91, the minimum required information to describe the identity of a project is the groupId, the artifactId, the version, and the packaging type.

Listing 91. Header of a Maven Project Descriptor

```xml
<?xml version="1.0" encoding="UTF-8"?>
<project xmlns:xsi="http://www.w3.org/2001/XMLSchema-instance"
         xmlns="http://maven.apache.org/POM/4.0.0"
         xsi:schemaLocation="http://maven.apache.org/POM/4.0.0
http://maven.apache.org/xsd/maven-4.0.0.xsd">

  <modelVersion>4.0.0</modelVersion>
  <groupId>org.agoncal.fascicle</groupId>
  <artifactId>chapter01</artifactId>
  <version>1.0-SNAPSHOT</version>
  <packaging>jar</packaging>
</project>
```

A project is often divided into different artifacts. These artifacts are then grouped under the same groupId (similar to packages in Java) and uniquely identified by the artifactId. Packaging allows Maven to produce each artifact following a standard format (jar, war, ear etc.). Finally, the version allows the identifying of an artifact during its lifetime (version 1.1, 1.2, 1.2.1 etc.). Maven imposes versioning so that a team can manage the life of its project development. Maven also introduces the concept of SNAPSHOT versions (the version number ends with the string -SNAPSHOT) to identify an artifact that is being developed and is not released yet.

The POM defines much more information about your project. Some aspects are purely descriptive (name, description etc.), while others concern the application execution such as the list of external libraries used, and so on. Moreover, the pom.xml defines environmental information to build the project (versioning tool, continuous integration server, artifact repositories), and any other specific process to build your project.

A.4.3. Managing Artifacts

Maven goes beyond building artifacts; it also offers a genuine approach to archive and share these artifacts. Maven uses a local repository on your hard drive (by default in ~/.m2/repository) where it stores all the artifacts that the project's descriptor references. The local repository is filled either by the local developer's artifacts (e.g. myProject-1.1.jar) or by external ones (e.g. javax.annotation-api-1.2.jar) that Maven downloads from remote repositories.

A Maven project can reference a specific artifact including the artifact's dependencies in the POM using groupId, artifactId, version and scope in a declarative way as shown in Listing 92. If necessary, Maven will download them to the local repository from remote repositories. Moreover, using the POM descriptors of these external artifacts, Maven will also download the artifacts they need (so-called "*transitive dependencies*"). Therefore, the development team doesn't have to manually add the project dependencies to the classpath. Maven automatically adds the necessary libraries.

Listing 92. Maven Dependencies

```
<dependencies>
  <dependency>
    <groupId>org.eclipse.persistence</groupId>
    <artifactId>javax.persistence</artifactId>
    <version>2.1</version>
    <scope>provided</scope>
  </dependency>
  <dependency>
    <groupId>org.glassfish</groupId>
    <artifactId>javax.ejb</artifactId>
    <version>3.2</version>
    <scope>provided</scope>
  </dependency>
</dependencies>
```

Dependencies may have limited visibility (called scope):

- `test`: The library is used to compile and run test classes but is not packaged in the produced artifact (e.g. war file).

- `provided`: The library is provided by the environment (persistence provider, application server etc.) and is only used to compile the code.

- `compile`: The library is necessary for compilation and execution. Therefore, it will be packaged as part of the produced artifact too.

- `runtime`: The library is only required for execution but is excluded from the compilation (e.g. Servlets).

A.4.4. Installing Maven on macOS

The examples of this fascicle have been developed with Apache Maven 3.8.3. Once you have installed the JDK 11.0.13, make sure the `JAVA_HOME` environment variable is set. Then, check if you already have the Maven formula installed on your machine:

```
$ brew list maven
Error: No such keg: /usr/local/Cellar/maven
```

If the Maven formula is not installed, execute the following Homebrew command to install it:

```
$ brew install maven
...
maven was successfully installed!
```

You should now see the Maven formula in Homebrew:

```
$ brew list maven
/usr/local/Cellar/maven/3.8.3/bin/mvn
/usr/local/Cellar/maven/3.8.3/bin/mvnDebug
/usr/local/Cellar/maven/3.8.3/bin/mvnyjp
```

A.4.5. Checking for Maven Installation

Once you've got Maven installed, open a command line and enter mvn -version to validate your installation. Maven should print its version and the JDK version it uses (which is handy as you might have different JDK versions installed on the same machine).

```
$ mvn -version

Apache Maven 3.8.3
Maven home: /usr/local/Cellar/maven/3.8.3/libexec
```

Be aware that Maven needs Internet access so it can download plugins and project dependencies from the Maven Central[108] and/or other remote repositories. If you are behind a proxy, see the documentation to configure your settings.

A.4.6. Some Maven Commands

Maven is a command line utility where you can use several parameters and options to build, test or package your code. To get some help on the commands you can type, use the following command:

```
$ mvn --help

usage: mvn [options] [<goal(s)>] [<phase(s)>]
```

Here are some commands that you will be using to run the examples in the fascicle. Each invokes a different phase of the project life cycle (clean, compile, install etc.) and uses the pom.xml to download libraries, customise the compilation, or extend some behaviours using plugins:

- mvn clean: Deletes all generated files (compiled classes, generated code, artifacts etc.).

- mvn compile: Compiles the main Java classes.

- mvn test-compile: Compiles the test classes.

- mvn test: Compiles the main Java classes as well as the test classes and executes the tests.

- mvn package: Compiles, executes the tests and packages the code into an archive (e.g. a war file).

- mvn install: Builds and installs the artifacts in your local repository.

- mvn clean install: Cleans and installs (note that you can add several commands separated by spaces, like mvn clean compile test).

Maven allows you to compile, run, and package the examples of this fascicle. It decouples the fact that you need to write your code (within an IDE) and build it. To develop you need an *Integrated Development Environment* (IDE). I use IntelliJ IDEA from JetBrains, but you can use any IDE you like because this fascicle only relies on Maven and not on specific IntelliJ IDEA features.

A.5. Testing Frameworks

A.5.1. JUnit 5.x

All the examples of this fascicle are tested using JUnit 5.x. JUnit[109] is an open source framework to write and run repeatable tests. JUnit features include: assertions for testing expected results, fixtures for sharing common test data, and runners for running tests.

JUnit is the de facto standard testing library for the Java language, and it stands in a single jar file that you can download from https://junit.org/junit5 (or use Maven dependency management, which we do in this fascicle). The library contains a complete API to help you write your unit tests and execute them. Unit and integration tests help your code to be more robust, bug free, and reliable. Coming up, we will go through the above features with some examples but before that, let's have a quick overview of JUnit's history.

The code in this appendix can be found at https://github.com/agoncal/agoncal-fascicle-commons/tree/master/junit

A Brief History of JUnit

JUnit was originally written by Erich Gamma and Kent Beck in 1998. It was inspired by Smalltalk's SUnit test framework, also written by Kent Beck. It quickly became one of the most popular frameworks in the Java world. JUnit took an important step in achieving test-driven development (TDD). Let's see some of the JUnit features through a simple example.

Writing Tests

Listing 93 represents a `Customer` POJO. It has some attributes, including a date of birth, constructors, getters and setters. It also provides two utility methods to clear the date of birth and to calculate the age of the customer (`calculateAge()`).

Listing 93. A Customer Class

```java
public class Customer {

  private Long id;
  private String firstName;
  private String lastName;
  private String email;
  private String phoneNumber;
  private LocalDate dateOfBirth;
  private Integer age;

  // Constructors, getters, setters

  public void calculateAge() {
    if (dateOfBirth == null) {
      age = null;
      return;
    }

    age = Period.between(dateOfBirth, LocalDate.now()).getYears();
  }

  public void clear() {
    this.dateOfBirth = null;
  }
}
```

The calculateAge() method uses the dateOfBirth attribute to set the customer's age. It has some business logic and we want to make sure the algorithm calculates the age accurately. We want to test this business logic. For that, we need a test class with some JUnit test methods and assertions.

Test Class

In JUnit, test classes do not have to extend anything. To be executed as a test case, a JUnit test class needs at least one method annotated with @Test. If you write a class without at least one @Test method, you will get an error when trying to execute it (java.lang.Exception: No runnable methods). Listing 94 shows the CustomerTest class that initialises the Customer object.

Listing 94. A Unit Test Class for Customer

```java
public class CustomerTest {

  private Customer customer = new Customer();
```

Fixtures

Fixtures are methods to initialise and release any common object during tests. JUnit uses @BeforeEach and @AfterEach annotations to execute code before or after each test. These methods can be given any name (clearCustomer() in Listing 95), and you can have multiple methods in one test class. JUnit uses @BeforeAll and @AfterAll annotations to execute specific code only once, before or after the test suite is executed (CustomerTest in this case). These methods must be unique and static. @BeforeAll and @AfterAll can be very useful if you need to allocate and release expensive resources.

Listing 95. Fixture Executed Before Each Test

```
@BeforeEach
public void clearCustomer() {
    customer.clear();
}
```

Test Methods

A test method must use the @Test annotation, return void, and take no parameters. This is controlled at runtime and throws an exception if not respected. In Listing 96, the test method ageShouldBeGreaterThanZero creates a new Customer and sets a specific date of birth. Then, using the assertion mechanism of JUnit (explained in the next section), it checks that the calculated age is greater than zero.

Listing 96. Method Testing Age Calculation

```
@Test
public void ageShouldBeGreaterThanZero() {
    customer = new Customer("Rita", "Navalhas", "rnavalhas@gmail.com");
    customer.setDateOfBirth(LocalDate.of(1975, 5, 27));

    customer.calculateAge();

    assertTrue(customer.getAge() >= 0);
}
```

JUnit also allows us to check for exceptions. In Listing 97, we are trying to calculate the age of a null customer object so the call to the calculateAge() method should throw a NullPointerException. If it does, then the test succeeds. If it doesn't, or if it throws a different type of exception than the one declared, the test fails.

Listing 97. Method Testing Nullity

```
@Test
public void shouldThrowAnExceptionCauseDateOfBirtheIsNull() {

    customer = null;
    assertThrows(NullPointerException.class, () -> {
        customer.calculateAge();
    });
}
```

Listing 98 does not implement the shouldCalculateOldAge() method. However, you don't want the

213

test to fail; you just want to ignore it. You can add the `@Disable` annotation next to the `@Test` annotation. JUnit will report the number of disabled tests, along with the number of tests that succeeded and failed. Note that `@Disable` takes an optional parameter (a `String`) in case you want to record why a test is being disabled.

Listing 98. Disabling a Method for Testing

```
@Test
@Disabled("Test is not ready yet")
public void shouldCalculateOldAge() {
    // some work to do
}
```

JUnit Assertions

Test cases must assert that objects conform to an expected result, such as in Listing 96 where we assert that the age is greater than zero. For that, JUnit has an `Assertions` class that contains several methods. In order to use different assertions, you can either use the prefixed syntax (e.g. `Assertions.assertEquals()`) or import the `Assertions` class statically. Listing 99 shows a simplified subset of the methods defined in the `Assertions` class.

Listing 99. Subset of JUnit Assertions

```
public class Assertions {

    void assertTrue(boolean condition) { }
    void assertFalse(boolean condition) { }

    void assertNull(Object actual) { }
    void assertNotNull(Object actual) { }

    void assertEquals(Object expected, Object actual) { }
    void assertNotEquals(Object unexpected, Object actual) { }

    void assertArrayEquals(Object[] expected, Object[] actual) { }
    void assertLinesMatch(List<String> expectedLines, List<String> actualLines) { }

    void assertSame(Object expected, Object actual) { }
    void assertNotSame(Object unexpected, Object actual) { }
    void assertAll(Collection<Executable> executables) { }
    void assertTimeout(Duration timeout, Executable executable) { }

    <T extends Throwable> T assertThrows(Class<T> expectedType, Executable exec) { }
}
```

Executing Tests

JUnit is very well integrated with most IDEs (IntelliJ IDEA, Eclipse, NetBeans etc.). When working with these IDEs, in most cases, JUnit highlights in green to indicate successful tests and in red to indicate failures. Most IDEs also provide facilities to create test classes.

JUnit is also integrated with Maven through the Surefire[110] plugin used during the test phase of the build life cycle. It executes the JUnit test classes of an application and generates reports in XML and text file formats. That's mostly how we will be using JUnit in this fascicle: through Maven. To integrate JUnit in Maven, you just need the JUnit dependency and make sure to declare the Surefire plugin in the pom.xml as shown in Listing 100.

Listing 100. JUnit Dependencies in a Maven pom.xml

```xml
<dependencies>
  <dependency>
    <groupId>org.junit.jupiter</groupId>
    <artifactId>junit-jupiter-engine</artifactId>
    <version>5.6.0</version>
    <scope>test</scope>
  </dependency>
</dependencies>

<build>
  <plugins>
    <plugin>
      <groupId>org.apache.maven.plugins</groupId>
      <artifactId>maven-surefire-plugin</artifactId>
      <version>2.22.2</version>
    </plugin>
  </plugins>
</build>
```

The following Maven command runs the JUnit tests through the Surefire plugin:

```
$ mvn test
```

Then JUnit executes the tests and gives the number of executed tests, the number of failures and the number of disabled tests (through warnings).

```
[INFO] ------------------------
[INFO] Building Commons :: JUnit
[INFO] ------------------------
[INFO]
[INFO] --- maven-compiler-plugin:3.7.0:compile (default-compile)
[INFO]
[INFO] --- maven-surefire-plugin:2.22.2:test (default-test)
[INFO]
[INFO] ----------
[INFO]  T E S T S
[INFO] ----------
[INFO] Running org.agoncal.fascicle.commons.junit.CustomerTest
[WARNING] Tests run: 3, Failures: 0, Errors: 0, Skipped: 1, Time elapsed: 0.032 s
[INFO]
[INFO] Results:
[INFO]
[WARNING] Tests run: 3, Failures: 0, Errors: 0, Skipped: 1
[INFO]
[INFO] -------------
[INFO] BUILD SUCCESS
[INFO] -------------
[INFO] Total time:  1.824 s
[INFO] Finished at: 2020-03-04T11:51:34+01:00
[INFO] -------------
```

A.5.2. REST Assured 4.4.x

All the examples of this fascicle containing REST resources are tested using REST Assured 4.4.x. *REST Assured*[111] is an open source Java library that provides a *Domain Specific Language* (DSL) for writing powerful and maintainable tests for RESTful APIs. It supports POST, GET, PUT, DELETE, OPTIONS, PATCH and HEAD requests and can be used to validate and verify the response of these requests.

Listing 101 uses REST Assured to execute an HTTP GET on a resource and check that the return code is 200.

Listing 101. Simple HTTP GET Test

```
given().
when()
  .get("/customers").
then()
  .statusCode(200);
```

Listing 102 and Listing 101 are quite similar. Listing 102 uses the REST Assured DSL to pass certain parameters to the HTTP GET such as the ACCEPT header.

Listing 102. HTTP GET Test Given Certain Parameters

```
given()
  .baseUri("http://localhost:8081")
  .header(ACCEPT, APPLICATION_JSON).
when()
  .get("/customers").
then()
  .statusCode(200);
```

As you can see in Listing 103, REST Assured can then help to easily make the GET request and verify the response as well as its content (thanks to the body() method).

Listing 103. HTTP GET Test Checking Response Body

```
given()
  .pathParam("id", 1L).
when()
  .get("/customers/{id}").
then()
  .statusCode(200)
  .contentType(APPLICATION_JSON)
  .body("first-name", is("John"))
  .body("last-name", is("Lennon"));
```

Listing 104 shows how to invoke an HTTP POST passing a Customer object and then check that the response code is a 201 (created).

Listing 104. HTTP POST Test Passing a Body

```
Customer customer = new Customer().firstName("John").lastName("Lennon");

given()
  .body(customer)
  .header(CONTENT_TYPE, APPLICATION_JSON)
  .header(ACCEPT, APPLICATION_JSON).
when()
  .post("/customers").
then()
  .statusCode(201);
```

A.5.3. Hamcrest 2.2.x

Hamcrest[112] is a framework for writing matcher objects allowing "*match*" rules to be defined declaratively. When writing tests it is sometimes difficult to get the balance right between overspecifying the test, and not specifying enough. Hamcrest allows you to pick out precisely the aspect being tested and to describe the values it should have.

Listing 105 shows a very simple JUnit test. Instead of using JUnit's assertEquals() methods, we use

Hamcrest's `assertThat` construct and the standard set of matchers, both of which we statically import.

Listing 105. Simple Hamcrest Assertion

```java
import static org.hamcrest.MatcherAssert.assertThat;
import static org.hamcrest.Matchers.equalTo;

class BookTest {

  @Test
  public void shouldTestEquals() {
    Book oneBook = new Book("H2G2");
    Book anotherBook = new Book("H2G2");
    assertThat(oneBook, equalTo(anotherBook));
  }
}
```

The `assertThat()` method is a stylised sentence for making a test assertion. You can write simple assertions that are easy to read such as:

```java
assertThat(book.getTitle(), equalTo("H2G2"));
assertThat(book.getYearOfPublication(), equalTo(1979));
assertThat(book, equalTo(anotherBook));
```

If you want to be even more expressive, you can use some sugar syntax. For example, Hamcrest has an `is` matcher that doesn't add any extra behaviour to the underlying matcher. So the following assertions are equivalent to the previous ones:

```java
assertThat(book.getTitle(), is(equalTo("H2G2")));
assertThat(book.getYearOfPublication(), is(equalTo(1979)));
assertThat(book, is(anotherBook));
assertThat(book.getTitle(), is(not(nullValue())));
assertThat(book.getIsbn10(), is(nullValue()));
assertThat(book.getNbOfPages(), is(greaterThan(100)));
```

Hamcrest comes with a library of useful matchers. Table 27 shows some of the most important ones.

Table 27. Main Hamcrest Matchers

Matchers	Description
anything	Always matches, useful if you don't care what the object under test is
is	Decorator to improve readability
allOf	Matches if all matchers match (like Java &&)

Matchers	Description
anyOf	Matches if any matchers match (like Java ||)
not	Matches if the wrapped matcher doesn't match and vice versa
equalTo	Tests object equality using Object.equals()
notNullValue, nullValue	Tests for null
greaterThan, greaterThanOrEqualTo, lessThan, lessThanOrEqualTo	Tests ordering
equalToIgnoringCase	Tests string equality ignoring case
equalToIgnoringWhiteSpace	Tests string equality ignoring differences in runs of whitespace
containsString, endsWith, startsWith	Tests string matching

A.5.4. TestContainers 1.16.x

TestContainers[113] is a Java library that supports JUnit tests, providing lightweight, throwaway instances of common Docker images. It allows us to use Docker containers within our tests. For example, it can use a containerised instance of a PostgreSQL database to test a data access layer but without requiring a complex setup on the developer's machine. The pre-requisites of using TestContainers are to have Docker installed and to use a supported JVM testing framework (such as JUnit or TestNG).

Let's say our application uses PostgreSQL as a relational database and we want to run some tests with a running PostgreSQL. With TestContainers it's easy to make such a test. As you can see in Listing 106, JUnit integration is provided by means of the @org.testcontainers.junit.jupiter.Testcontainers annotation. This JUnit extension finds all fields that are annotated with @Container (PostgreSQLContainer in our example) and calls their container life cycle methods (e.g. start(), stop()). Containers declared as static fields will be shared between test methods. They will be started only once before any test method is executed and stopped after the last test method has executed. Containers declared as instance fields will be started and stopped for every test method.

Listing 106. PostgreSQL TestContainers Test

```
@Testcontainers
public class PingPostgreSQLTest {

  @Container
  public static PostgreSQLContainer pg = new PostgreSQLContainer<>("postgres:12.4")
    .withDatabaseName("vintageStoreDB")
    .withUsername("vintage")
    .withPassword("vintage")
    .withExposedPorts(5432);

  @Test
  public void shouldPingPostgreSQL() throws Exception {
    pg.start();

    try (Connection con = DriverManager.getConnection(pg.getJdbcUrl(), pg.getUsername
(), pg.getPassword());
         Statement st = con.createStatement();
         ResultSet rs = st.executeQuery("SELECT VERSION()")) {

      if (rs.next()) {
        assertTrue(rs.getString(1).contains("PostgreSQL 12"));
      } else {
        throw new Exception();
      }
    }

    pg.stop();
  }
}
```

TestContainers will try to connect to a Docker daemon. So, to execute the test in Listing 106, make sure Docker is up and running. If that's not the case, you will get the following exception:

```
IllegalStateException: Could not find a valid Docker environment.
```

With Docker up and running, TestContainers will first download the PostgreSQL image from Docker Hub[114] if not available locally on your machine. Then, it starts the PostgreSQL container, executes the test, and stops the PostgreSQL container. The output looks like this:

```
INFO --- maven-surefire-plugin:test @ testcontainers ---
--------------------
 T E S T S
--------------------
Running org.agoncal.fascicle.PingPostgreSQLTest

INFO Accessing docker with local Unix socket
INFO Found Docker environment with local Unix socket
INFO Docker host IP address is localhost
INFO Connected to docker:
INFO Checking the system...

INFO [postgres] - Pulling docker image: postgres. Please be patient;
INFO [postgres] - Starting to pull image
INFO [postgres] - Pulling image layers:  0 pending,  0 downloaded,  0 extracted
INFO [postgres] - Pulling image layers: 13 pending,  1 downloaded,  0 extracted
INFO [postgres] - Pulling image layers: 10 pending,  4 downloaded,  0 extracted
INFO [postgres] - Pulling image layers:  7 pending,  7 downloaded,  2 extracted
INFO [postgres] - Pulling image layers:  6 pending,  8 downloaded,  3 extracted

INFO [postgres] - Creating container for image: postgres
INFO [postgres] - Starting container with ID: 77a1669fe4bb3f7f
INFO [postgres] - Container postgres is starting: 77a1669fe4bb3f7f
INFO [postgres] - Container postgres started

Tests run: 1, Failures: 0, Errors: 0, Skipped: 0
INFO --------------------
INFO BUILD SUCCESS
INFO --------------------
```

A.6. cURL 7.x

To invoke the REST Web Services described in this fascicle, we often use cURL. cURL[115] is a command line tool for transferring files with url syntax via protocols such as HTTP, FTP, SFTP, SCP, and many more. It is free, open source (available under the MIT Licence) and has been ported to several operating systems. You can send HTTP commands, change HTTP headers, and so on. It is a good tool for simulating a user's actions in a web browser.

A.6.1. A Brief History of cURL

cURL was first released in 1997. The name stands for *Client URL*, that's why you can stumble on the spelling *cURL* instead of *Curl* or *CURL*. The original author and lead developer is the Swedish developer Daniel Stenberg[116].

A.6.2. Installing cURL on macOS

Usually macOS already provides cURL and installing another version in parallel can cause all kinds of trouble. So first, double check if cURL is already installed just by executing the following cURL command:

```
$ curl --version
```

If cURL is not installed, then it is just a matter of installing it with a single Homebrew command:

```
$ brew install curl
```

A.6.3. Checking for cURL Installation

Once installed, check for cURL by running `curl --version` in the terminal. It should display cURL version:

```
$ curl --version

curl 7.64.1 (x86_64-apple-darwin18.0) libcurl/7.64.1 LibreSSL/2.6.5 zlib/1.2.11
nghttp2/1.24.1
Protocols: dict file ftp ftps gopher http https imap imaps ldap ldaps pop3 pop3s rtsp
smb smbs smtp smtps telnet tftp
Features: AsynchDNS IPv6 Largefile GSS-API Kerberos SPNEGO NTLM NTLM_WB SSL libz HTTP2
UnixSockets HTTPS-proxy
```

A.6.4. Some cURL Commands

cURL is a command line utility where you can use several parameters and options to invoke URLs. You invoke `curl` with zero, one or several command lines and a URL (or set of URLs) to which the data should be transferred. cURL supports over two hundred different options and I would recommend reading the documentation for more help. To get some help on the commands[117] and options, you can use the following command:

```
$ curl --help

Usage: curl [options...] <url>
```

You can also opt to use `curl --manual` which will output the entire man page for cURL plus an appended tutorial for the most common use cases.

Here are some sample cURL commands that you will be using to invoke the RESTful web service examples in this fascicle.

- `curl http://localhost:8080/authors`: HTTP GET on a given URL.
- `curl -X GET http://localhost:8080/authors`: Same effect as the previous command, an HTTP GET on a given URL.
- `curl -v http://localhost:8080/authors`: HTTP GET on a given URL with verbose mode on.

- `curl -H 'Content-Type: application/json' http://localhost:8080/authors`: HTTP GET on a given URL passing the JSON Content Type in the HTTP Header.

- `curl -X DELETE http://localhost:8080/authors/1`: HTTP DELETE on a given URL.

A.6.5. Formatting the cURL JSON Output with JQ

Very often when using cURL to invoke a RESTful web service, we get some JSON payload in reply. cURL does not format this JSON, so you will get a flat String such as:

```
$ curl http://localhost:8080/vintage-store/artists
[{"id":"1","firstName":"John","lastName":"Lennon"},{"id":"2","firstName":"Paul","lastN
ame":"McCartney"},{"id":"3","firstName":"George","lastName":"Harrison"},{"id":"4","fir
stName":"Ringo","lastName":"Starr"}]
```

But what we really want is to format the JSON payload to make it easier to read. For that, there is a neat utility tool called jq[118]. It is a tool for processing JSON inputs, applying the given filter on them and producing the filtered results as JSON on standard output. You can install it on macOS with a simple `brew install jq`. Once installed, it's just a matter of piping the cURL output to jq like this:

```
$ curl http://localhost:8080/vintage-store/artists | jq
[
  {
    "id": "1",
    "firstName": "John",
    "lastName": "Lennon"
  },
  {
    "id": "2",
    "firstName": "Paul",
    "lastName": "McCartney"
  },
  {
    "id": "3",
    "firstName": "George",
    "lastName": "Harrison"
  },
  {
    "id": "4",
    "firstName": "Ringo",
    "lastName": "Starr"
  }
]
```

A.7. Docker

Docker[119] is a set of *Platform-as-a-Service* (PaaS) products that use OS-level virtualisation to deliver software. It makes it easier to create, deploy and run applications by using containers. Containers are isolated from one another and bundle their own software, libraries and configuration files; they can communicate with each other through well-defined channels. Containers allow developers to package an application with all its dependencies and ship it all out as one package.

A.7.1. A Brief History of Docker

Docker was founded by Solomon Hykes and Sebastien Pahl during the Y Combinator Summer 2010 startup incubator group and launched in 2011[120]. Hykes started the Docker project in France as an internal project within dotCloud (a *Platform-as-a-Service* company). Docker debuted to the public in Santa Clara at PyCon in 2013. It was released as open source in March 2013. At the time, it used LXC as its default execution environment. One year later, with the release of version 0.9, Docker replaced LXC with its own component, which was written in the Go programming language.

A.7.2. Installing Docker on macOS

The infrastructure in this fascicle uses Docker to ease the installation of the different technical services (database, monitoring, etc.). So for this, we need to install the docker command line. First of all, check if you already have the Docker formula installed on your machine:

```
$ brew cask list docker
Error: Cask 'docker' is not installed.
```

If the Docker formula is not installed, execute the following Homebrew command to install it:

```
$ brew cask install docker
...
docker was successfully installed!
```

You should now see the Docker formula in Homebrew:

```
$ brew cask list docker
==> App
/Applications/Docker.app
```

A.7.3. Checking for Docker Installation

After installing Docker, you should have docker available in your PATH. But the command docker should not be able to connect to the Docker daemon. You should have the following error:

```
$ docker version

Cannot connect to the Docker daemon at unix:///var/run/docker.sock.
        Is the docker daemon running?
```

That's because you need to launch the Docker Desktop application. To do that, you can either click on the Docker.app icon located under /Applications, launch it using Spotlight or execute the following command:

```
$ open -a Docker
```

On your Mac top menu bar you should see the logo of a whale. Click on it and you should see a menu that looks like Figure 37.

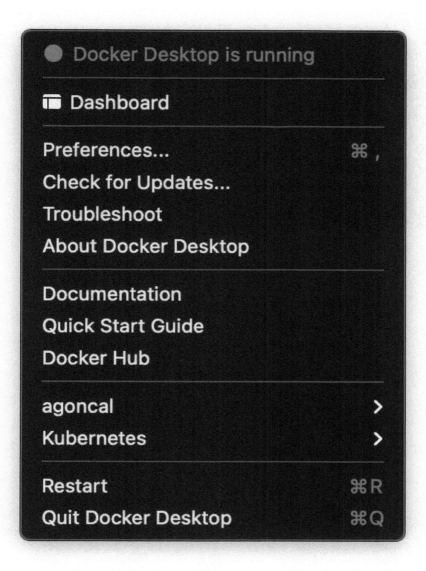

Figure 37. Docker icon on the menu bar

Click on the **About** menu, a window that looks like Figure 38 should give you the versions of the installed Docker tools.

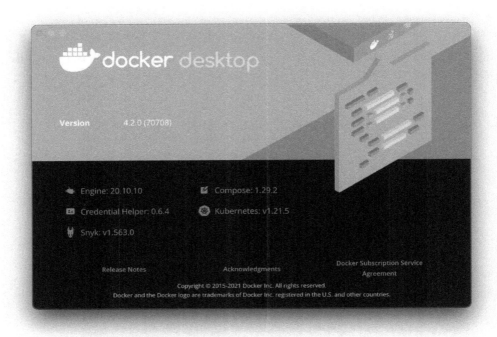

Figure 38. About Docker desktop

Now, if you type the same Docker command, it should connect to the daemon:

```
$ docker version

Client:
 Cloud integration: v1.0.20
 Version:           20.10.10
 API version:       1.41
 Go version:        go1.16.9
 Git commit:        b485636
 Built:             Mon Oct 25 07:43:15 2021
 OS/Arch:           darwin/amd64
 Context:           default
 Experimental:      true

Server: Docker Engine - Community
 Engine:
  Version:          20.10.10
  API version:      1.41 (minimum version 1.12)
  Go version:       go1.16.9
  Git commit:       e2f740d
  Built:            Mon Oct 25 07:41:30 2021
  OS/Arch:          linux/amd64
  Experimental:     true
 containerd:
  Version:          1.4.11
  GitCommit:        5b46e404f6b9f661a205e28
 runc:
  Version:          1.0.2
  GitCommit:        v1.0.2-0-g52b36a2
 docker-init:
  Version:          0.19.0
  GitCommit:        de40ad0
```

Finally, you can run your first container. The `docker container run` command will execute a container that is located on your computer. If not, it will pull the image from the Docker Hub[121] registry and then execute it. That's what happens when you execute an image for the very first time.

Below, the `docker container run` method wants to execute the Docker image called `hello-world`. It doesn't find the image locally, therefore it pulls the image from the default Docker Hub registry: https://hub.docker.com/_/hello-world. Then it executes it:

```
$ docker container run hello-world

Unable to find image 'hello-world:latest' locally
latest: Pulling from library/hello-world
Pull complete
Status: Downloaded newer image for hello-world:latest

Hello from Docker!
This message shows that your installation appears to be working correctly.

To generate this message, Docker took the following steps:
 1. The Docker client contacted the Docker daemon.
 2. The Docker daemon pulled the "hello-world" image from the Docker Hub.
 3. The Docker daemon created a new container from that image which runs the
    executable that produces the output you are currently reading.
 4. The Docker daemon streamed that output to the Docker client, which sent it
    to your terminal.

To try something more ambitious, you can run an Ubuntu container with:
 $ docker run -it ubuntu bash

Share images, automate workflows, and more with a free Docker ID:
 https://hub.docker.com/

For more examples and ideas, visit:
 https://docs.docker.com/get-started/
```

A.7.4. Building, Running, Pushing and Pulling Images

Let's now see the typical flow on how to get started on using docker images and containers. Basically you create a Dockerfile, build it into a local Docker image and run it inside a container. To make your local image available to others (external team developers but also tools such as Kubernetes), push the image to a remote Docker registry (the default one being Docker Hub). Then, if your local image has been removed, just pull it from the remote repository and execute it again.

But first, you need to create an account on a remote Docker repository. Let's take the default one: Docker Hub.

Remote Docker Repository

Docker Hub[122] is a service provided by Docker for finding and sharing container images. It will be used to push and pull our Docker images.

To create a Docker account, sign up on https://hub.docker.com/signup. The name of the account is very important as it will be used to name the Docker images so they can be pushed to your remote repository (the image name and account name have to be the same). Figure 39 shows a Docker hub account called agoncal (you should have your own).

agoncal

👤 User   🕐 Joined November 13, 2014

Figure 39. Docker hub account

Now back to your local computer. You should be able to login to your newly created Docker hub account with the following command:

```
$ docker login

Login with your Docker ID to push and pull images from Docker Hub.
Username: agoncal
Password:
Login Succeeded
```

Dockerfile

Now, let's create a very simple Dockerfile. The Dockerfile below is based on the Alpine image which is a very lightweight Linux (only 5 MB in size). Then, it uses the echo command to display the message *Hello Fascicle*. Take any text editor, create a file called Dockerfile and add the following:

```
FROM alpine
CMD echo "Hello Fascicle"
```

This is a very simple Dockerfile that only uses two commands: FROM and CMD. But a Dockerfile is usually much richer than that and uses more commands. Table 28 shows a subset of Dockerfile commands that can be used.

Table 28. Some Docker Commands

Command	Description
ADD	Defines files to copy from the Host file system onto the container
CMD	Command that will run when the container starts
COPY	Copies files or directories from a source to a destination
ENTRYPOINT	Sets the default application used every time a container is created from the image
ENV	Sets/modifies the environment variables within containers created from the image
EXPOSE	Defines which container ports to expose
FROM	Selects the base image to build the new image on top of

Command	Description
USER	Defines the default user all commands will be run as within any container created from your image
RUN	Executes any commands in a new layer on top of the current image and commits the result
WORKDIR	Defines the default working directory for the command defined in the ENTRYPOINT or CMD instructions

Building the Docker Image

Now, using this Dockerfile, build the Docker image using the following command:

```
$ docker image build -t agoncal/hello-fascicle .

Sending build context to Docker daemon  2.048kB
Step 1/2 : FROM alpine
Step 2/2 : CMD echo "Hello Fascicle"
Successfully built a896f9983057
Successfully tagged agoncal/hello-fascicle:latest
```

The last message of the trace indicates that the Docker image has been successfully built and is called agoncal/hello-fascicle:latest. Notice that the prefix agoncal is the name of the Docker hub account (change it accordingly to yours). To check that this image is now locally installed, type the following command:

```
$ docker image ls --filter "reference=agoncal/hello-fascicle"

REPOSITORY              TAG       IMAGE ID       SIZE
agoncal/hello-fascicle  latest    d036b3b86cd4   5.57MB
```

Running the Docker Image

Now that the image is available locally, let's execute it. The following command executes our image which echoes a message to the console:

```
$ docker container run agoncal/hello-fascicle

Hello Fascicle
```

Pushing to a Docker Registry

Now that we know that our image runs as expected, let's make it available to others by pushing it to the remote Docker registry. This is done with a simple push command. For consuming existing public images from Docker Hub, you don't need to be authenticated. But for publishing your own images, you need to be authenticated. The docker image push command assumes that you've already authenticated with the remote registry (otherwise execute `docker login` before hand):

```
$ docker image push agoncal/hello-fascicle

The push refers to repository [docker.io/agoncal/hello-fascicle]
50644c29ef5a: Mounted from library/alpine
latest: digest: sha256:608aa60a8d32b6b3 size: 528
```

Go back to the Docker Hub website to see the newly-pushed image. It should look like the repository shown in Figure 40.

Figure 40. Docker image available on Docker Hub

Pulling from a Docker Registry

Now let's remove our image from our local system:

```
$ docker image rm agoncal/hello-fascicle -f

Untagged: agoncal/hello-fascicle:latest
Untagged: agoncal/hello-fascicle@sha256:608aa60a8d32b6b3
Deleted: sha256:d036b3b86cd4a2a82234202dac26ebbf39f8aae2

$ docker image ls --filter "reference=agoncal/hello-fascicle"
REPOSITORY              TAG              IMAGE ID        SIZE
```

The `docker image ls` command confirms that the `rm` command has been successful and that the image `agoncal/hello-fascicle` has been removed. This means that we can't execute our image anymore. Well, this is not exactly true. If we run our image again, Docker automatically downloads (pulls) the images that don't yet exist locally, creates a container, and starts it.

```
$ docker container run agoncal/hello-fascicle

Unable to find image 'agoncal/hello-fascicle:latest' locally
latest: Pulling from agoncal/hello-fascicle
df20fa9351a1: Already exists
Digest: sha256:608aa60a8d32b6b36ef595e1bf81c046bcf3504b06da787d1cbfe848e31da8db
Status: Downloaded newer image for agoncal/hello-fascicle:latest

Hello Fascicle
```

This has exactly the same effect as pulling the image first, and executing it after:

```
$ docker image pull agoncal/hello-fascicle

Using default tag: latest
latest: Pulling from agoncal/hello-fascicle
df20fa9351a1: Already exists
Digest: sha256:608aa60a8d32b6b36ef595e1bf81c046bcf3504b06da787d1cbfe848e31da8db
Status: Downloaded newer image for agoncal/hello-fascicle:latest
docker.io/agoncal/hello-fascicle:latest

$ docker container run agoncal/hello-fascicle

Hello Fascicle
```

A.7.5. Some Docker Commands

Docker is a command line utility where you can use several parameters and options to start/stop a container. You invoke docker with zero, one or several command line options with the container or image ID you want to work with. Docker comes with several options that are described in the documentation if you need more help. To get some help on the commands[123] and options, you can use the following command:

```
$ docker help

Usage:  docker [OPTIONS] COMMAND

$ docker help attach

Usage:  docker attach [OPTIONS] CONTAINER

Attach local standard input, output, and error streams to a running container
```

Here are some commands that you will be using to start/stop containers in this workshop.

- docker login: Logs into a Docker registry.

- `docker image ls`: Lists images.

- `docker image push`: Pushes a local Docker image to the remote Docker repository.

- `docker image pull`: Pulls a Docker image from the remote Docker repository to the local repository.

- `docker container ls`: Lists containers.

- `docker container run <CONTAINER>`: Starts one or more stopped containers.

- `docker container stop <CONTAINER>`: Stops one or more running containers.

- `docker compose -f docker-compose.yaml up -d`: Starts all containers defined in a Docker Compose file.

- `docker compose -f docker-compose.yaml down`: Stops all containers defined in a Docker Compose file.

A.8. Git

Git[124] is a free and open source distributed version control system designed for tracking changes in computer files and coordinating work on those files among multiple people. It is primarily used for source code management in software development, but it can be used to keep track of changes in any set of files. Git was created by Linus Torvalds in 2005 for the development of the Linux kernel, with other kernel developers contributing to its initial development.

Git is not really needed to run the samples in this fascicle. Even if the code is hosted on a public Git repository (https://github.com/agoncal/agoncal-fascicle-quarkus-pract/tree/2.0), you can either download the code as a zip file, or clone the repository. Only if you clone the repository will you need to have Git installed.

A.8.1. A Brief History of Git

Git development began in April 2005, after many developers in the Linux kernel gave up access to BitKeeper, a proprietary source-control management (SCM). Linus Torvalds wanted a distributed system that he could use, like BitKeeper, but none of the available free systems met his needs. So, Linus started the development of Git on 3rd April 2005, announced the project on 6th April and the first merge of multiple branches took place on 18th April. On 29th April, the nascent Git was benchmarked, recording patches to the Linux kernel tree at the rate of 6.7 patches per second[125].

A.8.2. Installing Git on macOS

On macOS, if you have installed Homebrew[126], then installing Git is just a matter of a single command. Open your terminal and install Git with the following command:

```
$ brew install git
```

A.8.3. Checking for Git Installation

Once installed, check for Git by running `git --version` in the terminal. It should display the git version:

```
$ git --version
git version 2.33.1
```

A.8.4. Cloning Repository

Once Git is installed, you can clone the code of the repository with a `git clone` on https://github.com/agoncal/agoncal-fascicle-quarkus-pract.git.

[86] Homebrew https://brew.sh

[87] Homebrew History https://en.wikipedia.org/wiki/Homebrew_(package_manager)#History

[88] Homebrew Cask https://github.com/Homebrew/homebrew-cask

[89] Java http://www.oracle.com/technetwork/java/javase

[90] Visual VM https://visualvm.github.io

[91] The Java HotSpot Performance Engine Architecture https://www.oracle.com/technetwork/java/whitepaper-135217.html

[92] Java History https://en.wikipedia.org/wiki/Java_(programming_language)#History

[93] Java Website http://www.oracle.com/technetwork/java/javase/downloads/index.html

[94] GraalVM https://www.graalvm.org

[95] SubstrateVM https://github.com/oracle/graal/tree/master/substratevm

[96] Sulong https://github.com/oracle/graal/tree/master/sulong

[97] Truffle https://github.com/oracle/graal/tree/master/truffle

[98] Graal Compiler https://github.com/oracle/graal/tree/master/compiler

[99] JVM Compiler Interface https://openjdk.java.net/jeps/243

[100] Substrate VM https://github.com/oracle/graal/tree/master/substratevm

[101] MaxineVM https://dl.acm.org/doi/10.1145/2400682.2400689

[102] OTN License https://www.oracle.com/downloads/licenses/graalvm-otn-license.html

[103] GraalVM Download https://www.graalvm.org/downloads

[104] GraalVM GitHub https://github.com/graalvm/graalvm-ce-builds/tags

[105] Native Image https://www.graalvm.org/reference-manual/native-image

[106] Maven https://maven.apache.org

[107] Maven History https://en.wikipedia.org/wiki/Apache_Maven#History

[108] Maven Central https://search.maven.org

[109] JUnit https://junit.org/junit5

[110] Maven Surefire Plugin https://maven.apache.org/surefire/maven-surefire-plugin

[111] REST Assured http://rest-assured.io

[112] Hamcrest http://hamcrest.org/JavaHamcrest

[113] TestContainers https://www.testcontainers.org

[114] Docker Hub https://hub.docker.com

[115] cURL https://curl.haxx.se

[116] Daniel Stenberg https://en.wikipedia.org/wiki/Daniel_Stenberg

[117] cURL commands https://ec.haxx.se/cmdline.html

[118] jq https://stedolan.github.io/jq

[119] Docker https://www.docker.com

[120] Docker History https://en.wikipedia.org/wiki/Docker_(software)#History

[121] Docker Hub https://hub.docker.com

[122] Docker Hub https://hub.docker.com

[123] Docker commands https://docs.docker.com/engine/reference/commandline/cli

[124] Git https://git-scm.com

[125] **History of Git** https://en.wikipedia.org/wiki/Git#History

[126] **Homebrew** https://brew.sh

Appendix B: Quarkus Versions

Quarkus[127] evolves at a fast pace. Below you will find a short recap of the latest major versions and their content. If you want to have more details on each release, you can browse the GitHub account.

B.1. Quarkus 2.5 (*November 2021*)

Quarkus 2.5.0.Final[128] comes with the following main improvements:

- Upgrade to GraalVM/Mandrel 21.3
- Support for JPA entity listeners for Hibernate ORM in native mode
- Ability to add HTTP headers to responses
- Various usability improvements in extensions and our dev mode/testing infrastructure

B.2. Quarkus 2.4 (*October 2021*)

Quarkus 2.4.0.Final[129] brings the following new features:

- Hibernate Reactive 1.0.0.Final
- Introducing Kafka Streams DevUI
- Support continuous testing for multi module projects
- Support AWT image resize via new AWT extension

B.3. Quarkus 2.3 (*October 2021*)

Version 2.3.0.Final[130] includes a lot of refinements and improvements and some new features:

- Dev Service for Neo4J
- Logging with Panache
- Testing support for CLI applications
- MongoDB Liquibase extension
- Support for Hibernate ORM interceptors

B.4. Quarkus 2.2.1 (*August 2021*)

Version 2.2.0.Final wasn't fully released because it suffered from a bug preventing dev mode to work on Windows. Thus 2.2.1.Final[131] was announced with the following changes:

- Upgrade to GraalVM 21.2
- Add global flag to disable Dev Services
- Change the default thread model for RESTEasy Reactive
- Introduce support for MongoDB service binding

- Extension for running Narayana LRA participants

B.5. Quarkus 2.1 (*July 2021*)

Quarkus 2.1[132] stabilizes the 2.0 version and brings new features:

- Add Dev Services support for Keycloak
- Add reactive MS SQL client extension
- Upgrade Kotlin dependency to 1.5.21
- Split out the WebSocket client

B.6. Quarkus 2.0 (*June 2021*)

Quarkus 2.0[133] with a ton of exciting new features. There is a migration guide[134] you can follow to make sure your code is up to date:

- JDK 11 as the minimum Java runtime
- Support for GraalVM 21.1
- Vert.x 4
- Eclipse MicroProfile 4 and updated SmallRye components
- Continuous Testing
- Quarkus CLI

B.7. Quarkus 1.13 (*March 2021*)

Quarkus 1.13[135] brings several new features:

- Dev Services simplifies testing with containers (automatically start containers for when testing so no need to configure anything).
- OpenTelemetry is now supported via two new extensions.
- Kubernetes Service Binding simplifies the deployment on Kubernetes.
- MicroProfile REST Client is now based on RESTEasy Reactive.
- `quarkus-jacoco` can generate test coverage reports.

B.8. Quarkus 1.12 (*February 2021*)

Quarkus 1.12[136] comes with some significant changes:

- Fast-JAR is now the default packaging when you build a jar.
- RESTEasy Reactive keeps improving and it now has support for multipart.
- Vert.x Axle and RX Java managed instances have been dropped.
- We upgraded to GraalVM 21.0.

B.9. Quarkus 1.11 (*January 2021*)

Quarkus 1.11[137] is a very important release because it brings reactive programming to RESTEasy. The major new features are:

- RESTEasy Reactive[138]
- Development console
- Improved Micrometer support
- Spring Data REST extension
- Non application endpoints moved to /q/ path
- jbang dev mode & platform support
- Recommended version of GraalVM is 20.3

B.10. Quarkus 1.10 (*December 2020*)

Quarkus 1.10[139] comes with a lot of improvements and new features:

- Default media type is now JSON
- The Micrometer extension got its fair share of improvements (e.g. new registries)
- New Qute error pages
- Swagger/GraphQL/Health/OpenAPI UIs and Swagger UI configuration
- Part of the Hibernate ORM configuration is now overridable at runtime
- SmallRye Reactive Messaging 2.5.0 and Mutiny 0.11.0
- Reactive SQL Clients support multiple datasources
- New Amazon IAM extension

B.11. Quarkus 1.9 (*October 2020*)

Quarkus 1.9[140] comes with a lot of improvements on top of our existing feature set:

- The Micrometer extension is maturing
- Kafka now has metrics
- Multiple Redis clients are supported (as well as Sentinel connections)
- Bean Validation is supported by Reactive Routes
- SmallRye Reactive Messaging upgraded to 2.4.0 and Mutiny to 0.9.0
- Creation of the Quarkiverse initiative[141], the extension ecosystem.

B.12. Quarkus 1.8 (*September 2020*)

Quarkus 1.8[142] comes with bug fixes, improvements, as well as some notable new features:

- Multiple persistence units support for the Hibernate ORM extension
- A new Micrometer extension
- jbang integration for easy Quarkus-based scripting
- An update to GraalVM 20.2

B.13. Quarkus 1.7 (*August 2020*)

Quarkus 1.7[143], with more than 300 pull requests merged, was released with Elasticsearch and Redis clients, Reactive routes and Funqy improvements. The most prominent new features are:

- New extensions for the low-level and high level Elasticsearch REST clients
- An extension for the Vert.x Redis client
- An Hibernate Envers extension
- Support for the JDBC Db2 driver
- A lot of improvements to the Reactive routes feature
- The Funqy serverless framework got some interesting new features

B.14. Quarkus 1.6 (*July 2020*)

Quarkus 1.6[144] released with AppCDS, Google Cloud Functions, GraalVM 20.1.0 and more.

- Integrated generation of AppCDS archives to improve startup time in JVM mode
- Support for Google Cloud Functions - joining the existing Amazon Lambda and Azure Functions support
- Reactive IBM Db2 client (the Db2 JDBC driver is coming in 1.7)
- An Apache Cassandra client
- WebJars locator extension and Spring @Scheduled support
- Better tools to troubleshoot your applications
- Upgrade to GraalVM 20.1.0

B.15. Quarkus 1.5 (*June 2020*)

Quarkus 1.5[145] introduces the fast-jar packaging as an option.

- New fast-jar packaging format to bring faster startup times
- Quarkus 1.4 introduced command mode and 1.5 added a Picocli[146] extension
- Adds gRPC extension
- Implements Eclipse MicroProfile GraphQL extension
- Supports more Amazon Services (DynamoDB, KMS, S3, SES, SNS, SQS)
- Hibernate ORM REST Data with Panache extension

- Spring Cache compatibility layer

B.16. Quarkus 1.4 (*April 2020*)

Quarkus 1.4[147] brings some major updates.

- Deprecates support for Java 8 as Java 11 is recommended
- Introduces *Command mode* (how to build command line applications with Quarkus)
- Introduces *Funqy*, the new FaaS framework, to improve function front (AWS Lambdas and Azure Functions)
- Adds support for HTTP/2
- Quarkus Security 1.1.0.Final
- Moves the Security API to Mutiny
- Improved mocking (add support for @InjectMock and Mockito)
- Adds support for SmallRye Reactive Messaging 2.0
- Update to SmallRye Health 2.2.0

B.17. Quarkus 1.3 (*March 2020*)

Quarkus 1.3[148] passed the TCKs of all Eclipse MicroProfile 3.3 specifications. MicroProfile 3.3 includes the following specification updates:

- Config 1.4
- Fault Tolerance 2.1
- Health 2.2
- Metrics 2.3
- REST Client 1.4

In addition to the specifications within the MicroProfile platform, Quarkus also includes implementations of Reactive Streams Operators, Reactive Messaging, and Context Propagation. This version also brings GraalVM 20.0 support and a new class loader infrastructure[149].

B.18. Quarkus 1.2 (*January 2020*)

Quarkus 1.2[150] was released with GraalVM 19.3.1 support, Metrics, Cache extension, and much more.

- Supports three flavors of GraalVM:
  - GraalVM 19.2.1 - JDK 8
  - GraalVM 19.3.1 - JDK 8
  - GraalVM 19.3.1 - JDK 11
- Adds a brand new Cache extension

- Adds metrics for Agroal (the database connection pool) and Hibernate ORM
- New SmallRye Fault Tolerance v4.0.0 that replaces Hystrix

B.19. Quarkus 1.1 (*December 2019*)

Quarkus 1.1[151] released with a template engine and YAML configuration.

- Adds Qute template engine
- YAML support for configuration file
- Adds health checks for Kafka, Kafka Streams, MongoDB, Neo4j and Artemis
- Adds Quartz extension

B.20. Quarkus 1.0 (*November 2019*)

First final version[152] of Quarkus.

- Creation of a Platform BOM
- Upgrades SmallRye OpenAPI and Swagger UI
- Updates to GraalVM SDK 19.2.1
- Replace usage of java.util.logging by JBoss logging
- Upgrade to Hibernate ORM 5.4.9.Final
- Quarkus HTTP 3.0.0.Final
- Quarkus Security 1.0.0.Final

B.21. Quarkus 0.0.1 (*November 2018*)

Very first commit[153] of the Quarkus code. Tag 0.0.1 was created[154].

[127] **Quarkus Releases** https://github.com/quarkusio/quarkus/releases

[128] **Quarkus 2.5** https://quarkus.io/blog/quarkus-2-5-0-final-released

[129] **Quarkus 2.4** https://quarkus.io/blog/quarkus-2-4-0-final-released

[130] **Quarkus 2.3** https://quarkus.io/blog/quarkus-2-3-0-final-released

[131] **Quarkus 2.2.1** https://quarkus.io/blog/quarkus-2-2-1-final-released

[132] **Quarkus 2.1** https://quarkus.io/blog/quarkus-2-1-0-final-released

[133] **Quarkus 2.0** https://quarkus.io/blog/quarkus-2-0-0-final-released

[134] **Migration Guide Quarkus 2.0** https://github.com/quarkusio/quarkus/wiki/Migration-Guide-2.0

[135] **Quarkus 1.13** https://quarkus.io/blog/quarkus-1-13-0-final-released

[136] **Quarkus 1.12** https://quarkus.io/blog/quarkus-1-12-0-final-released

[137] **Quarkus 1.11** https://quarkus.io/blog/quarkus-1-11-0-final-released

[138] **RESTEasy Reactive** https://quarkus.io/blog/resteasy-reactive

[139] **Quarkus 1.10** https://quarkus.io/blog/quarkus-1-10-2-final-released

[140] **Quarkus 1.9** https://quarkus.io/blog/quarkus-1-9-0-final-released

[141] **Quarkiverse** https://github.com/quarkiverse

[142] **Quarkus 1.8** https://quarkus.io/blog/quarkus-1-8-0-final-released

[143] **Quarkus 1.7** https://quarkus.io/blog/quarkus-1-7-0-final-released

[144] **Quarkus 1.6** https://quarkus.io/blog/quarkus-1-6-0-final-released

[145] **Quarkus 1.5** https://quarkus.io/blog/quarkus-1-5-final-released

[146] **Picocli** https://picocli.info

[147] **Quarkus 1.4** https://quarkus.io/blog/quarkus-1-4-final-released

[148] **Quarkus 1.3** https://quarkus.io/blog/quarkus-eclipse-microprofile-3-3

[149] **Quarkus Class Loader** https://quarkus.io/guides/class-loading-reference

[150] **Quarkus 1.2** https://quarkus.io/blog/quarkus-1-2-0-final-released

[151] **Quarkus 1.1** https://quarkus.io/blog/quarkus-1-1-0-final-released

[152] **Quarkus 1.0** https://quarkus.io/blog/quarkus-1-0-0-Final-bits-are-here

[153] **Quarkus 1st commit** https://github.com/quarkusio/quarkus/commit/161cfa303b4ea366dbd07e54bf4fe5a67ddec497

[154]   **Quarkus   Tag   0.0.1**   https://github.com/quarkusio/quarkus/commits/0.0.1?
after=1200367b8ddbe5605d8219c4994205f6c1d7af50+1084

Appendix C: Eclipse MicroProfile Specification Versions

The MicroProfile[155] specification evolves at a fast pace. Below you will find a short recap of the latest versions and which sub-specification has been updated for a specific version. If you want to have more details on each specification, you can browse the GitHub account.

C.1. MicroProfile 4.1 (*July 2021*)

MicroProfile 4.1[156] brings the following updates:

- Health 3.1

C.2. MicroProfile 4.0 (*December 2020*)

MicroProfile 4.0[157] is a major release. It is the first version released by the recently-formed *MicroProfile Working Group*[158] within the Eclipse Foundation. It includes updates to:

- Configuration 2.0
- Health 3.0
- Eclipse MicroProfile JWT Auth 1.2
- Metrics 3.0
- REST Client 2.0
- Fault Tolerance 3.0
- Eclipse MicroProfile OpenAPI 2.0
- OpenTracing 2.0

C.3. MicroProfile 3.3 (*February 2020*)

MicroProfile 3.3[159] is an incremental release. It includes an update to:

- Configuration 1.4
- Fault Tolerance 2.1
- Health 2.2
- Metrics 2.3
- REST Client 1.4

C.4. MicroProfile 3.2 (*November 2019*)

MicroProfile 3.2[160] is an incremental release. It includes an update to:

- Metrics 2.2

- Health 2.1

C.5. MicroProfile 3.1 (*October 2019*)

MicroProfile 3.1[161] is an incremental release. It includes an update to:

- Health 2.1
- Metrics 2.1

C.6. MicroProfile 3.0 (*June 2019*)

MicroProfile 3.0[162] is a major release. It consists of:

- Eclipse MicroProfile Configuration 1.3
- Eclipse MicroProfile Fault Tolerance 2.0
- Eclipse MicroProfile Health 2.0
- Eclipse MicroProfile JWT Auth 1.1
- Eclipse MicroProfile Metrics 2.0
- Eclipse MicroProfile OpenAPI 1.1
- Eclipse MicroProfile OpenTracing 1.3
- Eclipse MicroProfile REST Client 1.3
- Context and Dependency Injection 2.0
- Common Annotations 1.3
- Java API for RESTful Web Services 2.1
- JSON Binding 1.0
- JSON Processing 1.1

C.7. MicroProfile 2.2 (*February 2019*)

MicroProfile 2.2[163] is an incremental release. It includes an update to:

- Fault Tolerance 2.0
- OpenAPI 1.1
- OpenTracing 1.3
- REST Client 1.2

C.8. MicroProfile 2.1 (*October 2018*)

MicroProfile 2.1[164] is an incremental release. It includes an update to:

- OpenTracing 1.2

C.9. MicroProfile 2.0.1 (*July 2018*)

MicroProfile 2.0.1[165] is a patch release to correct an issue with the JSON-B maven dependency in the `pom.xml`. The defined content for MicroProfile 2.0 did not change.

C.10. MicroProfile 2.0 (*June 2018*)

MicroProfile 2.0[166] is a major release since the subset of Java EE dependencies are now based on Java EE 8. It consists of:

- Eclipse MicroProfile Configuration 1.3
- Eclipse MicroProfile Fault Tolerance 1.1
- Eclipse MicroProfile Health 1.0
- Eclipse MicroProfile JWT Auth 1.1
- Eclipse MicroProfile Metrics 1.1
- Eclipse MicroProfile OpenAPI 1.0
- Eclipse MicroProfile OpenTracing 1.1
- Eclipse MicroProfile REST Client 1.1
- Context and Dependency Injection 2.0
- Common Annotations 1.3
- Java API for RESTful Web Services 2.1
- JSON Binding 1.0
- JSON Processing 1.1

C.11. MicroProfile 1.4 (*June 2018*)

MicroProfile 1.4[167] is an incremental release. It includes an update to:

- Configuration 1.3
- Fault Tolerance 1.1
- JWT 1.1
- OpenTracing 1.1
- REST Client 1.1

C.12. MicroProfile 1.3 (*January 2018*)

MicroProfile 1.3[168] is an incremental release. It includes an update to:

- Configuration 1.2
- Metrics 1.1

It adds:

- OpenAPI 1.0
- OpenTracing 1.0
- REST Client 1.0

C.13. MicroProfile 1.2 (*September 2017*)

MicroProfile 1.2[169] is an incremental release. It includes an update to:

- Common Annotations 1.2
- Configuration 1.1

It adds:

- Fault Tolerance 1.0
- Health 1.0
- Metrics 1.0
- JWT 1.0

C.14. MicroProfile 1.1 (*August 2017*)

MicroProfile 1.1[170] is an incremental release. It adds:

- Configuration 1.0

C.15. MicroProfile 1.0

MicroProfile 1.0 is the first major release and is based on Java EE 7 specifications. It consists of:

- Context and Dependency Injection 1.2
- Java API for RESTful Web Services 2.0
- JSON Processing 1.0

[155] **MicroProfile Releases** https://github.com/eclipse/microprofile/releases
[156] **MicroProfile 4.1** https://github.com/eclipse/microprofile/releases/tag/4.1
[157] **MicroProfile 4.0** https://github.com/eclipse/microprofile/releases/tag/4.0
[158] **MicroProfile Working Group 4.0** https://microprofile.io/workinggroup
[159] **MicroProfile 3.3** https://github.com/eclipse/microprofile/releases/tag/3.3
[160] **MicroProfile 3.2** https://github.com/eclipse/microprofile/releases/tag/3.2
[161] **MicroProfile 3.1** https://github.com/eclipse/microprofile/releases/tag/3.1
[162] **MicroProfile 3.0** https://github.com/eclipse/microprofile/releases/tag/3.0
[163] **MicroProfile 2.2** https://github.com/eclipse/microprofile/releases/tag/2.2
[164] **MicroProfile 2.1** https://github.com/eclipse/microprofile/releases/tag/2.1
[165] **MicroProfile 2.0.1** https://github.com/eclipse/microprofile/releases/tag/2.0.1
[166] **MicroProfile 2.0** https://github.com/eclipse/microprofile/releases/tag/2.0

[167] **MicroProfile 1.4** https://github.com/eclipse/microprofile/releases/tag/1.4

[168] **MicroProfile 1.3** https://github.com/eclipse/microprofile-bom/releases/tag/1.3

[169] **MicroProfile 1.2** https://github.com/eclipse/microprofile-bom/releases/tag/1.2

[170] **MicroProfile 1.1** https://github.com/eclipse/microprofile-bom/releases/tag/1.1.0

Appendix D: References

- Quarkus https://quarkus.io
- Quarkus developers' guides https://quarkus.io/guides
- Quarkus Super Hero Workshop https://quarkus.io/quarkus-workshops/super-heroes
- SmallRye https://github.com/smallrye
- MicroProfile https://microprofile.io
  - **Config** https://github.com/eclipse/microprofile-config
  - **Fault Tolerance** https://github.com/eclipse/microprofile-fault-tolerance
  - **Health** https://github.com/eclipse/microprofile-health
  - **JWT** https://github.com/eclipse/microprofile-jwt-auth
  - **Metrics** https://github.com/eclipse/microprofile-metrics
  - **OpenApi** https://github.com/eclipse/microprofile-open-api
  - **OpenTracing** https://github.com/eclipse/microprofile-opentracing
  - **Reactive Messaging** https://github.com/eclipse/microprofile-reactive-messaging
  - **Reactive Streams Operators** https://github.com/eclipse/microprofile-reactive-streams-operators
  - **REST-Client** https://github.com/eclipse/microprofile-rest-client

Appendix E: Revisions of the Fascicle

E.1. 2021-11-29

- Content
  - Updated book title to "Practising Quarkus 2.x"
  - Fixed typos
  - Improved footnote references
  - Added Continuous Testing
  - Added Dev Services
- Code
  - Bumped from Quarkus 1.13.x to 2.5.x
  - Bumped from Maven 3.6.x to 3.8.x
  - Bumped from GraalVM 21.0.x to 21.3.x
  - Bumped from Docker 19.x to 20.x
  - Bumped from PostgreSQL 12.1 to 14.1
  - Bumped from Prometheus v2.25.1 to v2.31.1
  - Split PostgreSQL and Prometheus Docker Compose files
  - Replace `/mp-rest/url` property with `quarkus.rest-client." ".uri`

E.2. 2021-05-03

- eBook published on agoncal.teachable.com
- Paper book published on Amazon KDP[171] (*Kindle Direct Publishing*)
- Structure
  - Added 💻 **Call to Action**
- Content
  - Bootstrapping the microservices' code with the Quarkus plugin instead of downloading it
- Code
  - Changed the *Number* microservice path from /api/numbers/book to /api/numbers
  - Bumped from Quarkus 1.9.x to 1.13.x
  - Bumped from GraalVM 20.x to 21.x

E.3. 2020-11-02

- Book published on Red Hat Developer Portal[172]

[171] **KDP** https://kdp.amazon.com

Appendix F: Resources by the Same Author

F.1. Fascicles

The *agoncal fascicle* series contains two types of fascicles. The *Understanding* collection is about fascicles that dive into a specific technology, explain it, and show different aspects of it as well as integrating it with other external technologies. On the other hand, the *Practising* collection is all about coding. So you are supposed to already know a little bit of this technology and be ready to code in order to build a specific application. Below the list of fascicles I have written.

F.1.1. Understanding Bean Validation 2.0

Validating data is a common task that Java developers have to do and it is spread throughout all layers (from client to database) of an application. This common practice is time-consuming, error prone, and hard to maintain in the long run. Besides, some of these constraints are so frequently used that they could be considered standard (checking for a null value, size, range, etc.). It would be good to be able to centralise these constraints in one place and share them across layers.

That's when Bean Validation comes into play.

In this fascicle, you will learn Bean Validation and use its different APIs to apply constraints on a bean, validate all sorts of constraints, write your own constraints and a few advanced topics such as integrating Bean Validation with other frameworks (JPA, JAX-RS, CDI, Spring).

You can find two different formats of this fascicle:

- eBooks (PDF/EPUB) at https://agoncal.teachable.com/p/ebook-understanding-bean-validation
- Paper book (ISBN: 9781980399025) and eBooks at https://www.amazon.com/gp/product/B07B2KJ41R

F.1.2. Understanding JPA 2.2

Applications are made up of business logic, interaction with other systems, user interfaces etc. and data. Most of the data that our applications manipulate have to be stored in datastores, retrieved, processed and analysed. If this datastore is a relational database and you use an object-oriented programming language such as Java, then you might want to use an Object-Relational Mapping tool.

That's when Java Persistence API comes into play.

In this fascicle, you will learn JPA, the standard ORM that maps Java objects to relational databases. You will discover its annotations for mapping entities, as well as the Java Persistence Query Language, entity life cycle and a few advanced topics such as integrating JPA with other frameworks (Bean Validation, JTA, CDI, Spring).

You can find two different formats of this fascicle:

- eBooks (PDF/EPUB) at https://agoncal.teachable.com/p/ebook-understanding-jpa
- Paper book (ISBN: 9781093918977) and eBooks at https://www.amazon.com/gp/product/B0993R88N3

F.1.3. Understanding Quarkus 2.x

Microservices is an architectural style that structures an application as a collection of distributed services. Microservices are certainly appealing but there are many questions that should be asked prior to diving into this architectural style: How do I deal with an unreliable network in a distributed architecture? How do I test my services? How do I monitor them? How do I package and execute them?

That's when Quarkus comes into play.

In this fascicle, you will learn Quarkus but also its ecosystem. You will discover Quarkus internals and how you can use it to build REST and reactive microservices, bind and process JSON or access datastores in a transactional way. With Cloud Native and GraalVM in mind, Quarkus makes packaging and orchestrating your microservices with Docker and Kubernetes easy.

This fascicle has a good mix of theory and practical examples. It is the companion book of *Practising Quarkus 2.x* where you learn how to develop an entire microservice architecture.

You can find two different formats of this fascicle:

- eBooks (PDF/EPUB) at https://agoncal.teachable.com/p/ebook-understanding-quarkus
- Paper book (ISBN: 9798775773083) and eBooks at https://www.amazon.com/gp/product/B0993R88N3

F.1.4. Practising Quarkus 2.x

Microservices is an architectural style that structures an application as a collection of distributed services. Microservices are certainly appealing but there are many questions that should be asked prior to diving into this architectural style: How do I deal with an unreliable network in a distributed architecture? How do I test my services? How do I monitor them? How do I package and execute them?

That's when Quarkus comes into play.

In this fascicle you will develop an entire microservice application using Quarkus as well as MicroProfile. You will expose REST endpoints using JAX-RS and OpenAPI, customise the JSON output thanks to JSON-B and deal with persistence and transaction with Hibernate ORM with

Panache and JTA. Having distributed microservices, you will implement health checks and add some metrics so you can monitor your microservice architecture. Finally, thanks to GraalVM you will build native executables, and package and execute them with Docker.

This fascicle is very practical. It is the companion book of the more theoretical *Understanding Quarkus 2.x* where you'll learn more about Quarkus, MicroProfile, REST and reactive microservices, as well as Cloud Native and GraalVM.

You can find two different formats of this fascicle:

- eBooks (PDF/EPUB) at https://agoncal.teachable.com/p/ebook-practising-quarkus
- Paper book (ISBN: 9798775794774) and eBooks at https://www.amazon.com/gp/product/B0993RBKKR

F.2. Online Courses

Online courses are a great way to learn a new technology or dive into one that you already know. Below the list of online courses I have created.

F.2.1. Starting With Quarkus

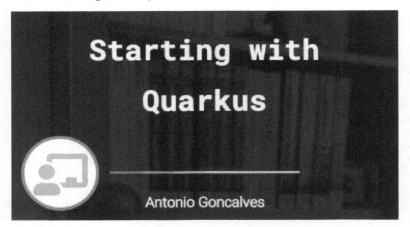

This course[173] is for Java developers who want to discover Quarkus. It's a mixture of slides and code so you can "Understand and Practice" at the same time. This way, you learn the theory, and then put it into practice by developing an application step by step.

In this course you will go through an entire development cycle. After introducing Quarkus, you will make sure your development environment is set up, and you will go from bootstrapping a Quarkus application, to running it as a Docker container.

F.2.2. Building Microservices With Quarkus

This course[174] is for Quarkus developers who want to discover how Quarkus and MicroProfile handle microservices. It's a mixture of slides and code so you can "Understand and Practice" at the same time. This way, you learn the theory, and then put it into practice by developing a microservice architecture step by step.

In this course you will develop two microservices that talk to each other. After introducing Microservices and MicroProfile, you will make sure your development environment is set up, and you will go from bootstrapping two Quarkus microservices, to running them as Docker containers.

F.2.3. Accessing Relational Databases with Quarkus

This course[175] is for Quarkus developers who want to discover how Quarkus handles relational databases. It's a mixture of slides and code so you can "Understand and Practice" at the same time. This way, you learn the theory, and then put it into practice by developing a microservice architecture step by step.

In this course you will develop a Quarkus applications maps and queries different kind of persistent objects to several relational databases. After introducing JDBC, JPA and Panache ORM, you will make sure your development environment is set up, and you will go from bootstrapping three Quarkus applications, developing and refactoring a rich business model, map and query these objects to a PostgreSQL database.

F.2.4. Quarkus: Fundamentals (*PluralSight*)

Quarkus is said to be a Supersonic Subatomic Java toolkit. But what does this mean? This course[176] explains what Quarkus is so you can decide if it's suited for your project.

F.2.5. Microservices: The Big Picture (*PluralSight*)

Microservices are quickly being adopted by companies worldwide. This course[177] teaches you the basics of microservice architectures from a 10,000-foot high view.

F.2.6. Java EE: The Big Picture (*PluralSight*)

This course[178] functions as a technical and business overview of Java Enterprise Edition.

F.2.7. Java EE: Getting Started (*PluralSight*)

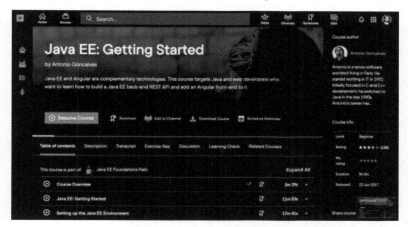

Java EE and Angular are complementary technologies. This course[179] targets Java and web developers who want to learn how to build a Java EE back-end REST API and add an Angular front-end to it.

F.2.8. Java EE 7 Fundamentals (*PluralSight*)

Developing web apps just got easier. In this course[180], you'll learn the essentials of developing web applications with Java EE 7.

F.2.9. Java Persistence API 2.2 (*PluralSight*)

In this course[181] you will learn how to map and query Java objects to a relational database in your Java SE and Java EE applications.

F.2.10. Context and Dependency Injection 1.1 (*PluralSight*)

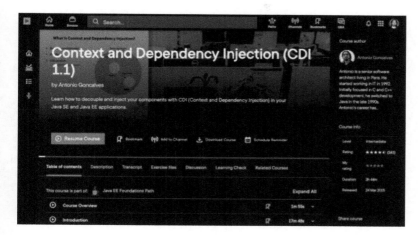

In this course[182] you will learn how to decouple and inject your components with CDI (Context and Dependency Injection) in your Java SE and Java EE applications.

F.2.11. Bean Validation 1.1 (*PluralSight*)

In this course[183] you will learn how to create and add business constraints to your Java SE and Java EE applications.

[173] **Starting With Quarkus** https://agoncal.teachable.com/p/course-starting-with-quarkus

[174] **Building Microservices With Quarkus** https://agoncal.teachable.com/p/course-building-microservices-with-quarkus

[175] **Accessing Relational Databases with Quarkus** https://agoncal.teachable.com/p/course-accessing-databases-with-jpa-and-panache-in-quarkus

[176] **Quarkus: Fundamentals** https://app.pluralsight.com/library/courses/quarkus-fundamentals/table-of-contents

[177] **Microservices: The Big Picture** https://app.pluralsight.com/library/courses/microservices-big-picture/table-of-contents

[178] **Java EE: The Big Picture** https://app.pluralsight.com/library/courses/java-ee-big-picture/table-of-contents

[179] **Java EE: Getting Started** https://app.pluralsight.com/library/courses/java-ee-getting-started/table-of-contents

[180] **Java EE 7 Fundamentals** https://app.pluralsight.com/library/courses/java-ee-7-fundamentals/table-of-contents

[181] **Java EE: The Big Picture** https://app.pluralsight.com/library/courses/java-persistence-api-21/table-of-contents

[182] **Context and Dependency Injection 1.1** https://app.pluralsight.com/library/courses/context-dependency-injection-1-1/table-of-contents

[183] **Bean Validation 1.1** https://app.pluralsight.com/library/courses/bean-validation/table-of-contents

Appendix G: Printed Back Cover

Antonio Goncalves is a senior software architect and Java Champion. Having been focused on Java development since the late 1990s, his career has taken him to many different countries and companies. For the last few years, Antonio has given talks at international conferences, mainly on Java, distributed systems and microservices. This fascicle stems from his extensive experience in writing books, blogs and articles.

Microservices is an architectural style that structures an application as a collection of distributed services. Microservices are certainly appealing but there are many questions that should be asked prior to diving into this architectural style: How do I deal with an unreliable network in a distributed architecture? How do I test my services? How do I monitor them? How do I package and execute them?

That's when Quarkus comes into play.

In this fascicle you will develop an entire microservice application using Quarkus as well as MicroProfile. You will expose REST endpoints using JAX-RS and OpenAPI, customise the JSON output thanks to JSON-B and deal with persistence and transaction with Hibernate ORM with Panache and JTA. Having distributed microservices, you will implement health checks and add some metrics so you can monitor your microservice architecture. Finally, thanks to GraalVM you will build native executables, and package and execute them with Docker.

This fascicle is very practical. It is the companion book of the more theoretical *Understanding Quarkus 2.x* where you'll learn more about Quarkus, MicroProfile, REST and reactive microservices, as well as Cloud Native and GraalVM.

You can find two different formats of this fascicle:

- eBooks (PDF/EPUB) at https://agoncal.teachable.com/p/ebook-practising-quarkus
- Paper book (ISBN: 9798775794774) and eBooks at https://www.amazon.com/gp/product/B0993RBKKR